T0247914

Social Ethics and Governance in Contemporary African Writing

BLACK LITERARY AND CULTURAL EXPRESSIONS

Bloomsbury's **Black Literary and Cultural Expressions** series provides a much-needed space for exploring dimensions of Black creativity as its local expressions in literature, music, film, art, etc., interface with the global circulation of culture. From contemporary and historical perspectives, and through a multidisciplinary lens, works in this series critically analyze the provenance, genres, aesthetics, intersections, and modes of circulation of works of Black cultural expression and production.

Series Editors

Toyin Falola and Abimbola A. Adelakun, University of Texas at Austin, USA

Advisory Board

Nadia Anwar, University of Management and Technology, Lahore, Pakistan
Adriaan van Klinken, University of Leeds, UK
Alain Lawo-Sukam, Texas A&M University, USA
Nathaniel S. Murrell, University of North Carolina, Wilmington, USA
Mukoma wa Ngugi, Cornell University, USA
Bode Omojola, Mount Holyoke and the Five College Consortium, USA
Nduka Otiono, Carleton University, Canada
Bola Sotunsa, Babcock University, Nigeria
Nathan Suhr-Sytsma, Emory University, USA

Volumes in the Series:

Wole Soyinka: Literature, Activism, and African Transformation
by Bola Dauda and Toyin Falola
Social Ethics and Governance in Contemporary African Writing:
Literature, Philosophy, and the Nigerian World by Nimi Wariboko
The Birth of Breaking: Hip Hop History from the Floor Up
by Serouj "Midus" Aprahamian (forthcoming)
The Epic Poetry of Mazisi Kunene by Dike Okoro (forthcoming)
The Decolonizing Work of Jessica Huntley: The Political Roots of a
Radical Black Activist by Claudia Tomlinson (forthcoming)

Social Ethics and Governance in Contemporary African Writing

Literature, Philosophy, and the Nigerian World

Nimi Wariboko

BLOOMSBURY ACADEMIC
NEW YORK • LONDON • OXFORD • NEW DELHI • SYDNEY

BLOOMSBURY ACADEMIC
Bloomsbury Publishing Inc
1385 Broadway, New York, NY 10018, USA
50 Bedford Square, London, WC1B 3DP, UK
29 Earlsfort Terrace, Dublin 2, Ireland

BLOOMSBURY, BLOOMSBURY ACADEMIC and the Diana logo
are trademarks of Bloomsbury Publishing Plc

First published in the United States of America 2023

Cover design by Eleanor Rose
Cover image © David Sanger Photography / Alamy

Library of Congress Cataloging-in-Publication Data

Names: Wariboko, Nimi, 1962- author.
Title: Social ethics and governance in contemporary African writing :
literature, philosophy, and the Nigerian world / Nimi Wariboko.
Other titles: Black literary and cultural expressions.
Description: New York : Bloomsbury Academic, 2023. | Series: Black literary
and cultural expressions | Includes bibliographical references and index. |
Summary: "Using cutting-edge philosophical analyses, this book
highlights Nigerian literature's contributions to moral imagination,
ethical discourse, postcolonial studies, and emancipatory politics"–Provided by publisher.
Identifiers: LCCN 2022025133 (print) | LCCN 2022025134 (ebook) |
ISBN 9781501398087 (hardback) | ISBN 9781501398070 (paperback) |
ISBN 9781501398094 (epub) | ISBN 9781501398100 (pdf) | ISBN 9781501398117
Subjects: LCSH: Nigerian fiction–History and criticism. |
Nigerian fiction–Philosophy. | Literature and society–Nigeria. |
Social ethics in literature.
Classification: LCC PR9387.05 .W37 2023 (print) | LCC PR9387.05 (ebook) |
DDC 823.009969–dc23/eng/20220525
LC record available at https://lccn.loc.gov/2022025133
LC ebook record available at https://lccn.loc.gov/2022025134

ISBN: HB: 978-1-5013-9808-7
PB: 978-1-5013-9807-0
ePDF: 978-1-5013-9810-0
eBook: 978-1-5013-9809-4

Series: Black Literary and Cultural Expressions

Typeset by Integra Software Services Pvt. Ltd.
Printed and bound in Great Britain

To find out more about our authors and books visit www.bloomsbury.com
and sign up for our newsletters.

To Uncle
Azubuike (Wright) Wariboko Jack (1927–1979)

CONTENTS

ACKNOWLEDGMENTS

Writing an acknowledgment is like living in three times at once. The writing at once engages the present, calls up a retrospective perspective, and conjures a prospective process. The present records the words to articulate the essential patterns of benefits one received while working on the manuscript. This present unfolds with the expectation of the words which are to come as the matrices in which one's gratitude appears—all the while presupposing that one knows the highest and unifying telos of the words by virtue of the art or compulsion of writing an acknowledgment. The telos of every acknowledgment is the expression, "thank you."

These three times also bear witness in the creation and production of any book. Thus, there are three sets of benefactors to acknowledge or accredit here. The retrospective segment belongs to the editors of *Black Literary and Cultural Expressions* series, Professors Toyin Falola and Abimbola Adunni Adelakun, who shepherded this project from the proposal stage to the issuance of contract by Bloomsbury. The present segment is the house of Bloomsbury's editors and staff (including Amy Martin and Hali Han) whose "eternal presence" of production and marketing will help keep the book in perpetual circulation. This author and the Bloomsbury team while eagerly expecting the publication and marketing of the book presupposed that the telos has already been reached: a great number of people will read it. Without this teleological ruse, I doubt there would have been any energy or desire to embark on the writing or publication of this book.

Finally, let me thank the University of Rochester Press for permission to reuse revised portions (pp. 35–50, 73–8, and 94) of my book *Ethics and Society in Nigeria: Identity, History, Political Theory* (2019). Portion (pp. 126–40) of my 2013 *Methods of Ethical Analysis: Between Theology, History, and Literature* is used by permission of Wipf and Stock Publishers, www.wipfandstock.com. Thanks to Dr. Hyunwoo Hans Koo of Boston University School of Theology for preparing the bibliography.

Introduction

Hear Word: Literature as Philosophy

On Friday, February 9, 2018, at Harvard University, I saw the play *Hear Word: Naija Woman Talk True*, cowritten and directed by Ifeoma Fafunwa.[1] For about 100 minutes, the audience was held spellbound, occasionally clapping; they rose in a standing ovation when the play came to an end.

The play highlights the sufferings of women in Nigeria and in so doing raises fundamental questions about nation-building and social ethics. The play is as deeply entertaining as it is profoundly philosophical. Take, for instance, the issue of adultery. Without being didactic, the play leads the audience into deep philosophical ruminations about adultery in ways that speak beyond Nigerian culture. The deep structure of the play rests on four types or levels of adultery. (These types were not presented as separate scenes in the play. I grasped the four types after a period of reflection on how adultery was discussed throughout the play.) Ultimately, Fafunwa's play shows that adultery is not just a sex act outside marriage but also a theoretical scaffold on which to organize our thoughts about gender discriminations in Nigerian culture.

First, *Hear Word* presents adultery as a husband sleeping with women outside the matrimonial home. The Nigerian woman endures insults and humiliations because of this. Second, the play expands the definition of adultery beyond sex outside marriage. The way this was done reminded me of how Jesus Christ expanded the Mosaic understanding of adultery. He

---

[1] The other co-writers are Tunde Aladesa, Wole Oguntokun, Mojisola Ajibola, and Ijeoma Ogwuegbu.

says that to look lustfully after a woman is as much adultery as the actual act of having sex with a woman outside wedlock. The play raises this point in the form of complaint about the eyes of Nigerian husbands darting to and fro, always looking for new wives to replace, displace, or substitute the ones at home. The third form of adultery *Hear Word* addresses might easily be missed. In his play, *Jesus of Nazareth*, Richard Wagner states that sex in a loveless marriage is adultery. Just as Jesus radicalizes the meaning of Moses's commandment, Wagner radicalizes the meaning of Jesus's commandment. Wagner writes, "The commandment saith: Thou shalt not commit adultery! But I say unto you: Ye shall not marry without love. A marriage without love is broken as soon as entered into, and who so hath wooed without love, already hath broken the wedding."[2] Nigerian women are forced to enter or stay in loveless marriages because of culture, religion, or economic necessity, or a combination of all three. By Wagner's definition, these women suffer the pain of adultery beyond their husbands having sex with or even lusting after other women. The pain of adultery here is, among others, the institutionalized stealing of a woman's right to basic decency, respect, and independence as they are forced to enter and stay in loveless marriages because of religio-economic and cultural pressures.

Finally, *Hear Word* points us to a final level of adultery, something bigger than the robbery of women's rights in the matrimonial home. In *Beggar's Opera*, Bertolt Brecht asks, "What is the burgling of a bank to the founding of a bank?"[3] In other words, if banks are founded on people's stolen money, then what does stealing from them really mean? Analogously, what is sex outside marriage when the legal basis of marriage is the robbery of a preteen girl's youth, education, destiny, and potentials? Why counsel a woman about obedience to her "lord and master" when her marriage was founded on violent disregard of her personhood or subjectivity? Is such a marriage not annulled even before it starts?

Indeed, *Hear Word* modifies our conception of adultery, even as it invites us to modify our understanding of gender roles. Does this line of deepening thought—going from the obvious, usual, normal understanding of adultery and gender inequality to the fundamental issue of constitutive violence at the root of every culture—not raise questions about the viability of Nigeria's social institutions? Do we only debate or quibble about the "surface" failures of Nigerian institutions or do we question their legitimacy? Indeed, the second half of the play relentlessly raises this deeper line of questioning. We must applaud the subversive reasoning of *Hear Word* and also think about how best to move into the new sites of gender equality it beckons.

---

[2]Richard Wagner, *Jesus of Nazareth and Other Writings* (Lincoln: University of Nebraska Press, 1995), 303.
[3]Bertolt Brecht, *The Threepenny Opera* (New York: Grove, 1994), 92.

Hear Word is full of dramatic shifts in meanings of inherited cultural notions as it presses to unleash the revolutionary potential of all Nigerian women. This tendency to subvert inherited cultural notion is obvious not only in the entire theme of the play but also in Fafunwa's deployment of long narratives, declarations, or women's monologues as fulcrums on which the play turns. The technique of long narration performs a theorization of women's subjective metamorphoses. *Hear Word* is not about events happening in the form of acting, actions, and narratives; rather, the play consists of long narratives that disrupt events onstage. Narratives recapitulate what happened in the past or what transpired before the play as a whole or before a particular scene. The audience hears, sees, and receives renderings of events through actors' narratives not their actions on stage.

It seems to me that Fafunwa carefully thought through this method of presenting the stories of Nigerian women, and the performative logic of her technique is powerful. Fafunwa is saying that the moment of truth, emancipation, and subjective transformation (will) happens when the oppressed woman acts and declares (recounts) her actions. Wagner also used this technique in his later operas. Here, contemporary radical philosopher Slavoj Žižek's comment on Wagner's style is helpful in interpreting the technique of long narration and declarations in *Hear Word*:

> One does something; one counts oneself as (declares oneself) the one who did it; and, on the basis of this declaration, one does something new—the proper moment of subjective transformation occurs at the moment of declaration, not at the moment of the act. In other words, the truly New emerges through narrative, the apparently purely reproductive retelling of what happened—it is this retelling that opens up the space (the possibility) of acting in a new way.[4]

The deep philosophical theory of subjectivity embedded in Fafunwa's vision of *Hear Word* is that the subjective transformation of Nigerian women into radical subjectivity will occur not only by taking actions but also, and more importantly, by retelling their acts of gender and class struggle. How can Nigeria hear word if Nigerian women do not speak up?

In *Hear Word*, literature is hermeneutical, interpreting the "situation" that is Nigeria. The play offers philosophical discourse as an interpretation of a *situation*, that is, positioning, qualifying, and criticizing the specific human condition in a given community, so as to point it to its "salvation" or "redemption," which requires nothing short of human flourishing for all its members.

---

[4]Slavoj Žižek, *Event: A Philosophical Journey through a Concept* (London: Penguin, 2014), 133.

Some of the deep sociocultural issues *Hear Word* brings up raise questions for the Nigerian philosopher concerning the role of literature in the Nigerian community. What is the philosophical significance of literature in Nigeria? What is the relationship between literature and philosophy in the Nigerian postcolony? The question of the relationship between philosophy and Nigerian literature is central to this book. Excellent books by intelligent and insightful people explore interpretation, history, style, themes, and other dimensions of Nigerian literature, but "philosophical" questions are not central to them. I am not saying that scholars have completely ignored the philosophical and theoretical aspects of Nigerian literature. However, this book is significant in the sense that it not only offers particular readings of some major works in Nigerian literature but also focuses specifically on what is philosophical in those works.[5] I take Nigerian novelists, playwrights, and comedians as serious thinkers and philosophers in their own right and merit and analyze their novels, stories, plays, and skits through a sophisticated philosophical lens. Something that could be called "philosophy" is at work in many Nigerian literary texts. I demonstrate that Nigerian literary stars often have discourses, excurses, analyses, and interpretations in their oeuvres that could be considered traditional (conventional) "philosophy" or included in works narrowly identified with philosophy.

I look to Nigerian literature for perspectives on public life, pluralism, and how to respond to the basic social ethical question. How can Nigerians live together as one nation marked and potholed with differences? Differences matter ultimately because pluralism matters. Often, good literary works offer the discerning reader a tutorial in ethical analysis and reasoning. Reading and learning from diverse writers is a way to develop one's socio-ethical analytical capability and acquire the skills and ethos necessary for public debates in modern pluralistic democracies. This is so because there is no single way to teach or learn such a set of capability, skills, and ethos. And there is no single theory of ethics that satisfies all. Thus, ethics and its methodology are better understood, and capabilities, skills, and ethos for ethical analysis are better gained by enabling citizens to view the common good or pressing social problems through multiple "windows." Literature enables one to learn to view social reality from different perspectives.

Meaningful ethical conception and practice often demand seeing things from others' points of view. All over the world, great novels, plays, poems, and films help those who read or watch them reach empathic perceptions of particular people and situations by involving their intellect and emotion.

---

[5]M. S. C. Okolo, *African Literature as Philosophy* (London: Zed Books Ltd., 2007) is also significant in this respect.

Novels, tragic dramas, and others can make readers identify with fictional characters in ways that reflect similar possibilities and potential vulnerabilities for themselves. This kind of empathic identification is important for good ethical practice in diverse and pluralistic communities. Narrative works of art are important for developing the human self-understanding critical for embodying certain political and ethical ideals. Powerful literary works help citizens deepen and broaden their ethical understandings in ways that involve and give priority to context-specific moral evaluation, compassion, similar possibilities and vulnerabilities, and eudaimonistic judgment, rather than abstract general principles for ethical judgment.

I promise nothing more in this book than the beginning of this adventure or engagement with Nigerian literature. It is neither a comprehensive study nor an exhaustive exploration of the connections between literature (novels, plays, and short stories) and philosophy (ethics). I am only trying to illustrate a method of philosophical analysis of Nigerian writers with the works of five artists (four authors and one comedian). This illustration moves in five ways. First, I use philosophy to cast light on the imaginative universe of Nigerian fictions. Second, I use the fictional worlds of Nigerian writers not only to interrogate the "real" Nigerian world but also to illustrate philosophical ideas and concepts as they relate to Nigeria. Third, I retrieve from the fictions and fictional intents of Nigerian writers such ideas, lessons, tools, sensibilities, and provocations that illuminate democratic politics or counter the politics of the present ruling class that have undermined the country's socioeconomic development. The goal of this exercise is to focus on some of the fictions and fictional intents of Nigerian writers that might ginger their fellow citizens to transform or revolutionize their polity and economy in ways that promote human flourishing for all citizens. Fourth, I construct a political philosophy from Nigerian literature. This book carefully demonstrates the profound contributions Nigerian literature can make toward (re)constructing a philosophy of social transformation for a humane world. Finally, my illustrative method will show how scholars can explore a fourth space beyond literature, philosophy, and the site of their intersection. This "beyond" is emptiness, zero, a place outside anything said or given in the texts. This place is one of the unsaid, absence, the site of all that is not in the texts. It is a zone of their nonbeing. From this possibility of emptiness, nothingness, one can inject new questions into the texts and their intersections. In the fourth space, the philosophical or ethical points of the literary and philosophical texts

> are made through what is *not* in them, rather than through anything they say explicitly.... [Often both philosophy and literature] are marked by absence. Both leave it to their readers to figure out how to learn something from that absence (of answers, explanations, resolution, or

straightforward teaching) by turning into something that transforms our understanding of the problems and mysteries[6] of social existence and the political in Nigeria. This is the site of openness to the new, creativity, new beginning, meaning that is beyond meaning.

In this book, I illustrate the five dimensions of the method of philosophical analysis of Nigerian writers. Once I have other participants or co-laborers who are willing to execute these five tasks, I can labor together with them to expand the focus of analysis to include many more writers, themes, and categories (such as more diversity in age, gender, and region) than what I can do in this one book.

The subtitle of this book, *Literature, Philosophy and the Nigerian World*, warrants a comment or two on the connections among the three terms. Philosophy is the mediator between or the medium through which I excavate and appropriate the deep thinking of the novels, plays, and skits I examine to identify what constitutes moral imagination in them, to recognize how it functions in them, and to explore how it might function in real-life ethical situations in Nigeria. Philosophy enables me to explore the connections between literature and social ethics in Nigeria: the relationship between creative imagination and moral imagination; the nature of moral attention and moral vision; and the role of context-specific judging in ethical decisions in the Nigerian world.

The middle term, *philosophy*, here speaks to my belief that literature can express philosophical insights and power. As I demonstrate throughout this book, there is a need in Nigerian studies for some kind of creative encounter of literature and the everyday Nigerian world to establish the nature or identity of the kind of philosophy underpinning literary works. Another way to see the juncture between literature and philosophy is to consider them both to be operating powers that can move Nigerian society toward a way of being more ethical than it is today. The middle term in *Literature, Philosophy, and the Nigerian World* expresses or articulates the forming and sustaining power of the coherence of that way of being, a way of being that can (re)form Nigeria as a place of social justice and unite the vital energy of its people around the goal of flourishing for all humans.[7] Philosophy helps me excavate the innermost radicial transformative possibilities of Nigerian literature.

My goal in this book is specific: to promote literature as an important dialogical partner in ethical discourse in the democratic, pluralistic society

---

[6]Karen Zumhagen-Yelpé, "The Everyday's Fabulous beyond: Nonsense, Parable, and the Ethics of the Literary in Kafka and Wittgenstein," in *Philosophy and Kafka*, ed. Brendan Moran and Carlo Salzan (Lanham, MD: Lexington, 2013), 75.
[7]This way of understanding the role of middle term was inspired by Mark Lewis Taylor, "Tillich's Ethics: Between Politics and Ontology," in *The Cambridge Companion to Paul Tillich*, ed. Russell Re Manning (Cambridge: Cambridge University Press, 2009), 203.

that is Nigeria, and to show how literature can inform the nature of public reason that guides ethical deliberation and moral judgment in a democratic public domain. The selection of the writers and works I discuss herein followed no pattern that may be described as a proper mapping of the site of intersection between literature and philosophy in the Nigerian world. To say this, however, is not to provide an excuse but to use differences and discontinuities to explore different aspects of ethical discourse. The variety of texts with which I engage also points to the key roles multiple forms of literary imagination play in the study of the Nigerian world and its ethical tensions. The existential survival and flourishing of the Nigerian way of life and the process of learning to appropriate its "truths," mores, and goodly powers for public policies will always demand that we listen to many voices and examine multiple perspectives on social issues in our communities.

A Map

In Chapter 1 ("Theoretical Hesitations: Ibadan Brown Roofs' Rusty Revival of Desires"), I examine the sociological context of a Nigerian extended family (*agboole* in Ibadan) as the traditional *agboole* makes its forays into the world of Western education and puts the building blocks together to actualize its desire for modernity. It is within the general framework of a "traditional society" modernizing its ways of educating its youths that Abimbola Adunni Adelakun crafts a philosophy of agonistic communitarianism in her 2011 novel, *Under the Brown Rusted Roofs*.[8] She helps me address the question, How does a community coordinate individual desires to produce and sustain the collective socioeconomic order for the sustenance of human flourishing? In the novel, Adelakun intuitively combines ideas about communalism and individualism in twentieth-century Ibadan to create what I would name *agonistic communitarianism* as a way to demonstrate how Nigerian communities can engage modernity.[9] This modernity is primarily located outside the *agbooles* in the traditional Ibadan society.

---

[8] Abimbola Adunni Adelakun, *Under the Brown Rusted Roofs: Fiction* (Ibadan: Kraft, 2011).
[9] *Agonistic communitarianism*, as I am using the term here, is individualism (not selfishness) that is framed within the communitarianism that undergirds and propels it. Individualism (an inadequate word chosen for a lack of a better term) in the context of agonistic communitarianism is not set as an opposite or rejection of communitarianism. It is an exfoliation of the abiding care and concern for individuality in African communitarianism, the individual-in-communion given an ample space better to actualize her potentiality for the flourishing of the self and what transcends it. See Nimi Wariboko, "Between Community and My Mother: A Theory of Agonistic Communitarianism," in *The Palgrave Handbook of African Social Ethics*, ed. Nimi Wariboko and Toyin Falola (Cham, Switzerland: Palgrave Macmillan, 2020), 147–63.

The road that leads to modernity outside the purview of traditional African institutions has created a crisis of identity for many Nigerian youths. Some among them want to be white, because the adults before them have created a nation whose citizens prefer whiteness to blackness. So, in Chapter 2 ("The Black Moon on the White Surface: A Philosophical Analysis of A. Igoni Barrett's *Blackass*"), I discuss the character Furo, who miraculously turned into a white man in A. Igoni Barrett's 2015 *Blackass*.[10] Barrett's novel offers an excellent lens through which to examine the crisis of identity that has engulfed Nigerian youths in the postcolony.

Identity crisis is just one of the millions of problems young people in Nigeria endure every day. Chris Abani's 2004 *GraceLand* reveals the sheer humanitarian crises of existence, uncertainty, and trauma that perennially define and limit the lives of young men and women in Nigeria.[11] They live in a world of the *postcolonial incredible*. Tejumola Olaniyan describes the reign of the incredible in the Nigerian postcolony in these words:

> The "incredible" inscribes that which cannot be believed; that which is too improbable, astonishing, and extraordinary to be believed. The incredible is not simply a breach but an outlandish infraction of "normality" and its limits. If "belief," as faith, confidence, trust, and conviction, underwrites the certainty and tangibility of institutions and practices of social exchange, the incredible dissolves all props of stability, normality, and intelligibility (and therefore of authority) and engenders social and symbolic crisis.... A presupposed interregnum that increasingly threatens to become the norm, a norm with a rapidly consolidating hierarchy of privileges feeding on and dependent on the crisis for reproduction.[12]

This discourse of the postcolonial incredible, uncertainty, and trauma of existence is what I engage in Chapter 3 ("Bad Governance and Postcoloniality: Literature as Cultural Criticism").

In Chapter 4 ("From Executed God to Ozidi Saga: Ethos of Ijo Democratic Republicanism"), I direct attention to some of the resources scholars and laypeople alike can retrieve from history to address Nigeria's current sociopolitical crisis. I turn to stories of emancipatory politics and republican democratic ethos as revealed in the 1857 historical event of the Niger Delta Kalabari-Ijo's collective decision to kill one of their gods who stepped out of line and could not fulfill the covenant it had made to protect them. How can this tradition be retrieved to illuminate democratic politics or counter the politics of near-divine impunity that political leaders in

[10]A. Igoni Barrett, *Blackass* (Minneapolis, MN: Gray Wolf, 2015).
[11]Chris Abani, *GraceLand* (New York: Farrar, Straus, and Giroux, 2004).
[12]Tejumola Olaniyan, *Arrest the Music!: Fela and His Rebel Art and Politics* (Bloomington: Indiana University Press, 2004), 2.

Nigeria practice? What socio-ontological power did the revolutionary act of deicide recognize, reveal, or portray? What is the implication of all this for democratic sovereignty in Nigeria? In this chapter, I mobilize lessons from J. P. Clark-Bekederemo's *The Ozidi Saga*, an epic of the Ijo/Ijaw people, to buttress the Kalabari story and to draw the reader more fully into the theorization of emancipatory revolutionary politics.

In Chapter 5 ("Comedy as Dialectics: Laughing Nigeria to Human Flourishing"), I leave behind novelists and playwrights and turn to comedian Gbadamasi Abbonjor Jonathan (Mc Edo Pikin).[13] Here, I posit his comedic style as a philosophical template for analyzing the contemporary social situation in Nigeria. His comedy provides a remarkable dialectics of cultural criticism. If the earlier four chapters demonstrated particular case studies of the Nigerian situation, Chapter 5 offers a kind of "universal" or meta-perspective on how to search for appropriate responses to the challenges of any situation.

If in the first five chapters I examine individual works, then the last chapter finds me broadening the context in order to consider the role literature can play in democratic politics and in shaping social ethics in any modern society. Chapter 6 ("Literature and Ethics") examines the role of literature in teaching citizens how to live together or to enact the proper ethical praxis. The question here is: How can we interpret or deploy literature in the practical matter of conscientizing the hearts of Nigerians to struggle for social justice and better participate in public policy debates? How can (does) literature tug at the hearts of Nigerians and fire their creative and moral imagination? Is there a way, a method by which to teach ethics about Nigeria that can capture the moral imagination of citizens and their social consciousness? I believe that literature can enable us to find this method. Literature is a good tool toward developing the moral imagination of Nigerians. As Lionel Trilling once wrote, "I spoke of the novel as an especially useful agent of the moral imagination, as the literary form which most directly reveals to us the complexity, the difficulty, and the interest of life in society, and best instructs us in our human variety and contradiction."[14]

The six chapters of this book illustrate five different ways in which philosophy can engage literature. Combined, the first two chapters provide

---

[13]Here I have broadened the understanding of literature to include comedy/comedy skits as literary text. This expansion if taken to its logical conclusion would suggest that I include cinema among the "texts" I study in this book. But I have limited myself to areas of the imaginative literature that I have the requisite philosophical expertise to analyze. As it is by now obvious to the reader, I have not even included poetry in this work. It is not that poetry does not raise cogent philosophical issues. I have not spent the required time to master this genre so as to bring it into a rigorous philosophical analysis.

[14]Lionel Trilling, *The Moral Obligation to Be Intelligent: Selected Essays*, rev. ed. (Evanston, IL: Northwestern University Press, 2008), 510.

a straight up-and-down philosophical analysis of two novels. Chapter 3 then demonstrates literature as a witness of the flow of contemporary events—that is, literature as cultural criticism. Here, literature has something to offer philosophy. Without being didactic, good novels under the hammer of reconstruction of social ethics must subject today's stories to a process of radical questioning and reawakening. Literature aids the philosophical task of cultural criticism, which consists in interpreting social existence and the human condition to appropriate the existential possibilities for nation-building that emanate from that interpretation. The fourth chapter explores how scholars can ride on the back of history and literature (epics and age-old oral narratives) in order to retrieve meaningful resources from the Nigerian past. The reconstruction of Nigerian society demands that scholars unearth the emancipatory potentials of her past. In this chapter, philosophy and literature work together to analyze the country's socio-ethical identity, history of emancipatory politics, religions, and culture in order to frame a new way of imagining the nation and its democratic republicanism. Chapter 5 demonstrates how one can mine comedy and literature as a methodological tool for social analysis to interrogate, conceptualize, clarify, and rigorously analyze regnant debates, elements, themes, concerns, and practices in Nigeria, and to lift up the assumptions that inform them to intellectual scrutiny. In this task, comedy is not only a tool for critical intellectual scrutiny but also a methodology of interpretative understanding that aids me in grasping the subjective meaning of dominant social practices and ideas in Nigeria. Finally, literature can help "perform" Nigeria. The nation as a normative imaginary has a performative dimension; the "people" (who are still emerging) need to learn to perform the nation, their socio-ethical collectivity. I see this performativity in two ways: citizens as "subjects" draw on the normative force of nationhood while also contributing to the particular constellations of normative values against which their performance is understood. Thus, in helping one live into the ethos of a pluralistic democratic nation, literature assists Nigerian readers in performing Nigeria and actualizing the nation of their collective dream.

The essentiality of literature in forming community or national social imaginary is almost obvious. No one should undervalue the crucial role in a pluralistic and democratic society that can be played by those who have the power to mold the moral imaginations of our youths and train them into patriotic or subversive citizens. To ignore the vital role of literature would imperil the future of Nigeria. Writers and their intellectual interpreters must be encouraged to interrogate, scrutinize, subvert, study, and evaluate the Nigerian situation, to gain new insights and understanding on how to move the country forward; otherwise, our nation will decline and die.

There is, perhaps, a need for me to justify my choice of Adelakun, Barrett, Abani, Clark-Bekederemo, and Edo Pikin for study amid the plethora of old and young writers in Nigeria. In a literary field crowded with many excellent writers, selecting novels and plays to study is challenging. So, what accounts for my choices? First, I deliberately selected a small number of works that I think, put together, beautifully tell the story of the evolution of state and society in Nigeria; offer excellent insights into the challenges of governance, leadership, and development in postcolonial Nigeria; shed ample light on the deepening crisis in the nation; and also offer resources for ethical and policy reimagining of the polity. More importantly, the writers constructed the postcolonial picture of Nigeria and its ethical evaluation with the Occam razor, the principle of parsimony.

Second, the works that I selected generally end with characters advancing into new modes of existence, at the cusp of initiating something new amid ongoing social processes. They are moving forward and not returning to the status quo with which the novels (play, comedy) started. I interpret this form of ending as symbolically pointing to a new, different, and forward-looking Nigeria that most Nigerians desire for their country.

Third, I intentionally picked writers born after Nigeria's independence in October 1960, that is, those born in the postcolonial period that I am studying. African social tradition demands connecting one generation to the ones before it for the preservation of crucial communal wisdom and history for human flourishing. In Chapter 4, I brought in the voice of J. P. Clark-Bekederemo who was born before 1960 to show how younger generations of Nigerian citizens can draw resources from the past to shed light on how to move forward from the present existential predicament of their nation into its future of national flourishing. The play of Clark-Bekederemo that I selected to study along with the works of the younger writers and a comedian is an ancient Ijaw/Ijo epic, *The Ozidi Saga*. Clark-Bekederemo retrieved the play in the 1960s to point his generation of Nigerians to valuable resources in their past waiting for them to access to forge a way forward. The lesson he wanted to pass on was not embraced. Thus, I needed to revive that lesson—which is still relevant—for the new generations of Nigerians.

A question still remains: Are there not many writers born in the postcolonial period that are not included in my study? As I stated earlier, this study is an illustrative one. My study of the works of the selected authors is to enable me to demonstrate my theoretical perspectives and methodological approaches to the study of the intersection of literature and philosophy. If I am successful in this book, then other scholars and I too will be encouraged to extend the methodologies and theoretical perspectives to more writers and their works in the future. Literature is essential in forming the societal ethos Nigerians need to build a viable democratic, pluralistic society for their flourishing and nation-building.

Ultimately, this book offers the reader a way to enjoy both literature and its explorations of some of the great ideas of Nigerian novelists, dramatists, and comedians under the searching lights of philosophy. Since 2010, I have been teaching a graduate course on literature and ethics to master's and doctoral students in the United States. In this course, we subject literary works to intense philosophic and socio-ethical scrutiny. The goal is to learn from these works how citizens in democratic pluralistic communities can peacefully coexist. Aristotle said long ago that literature is one of the best tools for teaching ethics and developing moral imagination. Studying literary works has taught my students and me that the subtleties of complex ethical situations suggest a need to reject calculative, systematic scientific understanding as the best method of ethical reasoning. We have also learned that the focus of any socio-ethical decision should be on what is necessary for good human functioning of all persons. Authors of good literary works teach their readers to approximate this best method of ethical reasoning or base their public or social decisions on what is necessary for good human functioning and flourishing—in other words, to strive for *perceptive equilibrium* in one's moral imaginations and deliberations. According to American philosopher Martha Nussbaum, this is "an equilibrium in which concrete perceptions 'hang beautifully together,' both with one another and with agent's general principles; an equilibrium that is always ready to reconstitute itself in response to the new."[15]

More specifically, I designed the course with four specific outcomes in mind. First, students learn to identify what constitutes moral imagination and recognize not only how it functions in Greek tragedies and modern novels/plays but also how it might function in real-life ethical situations. Second, through analyzing literary works, students become better able to interpret the human emotions that underpin ethical decision-making and identify when empathy is enacted in ethical proposals. Third, students gain cross-cultural sensitivity as they engage with narrative works of art from cultures other than their own. Finally, students examine how literature can help an individual open, expand, and transcend the boundaries of him/herself. To many ethicists, the beginning of wisdom in the practice of compassion is the expansion of the boundaries of the self. I believe readers of this book might experience one or more of these four outcomes.

In the many years since I started teaching the "Literature and Ethics" course, I have always found it difficult to find rigorous book-length philosophical analyses (not literary criticism or analysis) of works by Nigerian (African) writers that I can use in the class. I wrote this book to address this gap and to encourage more philosophical discussions about and analyses of Nigerian writers. (Mary Stella C. Okolo's 2007 *African Literature as Political Philosophy* is a rare find that also addresses this gap. More on this book later.) There is an urgent need to consider some of our

---

[15]Martha C. Nussbaum, *Love's Knowledge: Essays on Philosophy and Literature* (Oxford: Oxford University Press, 1990), 182–3.

best writers, comedians, and producers as philosophers whose works are worthy of careful philosophical reflection. In this regard, permit me to join philosopher Adeshina Afolayan in challenging Nigerian philosophers and the academic departments in which they operate to initiate conversations across the disciplinary boundaries in the university. As Afolayan notes, "The logic of insularity at work in academic practice in Nigeria ensures that there is a glaring absence of dialogues, conversations and linkages that ensures cross-fertilization of ideas, insights, perspectives and paradigms across disciplines. And interestingly enough, philosophy seems most suitably placed to initiate these interdisciplinary engagements."[16]

This neglect or insularity need not continue any longer. Nigerian writers have what it takes to assist philosophers in arriving at meaningful interpretations of the existential tensions in particular contexts in the Nigerian postcolony. Today, many novels and plays engage in specific discussions about the "situation" of the Nigerian postcolony—that is, a diagnosis of the socio-political-economic situation of the postcolonial period. German American philosopher and theologian Paul Tillich argued that the "situation cannot be neglected in [philosophy] without dangerous consequences. Only a courageous participation in the 'situation,' that is, in all the various cultural forms which express modern man's interpretation of his existence," can uncover the possibilities of freedom and human flourishing in any given historical period.[17] The urgent task before African philosophers today is to identify the "situations" begging for radical transformation in the name of justice and human flourishing for all, and, if necessary, to engage in emancipatory politics to liberate their country from the clutches of its rapacious, unpatriotic ruling class.

Mary Stella C. Okolo in her 2007 book *African Literature as Political Philosophy* examined how two famous African writers, Chinua Achebe and Ngugi wa Thiong'o, in their novels (Achebe's *Anthills of the Savannah* and Ngugi's *Petals of Blood*) portrayed the "situations" in postcolonial African begging for social transformation. She focuses on foregrounding African conditions in the stories told by Achebe and Ngugi. The main thrust of her argument is that these two preeminent writers considered politics as the most important part of the African conditions. She proceeded to construct a philosophical framework (more on this later) to enable her readers reflect on the nature of African politics portrayed in the two novels. She did this by hypothesizing the relationship "between literary expression and political ideology" or focusing on the political contents and contexts of the novel.[18]

---

[16]Adeshina Afolayan, *Philosophy and National Development in Nigeria: Toward a Tradition of Nigerian Philosophy* (London: Routledge, 2018), 155.
[17]Paul Tillich, *Systematic Theology*, Vol. 1 (Chicago: University of Chicago Press, 1951), 5.
[18]Clive Barnett, "Review of African Literature as Political Philosophy by M. S. C. Okolo," *African Affairs* 109, no. 436 (July 2010): 503–5; quotation, 505.

She used Achebe's novel to highlight what she called the "reformist" political perspective and Ngugi's novel to accent the "revolutionary" viewpoint in African literature.

She began her book by defining some criteria for determining the definitive features of political philosophy. In her model or framework, the proper character of political philosophy is anchored around (a) universal themes, (b) critical reflection on ideal standards for society, and (c) comprehensive worldview. She then proceeded to fit Achebe's *Anthills of the Savannah* or Ngugi's *Petals of Blood* to this single model (monologic philosophic design). The insights of these famous writers are then subjected to the higher truth of her model of political philosophy.[19] How well did she execute her stated task? Barry Riddell offered this evaluation of her book:

> [T]he text suffers from a "*déjà vu*" reading. These texts by Ngugi and Achebe will be quite familiar to most readers of this journal [*Review of African Political Economy*]; it is quite well known that they depicted both Africa's ills and their causes. Further, the philosophical framework presented by Okolo is elementary…. And, the reader asks: Where are the novel insights resulting from political philosophy? And so too, her Marxism adds little that has not already been stated or analysed by others. In fact, the originality of the issues raised was a basic concern—many have commented on these texts previously, and so the author's critique is especially thoughtful—but it is mostly a revisit, a synthetic essay which collates what others have indicated previously.[20]

So how does *Literature, Philosophy and the Nigeria World* compare with *African Literature as Political Philosophy*? First, Okolo's book focuses on Africa, but philosophically interpreting only two writers. This book engages five writers/artists in Nigeria. Second, my methodology avoids the imposition of a forced framework on the five writers that I studied. My approach is to generate an intense dialogical conversation between the five writers and some of the leading thinkers in postmodern philosophy and in the process excavate the philosophies embedded in their (writers') works. I let the novels, play, and the comedy skits to speak in their ownmost (disruptive) philosophical voices, and as a result they offer us their original insights into political philosophy. My analyses of the various works are not mere repeats, revisits of earlier arguments others have made. They arose from an originality of insights and sophisticated diverse political frameworks.

---

[19]By the use of a single model, she inadvertently presented the outmoded view of philosophy as a master discourse which claims the supremacy of judging all other disciplines.
[20]Barry Riddell, "Review of African Literature as Political Philosophy by M. S. C. Okolo," *Review of African Political Economy* 35, no. 118 (December 2008): 681–2; quotation, 682.

In lifting up or excavating the philosophical voices of the five writers, I was careful to avoid two common errors in works like this. I did not present the writers as merely "in conversation" with philosophy and nothing more. I also did not present them as intentionally engaging in philosophical reflections. They are presented as writers who are (hermeneutically) engaging with some of the serious issues of Nigeria and doing so in ways that are generative of philosophical ideas. I focused my analytical attention on dimensions of this generativity.[21]

Third, the book's chapters are not intended to be well-rounded and systematically staged monologic wholes. They are an ever-becoming, developing idea.[22] I tried as much as possible not to impose a single authoritative voice on them. The chapters are constituted as fundamentally polyphonic, dialogical, and unfinalizable. I have created them as characters independent of myself. They are points of view on the world. Together, they are polyphonically pluralistic; none coincides with itself, each a play on freedom and unfinalizability of a point of view, opinion on the world and self. None of the chapters should be construed as sacrificing its full and valid open-endedness, dialogical perchance for the sake of monologic philosophic design. Each is best viewed as participation in an ongoing dialogue in philosophy and postcolonial studies.

Fourth, Okolo's *African Literature as Political Philosophy* is a straightforward application of a tape (in this case, classical political philosophy) to measure the fittingness of the two novels of Achebe and Ngugi. But in this book, there is no such tape. The purpose here is to interpret a diverse set of Nigerian writers as political philosophers in their own right. The method is to use whatever sophisticated tools necessary to rigorously excavate the nature, depth, and logic of each writer's philosophical thought and to let it stand, shine, or shiver on its own merit or strength. None of the five writers is portrayed as a reflector of other thinkers' thoughts, but as a creative originator of philosophical ideas. To the extent that I take the mirrors of others' thoughts to their works, it is only to enable me who can only see in part or dimly to see more fully. The guiding principle in this exercise (a flawed one; yes, all interpretative methods are fragmentary, none can boast of a God's eye view) is to measure the "soul" of each writer's work by the twinned tape of the writer's thought and the existential predicament of the Nigerian postcolony. I will have no greater joy about my methods than to hear that my readers looked upon my interpretations with ecstatic contentment and scholarly rigor.

---

[21]Philip S. Thomas, *In a Vision of the Night: Job, Cormac McCarthy, and the Challenge of Chaos* (Waco, TX: Baylor University Press, 2021), 6. This way of expressing my thoughts in this paragraph is indebted to Thomas.
[22]Mikhail Bakhtin, *Problems of Dostoevsky's Poetics* (Minneapolis: University of Minnesota Press, 1984), xxxiv.

Finally, Okolo's book is about how Achebe and Ngugi explored Africa's contemporary political situation. She examined or described how each of them did the exploration but did not attempt to excavate or make explicit their philosophical theories or craft any original theories at the provocations of their thoughts. *Social Ethics and Governance in Contemporary African Writing* crafts such theories with its ensemble of writers. Yet it avoids constructing an overarching thesis that corrals all five writers into the iron pen of the academic ranch of icy systemization.

A Framework for Philosophical Analysis of Nigerian Literature

I stated earlier that this book does not offer a theory or an overarching argument about Nigerian literature. So, you might ask, What holds the various chapters together as an integrated book? There are six commonalities or threads that run through the book. Together, they provide a hexagramatic framework for philosophical analysis of novels, plays, stories, and comedy. The six-sided framework is storied (in the triple senses of the term[23]): (a) it speaks to the beginnings, middles, and possible ends of the processual predicament of the Nigerian postcolony; (b) it has layers of meanings and insights; and (c) it celebrates or reckons the philosophies at work in the novels (play and comedy skit) that are grasping at the meaning and "unmeaning" of a possible central character of Nigeria's self-defining myth.[24] The six commonalities constitute what I will call a philosophizing assemblage, which disciplines my interpretations into a social-ethical vision for (or conceptualization of) human flourishing in Nigeria's precarious postcolonial social formation.

First, each chapter offers a perspective on the Nigerian situation, and together they constitute an enriched study of the Nigerian postcolony. Second, every chapter demonstrates how to do philosophical analysis of Nigerian literature using what I will call the method of *polarity*. Each chapter has a polar character rather than a hierarchical structure of philosophy and literature. I have tried to hold the opposing polarity of literature and

---

[23]These are (a) narrative of beginnings and ends; (b) heights and depths. Example: a building with floors, (c) a person, institution, or period is celebrated or reckoned as having an interesting, illustrious feature. Example: storied past, institution. I added the last one to Green's dual senses. Chris E. W. Green, *All Things Beautiful: An Aesthetic Christology* (Waco, TX: Baylor University Press, 2021), 3.

[24]The term myth is used here in a special sense. "Myths are a means by which [a people] make sense of [their] shared history, working out [their] contradicting beliefs and incompatible convictions." Green, *All Things Beautiful*, 49.

philosophy in dynamic tension. I do not subordinate or reconcile the insights or "truths" of either literature or philosophy to some higher truth. At the same time, I do not give priority to one pole over the other. If either of the two poles is lost or ignored in my analysis, then the entire analysis falls apart. There is no two-truth theory that guides my reading of any of the works. I do not say, for instance, certain truths or views expressed in a novel are only preliminary or have restricted validity, which can be corrected by philosophy or some higher and ultimate truth. There is no hierarchical structure of account of truth or insights in my analysis.[25]

Third, as I stated above, each chapter carries forward the story of Nigeria from the initial traditional extended family's quest for Western education for its youths to the identity crisis that those same youths developed as they morphed into a hybridity of Africa-West, and to the life of meaninglessness and hopelessness that many of them now endure. I close the circle of the story by pointing Nigerian youths to resources they can retrieve from the nation's political history to address the crisis and trauma of governance in the nation. The book ends with a chapter that demonstrates how, in general, good literature conscientizes readers toward social justice and emancipatory politics.

Fourth, in this book I provide philosophical pictures of the novels (play and comedy). These pictures are not photographs of the authorial philosophical intents of the novels. They are also not idealized paintings that project any form of congruence between an ideal philosophical model and the "profound" philosophical minds of the writers. The philosophical picture of each novel that I provide is an "expressionist portrait." I have tried to enter into the deepest meanings of each novel, to profoundly "participate" in its reality, in its "inner life" to mine the deepest philosophical meanings embedded in its core. In every chapter, I will try to take the reader beyond the surface traits of a novel or an idealized version of them (the traits) according to a philosophical model, allowing the reader to experience the "being" of the novel through a personal participation in its deepest meanings.[26]

At the end the portrait that I paint of each novel, using the expressionistic style, carries the force of realism, impressionism, and expressionism. Realism: because the certitude of my interpretations of each novel are rooted in the inner reality or the narrative happenings in it—and not on mere abstract intellectual musings that do not reflect or do distort the narrative *reality*

---

[25]Paul Tillich made famous the method of polarity in his theology. I am deliberately extending this method outside the purview of his scholarship for its usefulness. See Tillich, *Systematic Theology*, Vol. 1, 169–99. See also John Thatamanil, *The Immanent Divine, God, Creation, and the Human Predicament: East–West Conversation* (Minneapolis, MN: Fortress, 2006), 103–5.

[26]Paul Tillich, *Systematic Theology, Vol. 2: Existence and Christ* (Chicago: University of Chicago Press, 1956), 115–16.

of the novel. There is enough force in the interpretation to leave the reader with an *impression* of rigorous philosophy in the novel. Lastly, there is a powerful witness to the narrative reality and philosophical impression in the portraits to impact the reader with the sense that an encounter with each of the portraits is an *expression* of a call to social justice or social transformation of the Nigerian postcolony.[27] The power of this call is a weak one; it is not a brute force. It summons or calls Nigerians to their greatness, to the promise ahead of today, and to their forgotten paths to national flourishing through the force of characterization, dialogue, action, and consequent reader's introspection. Each of the chosen novels (play and comedy) is an exemplar of soft power. As the philosopher John D. Caputo puts it:

> The weak force of a call is something we can (*posse*) or have the power to ignore—at our peril, perhaps, but just so. The call comes packing only a vocative power—not power pure and simple, but the powerless power of a provocation or a summon, a soliciting, seductive power—but it does not have an army to lend it support, and nothing stops us from turning a deaf ear to it. It lacks the sheer brawn to coerce or to translate what it calls for into fact. It must make do with the power of powerlessness, not the power of pure strength.[28]

The five novels, play, and comedy demonstrate the weak force that can conquer oppositions to human flourishing or can summon citizens to social transformation of their communities. This is the beauty of literature's power.

Before proceeding to the fifth dimension of my philosophizing assemblage for the analysis of Nigerian literature, it is germane for me to cast more light on the word, "mine." Two paragraphs above and earlier in this introductory chapter I have used the word to describe the extraction, excavation of the deepest philosophical meanings embedded in the chosen works. When I said I was mining novels I was not by any means positing that the ethical messages of the books were extricable from the interpretative stories themselves, from their narrative forms. Mine as a figure of speech is deployed here to point readers to the various ways the novels illustrate how Nigerians are living and how they can live well together, how they can live flourishing lives. The ethical or philosophical meanings I have analyzed in the following chapters to inform living and living well were abstracted from the novels with the understanding that the artistic qualities of the

---

[27]Terry Cross, "Tillich's Picture of Jesus as the Christ: Toward a Theology of the Spirit's Saving Presence," in *Paul Tillich and Pentecostal Theology: Spiritual Presence and Spiritual Power*, ed. Nimi Wariboko and Amos Yong (Bloomington, ID: Indiana University Press, 2015), 71–83.
[28]John D. Caputo, *The Weakness of God: A Theology of the Event* (Bloomington, IN: Indiana University Press, 2006), 13.

novels are more than the abstracted meanings.[29] In selecting, packaging, and presenting the philosophical meanings to my readers, I simultaneously paid special attention to the form of artistic creation (that is, the medium) and the contents (messages) of each novel.

In sum, the word mine (or excavate, for that matter) in the context of this book means I immersed myself in the narrative worlds of the novels, carefully journeyed through their structures of thoughts, and inhabited their inner lives long enough to receive certain gifts that I brought back to the everyday world of Nigerians that can inform how they can live flourishing lives. The gifts were not preexistent, waiting to be discovered by the reader. This is all the more so since none of the authors set out to illumine the consequences of a philosophical position in their novels. Besides, theirs are not cheap, didactic evangelizing novels. Thus, the gifts I have lifted are results of a retroactive process. Mining is a result of itself, its own becoming, its own product. The gifts the mining is finding are produced (put in place) by the very movement of this finding. Mining is fully performative; the movements and activities of mining create what they are mining. Simply put, my mining creates its own actualization.[30] Out of the gritty gumption of mining, the gifts rise up graciously and fragrantly.

Fifth, while there is no theory of Nigerian literature in the book, a power nonetheless emerges from it as the integrative spine of the corpus of literature-philosophy in Nigeria. This power has an "in spite of" character. This form of power affirms the manifestation of the "spirit" of philosophy grasping the narrative of each novel in spite of itself and driving it ecstatically beyond itself (into the fourth space) to actualize its existential philosophical "self" without destroying its essential literary "self."[31] Essential self represents the created nature of a work of arts—that is, what the writer meant it to be. The existential self refers to a novel as it "stands out" of its essential self, its created goodness to claim, grasp, or reach for its ambiguous philosophical nature.[32] The writer creates the essential self, and the philosopher discerns the existential self. A split always exists between the two selves of a novel. Addressing the split between the essence and existence is, in my opinion, the primary focus of philosophical analysis of literature. It has been my humble task in this book to remove any estrangement between the essential and existential selves of four Nigerian authors and one comedian.

---

[29]Thomas, *In a Vision of the Night*, 149–50.

[30]Slavoj Žižek, *The Parallax View* (Cambridge, MA: MIT Press, 2006), 46.

[31]By "spirit" of philosophy I mean the meaning-bearing power of concepts, patterns of thought, and fundamental truths about reality, self, self-world correlation, and self-other correlation. I borrowed "meaning-bearing power" from Paul Tillich, *Systematic Theology, Volume 3: Life and the Spirit, History and the Kingdom of God* (Chicago: University of Chicago Press, 1965), 115.

[32]This way of expressing my thoughts was inspired by Thatamanil, *Immanent Divine*, 114.

Finally, the last side of my hexagramatic framework is what for lack of a better word I would call *akwaletics* (akwa is a Kalabari, Niger Delta word for drum and it is pronounced "aqua"). Akwaletics is the art of connecting a novel (play, comedy, literary art) with the realities and prospects of human flourishing, moving from the insights of philosophical interpretations of the text (exegesis) to their application to ongoing social life in a community. Akwaletics not only roots my analyses in this book, but also sums up and ultimately organizes the depth meanings of the other five parts of the framework of which it is a part.

Awkaletics grew out of my understanding of how Kalabari people perform the interpretation of drum languages.[33] Drums and harps are particularly useful instruments of communication. Prominent individuals in Kalabari society have drum names, which are used to greet them, call them to an official function, or pass cryptic messages to them. Drums not only make men dance but also men "converse" with them. Immeasurable distances are conveyed by indicating at what point a person loses aural contact with the talking drum of his village—a distance of two to three miles. Tonye Erekosima et al. captured the importance of the Kalabari drum as a supplement to the human voice as thus:

> In peace-time, it could be used to inform members of the House group [a political and economic unit] or the city-state, not only of the imminence of an assembly, but also of the agenda of such an assembly. Again, it could be used to inform those concerned of some key event such as death. Both in naval warfare and in landings on enemy territory, it was the vital means whereby different units operating in different sectors of the battlefield were able to coordinate their actions.[34]

Learning to understand drum languages is not an easy undertaking; it requires long training and tutoring. Drum language consists essentially of "tone patterns extracted from speech" and its interpretation and understanding demand the acquisition of the "community's myth and history" and fluency in the ordinary Kalabari language and old Ijaw language. Most important, drum names "take the form of proverb or metaphor, learning them plunges one deep into traditional attitudes and imagery."[35] Interpretation of drum languages is a matter of technique: the person must

---

[33]Nimi Wariboko, "Senses and Legal expression in Kalabari Culture," in *The Foundations of Nigeria: Essays in Honor of Toyin Falola*, ed. Adebayo Oyebade (Trenton, NJ: African World Press, 2003), 305–31.

[34]Tonye V. Erekosima, W. H. Kio Lawson, and Obeleye Macjaja, *Hundred Years of Buguma History in Kalabari Culture* (Lagos: Sibon Books Limited, 1991), 120.

[35]Robin Horton, "Igbo: An Ordeal for the Aristocrats," *Nigeria Magazine* (September 1966): 168–83.

combine the competence in old and new Kalabari languages, exegesis of a drum's cryptic messages, the craft of responding to them appropriately, and often the skill of a dancer (that is, the dexterity of navigating ritual, physical, political, or intellectual spaces).

In 1879, a prominent Kalabari chief, Igbanibo Braide, had an irreconcilable disagreement with the Kalabari state. For this, the community decided to execute him. The chiefs that planned the execution swore to an oath of secrecy. Among these chiefs was an in-law of Braide. Kalabari custom taught that an in-law should not "spill the blood" of another in-law. Braide's in-law was therefore in a serious dilemma. Tradition forbade him from killing his in-law, while the oath of secrecy, which carried a penalty of death, prevented him from revealing the sinister plan to Braide. In order to climb down from this horn of a dilemma, he stayed up late into the middle of the night, after ordinary souls had gone to bed, picked up *his obo* (harp), and called the drum name of Chief Igbanibo Braide. Then he passed on this cryptic message, *akwa kiri poko fiete*, meaning, "the drum now gives an unusual tone." Braide, who was steeped in Kalabari language, imagery, myths, and history, correctly interpreted the "unusual sound of the drum" to mean he was to be executed that night. He quickly fled the town to save his life.[36]

My reading of the novels, plays, and comedy skit is akwaletic on three counts. First, it is a product of my application of the earlier five parts of the overall framework. The second is textual, reading the novels (play, comedy) as prominent documents for understanding contemporary Nigeria. Finally, my analysis plunges the reader deep into the nature, ideology, and functioning of Nigeria, interpreting the unusual sounds of the postcolonial drum which are nothing but the Sirens songs that are leading the country to disaster.

In spite of the six common threads in the book, I have written each chapter to stand on its own, to be easily pulled as a standalone to be studied in the classroom along with the novel it analyzes. From my experience teaching the course, "Literature and Ethics," this is the best way students and professors use books on philosophical analysis of novels. I hope the way I have organized this book would be helpful to teachers in the class.

The Academic Roadside Mechanic and Tokunbo Knowledges

In doing any philosophical work like this one, there is always a choice to be made. There is a decision on the selection of appropriate philosophical interlocutors or paradigms of thought. In any open knowledge society,

---

[36]Erekosima et al., *Hundred Years*, 88.

scholars work with whatever philosophical or methodological approaches that best suit their skill sets or best execute the tasks before them. After these scholars have done their works, there are always critics who come around to say they did not pay homage to certain schools of thought or have even not used some local epistemologies or native interlocutors they would prefer to interrogate. For instance, Mary Okolo was criticized for not including enough Africans as her interlocutors. A reviewer stated that her philosophical framework is "largely 'western,' other than Gandhi—where are Africa's thinkers?"[37] Okolo's *African Literature as Philosophy* engaged many African interlocutors, but perhaps the reviewer did a head count of interlocutors and dismissively labeled the work as "largely western." What is the right balance of interlocutors from different regions of the world, between local and global? What is the difference between uncritical appropriation of the concatenation of foreign ideas, epistemologies, and methods, and the realization that borrowing insights or perspectives from foreign sources might advance indigenous, homegrown intellectual discourse on a research topic?[38]

Given this debate, I need to justify my use of continental philosophy in Chapters 1 and 2, relating to the analyses of *Under the Brown Rusted Roofs* and *Blackass*. Continental philosophy is a body of ideas and analytical techniques that some African scholars consider as potentially "antagonistic" to indigenous cultural and philosophical paradigms, and as such should be avoided in the interpretation of African novels. There is less of the language of continental philosophy in Chapters 3–6. I also need to state why I used a mixture of Nigerian and foreign scholars as my interlocutors in the analyses of local writers. I will respond in different but related ways. There are five reasons that satisfy the needs of justification and the hybrid collection of interlocutors.

First, the theoretical natures of the chapters are different because I am purposely illustrating that philosophical analysis of literary works could be done with different levels or styles of sophistication. I reasoned that a problem is best tackled with a tool best fit for it. The specific tool might not be suitable to another problem. In fact, a particular novel might demand multiple interpretative techniques to unconceal its "truths" or messages. Barrett's novel particularly invites a mixed bag of interpretative tools, indigenous and foreign. *Blackass* is set in Franz Kafka's terms. Barrett quotes Kafka all through the novel. Kafka is a font of continental philosophical ideas. *Blackass* is stylized as some Nigerian version of Kafka's

---

[37]Riddell, "Review of African Literature as Political Philosophy," 682.
[38]Olufemi Taiwo, *Africa Must be Modern: A Manifesto* (Bloomington: Indiana University Press, 2014).

Metamorphosis, though I will demonstrate in Chapter 2 that it goes beyond the issues in Kafka's novella. The author deliberately set the novel to invite non-localized—indeed, multi-regional—tools of interpretation. Do we ignore the tools of continental philosophy when we are philosophically engaging *Blackass*?

Second, my purpose in this book is not to celebrate continental philosophy but to use it to illuminate the situation or problem in Nigeria. Despite employing this supposedly all too exotic tool, the African sense and sensibility of *Under the Brown Rusted Roofs* and *Blackass* came through in my analyses. Deploying continental philosophy as an interpretative tool in these Nigerian novels has not made them to be what they are not. This book does not conceal the works' literary and existential senses. Indeed, *Social Ethics and Governance in Contemporary African Writing* might stimulate other scholars to explore the novels for their capacity to hold important (universal) philosophical ideas in their African/Africanized bosoms.

Third, while it is arguable that African scholars should restrict themselves to ideas only generated by fellow Africans and shun engagement with the cutting-edge ideas of their times wherever they might have emerged, the first two chapters of this book employ continental philosophy to explore (and excavate) the hidden gems of the novels, and also lifted up their universal usefulness. *Under the Brown Rusted Roofs* and *Blackass* are particular works about Nigeria, but, to the credit of their authors, they speak to universal themes. They contribute to the intellectual debates of our times. The two novels throw brilliant light on international discussions on subjectivity and the challenges pertaining to engagement, confusion, and ambivalence with modernity, which is not a synonym for Westernization. This book clarifies these contributions. The insights of *Social Ethics and Governance in Contemporary African Writing* do not obviate or conceal the two novels' local contributions or provenance, even as they lift veils for readers to understand Nigeria in a global context. My preoccupation has been to expand the relevance or compass of the two novels so that people can either read them for their Africanity or globality. Globality? There is no harm in aspiring to make Nigerian literature into world literature. Currently, Nigerian literature is a Janus between the shores of Africa and the limits of the earth.

Fourth, I do not believe that African scholars should avoid continental philosophy because its epistemes originated outside their continent. Despite its foreign origins, Africans have made contributions to it, by either bending it to suit their purpose or appropriating it for other limited purposes. In writing *Social Ethics and Governance in Contemporary African Writing*, I resisted restricting myself to using only Africans' generated ideas to engage African novels that are in themselves telling stories about how Africans are grappling with the forces of globalization, Westernization, imperialism, global capitalism, and extra-territorial forces. For instance, Marxism, which originated outside Africa, influenced the ideas and narratives of Ngugi's *Petals of Blood*, and any analysis of the novel cannot do away with the theory. African writers have always interrogated or appropriated ideas from other worlds, and it is too late to argue for only African ideas to critique African writing. Philosophical analyses of African literature will flourish if they do not have to struggle against the boundary-making violence of an Authoritative Voice (Overarching Ideal) holding the dreaded *koboko* (horse whip) over ideas, hybridity, or difference. I worked through *Social Ethics and Governance in Contemporary African Writing* by drawing ideas from multiple places and disciplines to tackle the intellectual tasks at hand. If I succeeded in illuminating the two novels' recondite philosophical structures, supple logics, and robust arguments (stories) through my creative combination of transdisciplinary tools from all over the world, then I have succeeded in the tasks I set out to achieve.

Finally, in engaging continental philosophy—alongside African philosophy and local sociology of literature and knowledge—to shed light on Adelakun's *Under the Brown Rusted Roofs* and Barrett's *Blackass*, I planned to analyze these writers as philosophers in their own rights, at their theoretically most engaging angles. In reaching for this goal, I might have missed some of their most important literary ingenuity and aesthetics, their manifest features as imaginative writers, and their narrative perceptiveness. But alas, I am not a literary analyst, only a poor philosopher trying to make sense of them in the philosophical registers I understand best. *Social Ethics and Governance in Contemporary African Writing* is a book on philosophy that uses novels as resources for rigorous thinking and social-ethical deliberations. It is not a work of literature or literary criticism per se. In divining what social ethical lessons we can draw from these novels, I have lifted up local epistemologies as well as knowledges from any and everywhere useful. Like a West African roadside auto-mechanic, I vernacularized, "vulcanized," or panel-beat the *imported* knowledges (*Tokunbo* vehicles of wisdom) to suit my limited purposes in this book.

The academic roadside mechanic functions by rejecting or transcending two easy options and settling for a complicated one. He never accepts that his thought is already enmeshed in Western stream of thought and as such there is nothing that he can do about it.[39] He does not advocate for the

---

[39]This sentence and the next as ways of expressing my thought coquette with Tibebu's mode of expression. See Teshale Tibebus, *Hegel and the Third World: The Making of Eurocentrism in World History* (Syracuse, NY: Syracuse University Press, 2011), xix.

indigenously "authentic," epistemically pure, tension-free African mode of knowledge. This is to say he rejects the Talibanization of epistemes. His preferred option is the "synthetic ideal," converging epistemic pathways.[40] The dynamics of the synthetic ideal do not lead to any hegemonic, monocentric space of knowledge, but to polycentric, *worldization* (not globalization) of knowledge spaces.

---

[40]See Nimi Wariboko, "Kalabari: A Study of Synthetic Ideal," *Nordic Journal of African Studies* 8, no. 1 (1999): 80–93.

1

Theoretical Hesitations: Ibadan Brown Roofs' Rusty Revival of Desires

"Baami, why am I not in school?"
"Do you want to go to school?" his father asked.
He thought about it briefly and shook his head.
"No," he replied.
"So why did you ask?"
He shrugged. "Nothing. I know some people go to school
but we don't."
"If you want to go to school, tell me."
"No," he shook his head once more. "I don't want to go to school."
...
"What about them?" his father asked again.
"The roofs are rusty.
"Yes."
"The houses are old."
"Won't they collapse one day?"
His father paused. He did the same. The father took
a long look at him.
"Arigbabuwo, those brown rusted roofs you are looking at, the
house under them are strong."

—ABIMBOLA ADUNNI ADELAKUN,
UNDER THE BROWN RUSTED ROOFS, 7–8

Introduction

Abimbola Adunni Adelakun's novel, *Under the Brown Rusted Roofs*, is about a lack of fullness and desire.[1] Adelakun takes the reader on a journey of desire, showing the persistence of desire over time, its return to itself unsatisfied, its circling back to where it started, only to arise all over again. The novel begins with Father asking son Arigbabuwo if he wants to go to school. Arigbabuwo disavows the desire for school, though he was the one that had originally questioned his father about not being in school—a question which had provoked Father to make the offer (7–8). The novel ends with Arigbabuwo, now a father himself, walking with his own son, Kazeem, who has earned a college degree at a Western school. Now, Arigbabuwo expresses the desire for a Western education he gave up as a child. He now believes such an education would accomplish the fullness of being (human flourishing) for Kazeem and his other children. When Kazeem asks Arigbabuwo the same question about the rusted roofs of Ibadan threatening to collapse, Arigbabuwo responds to his son with the same words his own father spoke to him: "My son, those brown rusted roofs, the houses under them are strong" (249). Many other aspects of Arigbabuwo and Kazeem's walk mimic the earlier walk Father and Arigbabuwo took so many years before.

What this cyclical journey of desire demonstrates is not that desire can be obtained in time if only we avow it and pursue it but that desire is permanently unfulfilled because of time. Desire cannot be fulfilled, can never coincide with itself. It is always morning yet on desire. More importantly, desire is not self-identical because of temporal delay. As philosopher Martin Hägglund explains it,

Without a temporal delay there would be no desire, since there would be no time to reach out toward or aspire to anything whatsoever. Even if I only desire myself, auto-affection presupposes that I do not coincide with myself—otherwise I could never affect or be affected by myself. The point is thus not that the fulfillment of desire is impossible to attain. Rather, what is at stake is to rethink fulfillment as essentially temporal. Even the most ideal fulfillment is necessarily inhabited by non-fulfillment—not because fulfillment is lacking but because the state of fulfillment is temporal and thus altered from within. Even at the moment one *is* fulfilled, the moment is ceasing to be and opens the experience to loss.[2]

---

[1]Abimbola Adunni Adelakun, *Under the Brown Rusted Roofs* (Ibadan: Kraft, 2011). Throughout this chapter and at times in the notes, I use parenthetical citations for Adelukan's quotations; I use footnotes for other references.
[2]Martin Hägglund, *Dying for Time: Proust, Woolf, Nabokov* (Cambridge, MA: Harvard University Press, 2012), 3–4.

What Adelakun shows in her *Under the Brown Rusted Roofs* is how desire essentially lives on through the struggles and passions for survival. Desire lives through reproduction (sex, language, economics, politics, education, and culture), subtly demonstrating how life is inspired by different kinds of desire. The novel conveys the movement of desire from one generation to another in both the *agboole* (extended family) and the life of an individual, Arigbabuwo. Life in the *agboole* (as expressed in the passion for survival and the desire for political power, children, and sex) is an "organizational device"[3] for structuring the pursuit of actualization of desire into a consistent narrative, the desire for what is perceived as modernity, Western civilization, or participation in the magic of the Nigerian postcolony. The story of the novel is about how this desire lived on in a temporal process of change, desire's process of becoming in the Alabeni *agboole*.

Education—or broadly speaking, modernity—is the synecdoche of all desires in this novel. Ancient Greek philosophers generally considered wisdom (prudence) to be the key or the master of all other virtues. Wisdom enables one to make good judgments and to put the other virtues in proper or balanced practice. Wisdom directs all the other virtues for the sake of *eudaimonia* (human flourishing). The wisdom of modernity (knowledge of its ways and secrets) is the virtue that directs all other virtues in the novel. More precisely, it is the virtue of the written word as the anchor of prudence that puts all other virtues into practice. But this Yoruba wisdom of the written word is engrafted in the text of books and texts of flesh, *akosikun* (something written into the body, on the tablets of the inside) and *akosile* (something written down verbally, written on tablets on the outside). Afusa said to her son, Sikiru, "My son, it is only *akosikun*, the one that is written inside me that I can read, I don't know how to read *akosile* like those of you who go to school. But as long as you to go to school, I have done so as well" (184).

---

[3] As a character in this novel, the *agboole* is an "organizational device," a *ficelle*. An organizational device is a character around which story hangs together, unifies different raw materials in one character. The *agboole* is the character that is supposed to make everything clear about all other characters. The *agboole* is Adelakun's *point de capiton*, the "quilting point," which organizes the heterogeneous fantasies, hopes, morals, and histories of the other characters into a consistent narrative. According to Frederic Jameson, "Don Quixote is not really a character at all, but rather an organization device that permits Cervantes to write his book, serving as a thread that holds a number of different types of anecdotes together in a single form. (Thus Hamlet's madness permitted Shakespeare to piece together several heterogenous plot sources, and Goethe's Faust is an excuse for the dramatization of many different moods.)" (Frederic Jameson, *The Ideologies of Theory* [London: Verso, 2008], 9). Henry James termed this kind of narrative character whose actual function is to represent within the diegetic space its own process of enunciation—the discursive structure of the work itself—a *ficelle*. (Maria Gostrey in *The Ambassadors*, for example, is a *ficelle*). See Slavoj Žižek, *For They Know Not What They Do: Enjoyment as a Political Factor* (London: Verso, 1991), 18.

Afusa is portrayed throughout the novel as the one that has abundant wisdom. Her prudence, wisdom directs her properly in all her actions. She knows how to live peacefully with her co-wives in the polygamous home, knows how to cook well, knows when to talk to her husband to get what she wants, and knows how to operate her business profitably to support her husband and children. Afusa is generous in helping others—even the size of the chunks of meat in her soup is large. And she knows how to sexually fulfill her husband (40–1). Above all, in her wisdom, she managed to send all her children (Jimoh, Kazeem, and Sikiru) to school and steer them away from distractions, such as juju music, or professions with low prospects of sustainable long-term financial support. Afusa is the font of and embodiment of traditional Yoruba wisdom, the arrowhead of virtues that leads the *agboole* in sending her children to the university. Her basis of *akosikun* transforms into the triumph of her sons' *akosile*; "it is the combination of other people's wisdom that does not make an elder talk like a madman" (39). She is a kind of "synthetic ideal," the composite that is the mark of extraordinary beauty, intellect, or excellence.[4] In Afusa, we see the embodiment of wisdom as the key or master of all the virtues. In her dwells the "fullness" of bodily wisdom.

The characterization of Afusa is the key to understanding how the quest for knowledge in the *agboole* works and to grasping the celebration of wisdom (indigenous and foreign) as the red thread that holds the novel together. For instance, we can understand that Baba n'sale (the oldest man in the *agboole* and Arigbabuwo's cousin) who always speaks in sexual tropes is working from cultural wisdom, speech patterns, and metaphors that are written inside of him. Sikira (Arigbabuwo's third wife), the rascally woman, is a foil to well-behaved co-wife Afusa. Sikira's protofeminist ideas of resistance against patriarchy complement Afusa's deployment of wisdom, economic independence, and orientation to Western education; the juxtaposition of the two demonstrates different ways women in the *agboole* seek their own empowerment and assert themselves. Adelakun's understanding and portrayal of the social world of wives in Yoruba-Muslim polygynous homes are superb and illuminating. She complexifies things in ways that resist and appropriate some feminist understandings of polygyny in African societies.

My philosophical engagement with this novel is not directed at revealing the "purpose" for which the author constructed it. Instead, I focus on its intrinsic structures, the technique that brought it into being, and its production as a work of art. These three foci become the raw materials for, the gateway into, and the drive of my philosophical reflections on the

---

[4]See Nimi Wariboko, "Kalabari: A Study of Synthetic Ideal," *Nordic Journal of African Studies* 8, no. 1 (1999): 80–93.

novel. Thus, I will not tell you what this novel is all about. I am not going to tell you about its hidden meaning, even though I could try to unlock it for you if I wished. There is something about its irreducible integrity as a work that cannot be unlocked, all the more so with its complex use of metaphors, proverbs, and Yoruba-English.[5] I focus on how forms interact with contents throughout the novel, forms of exposition of philosophical ideas, and the forming power of words. I use forms or narrative structures to interrogate the philosophical exposition of the dynamic of desire in the novel.

First, a word or two about the major structuring forms that undergird the nuanced contents of this discerning novel. Three forces (paradigms) in the novel carefully mesh to tell a good story. For lack of better terms, I call them structuralism, poststructuralism, and complex adaptive network. The structuralism is graspable from the definite structures and codes that guide social life in Ibadan or *agboole*. (The way the novel started and ended, these structures could be interpreted to represent the strong houses under the brown rusted roofs to portray the determinate forms in the city/extended family.) The roofs (ever-rusting, turning brown) stand for the deconstructive forces, the *protestant principle*, that represent changes, ongoing transformation in the culture.[6] The fear that houses under the brown rusted roofs will collapse one day symbolizes the concern that the swirling powers of change might one day engulf an entire life or city. Poststructuralists tend to focus on the "roofs" in their inclination to focus on disruptive forces.[7] The third way connects the two not as binary forces but as forces of relationality. Ibadan and the lives lived in it form a kind of complex adaptive network: a network of meanings, emergent self-organizing networks of relationships that are both stabilizing and destabilizing.

Life in Ibadan as revealed in the novel is an interplay of stabilizing and disruptive forces. The life in the city/*agboole* is a creative process that figures and disfigures social existences, hence shaping the experience and pattern of the world of its inhabitants as they, in turn, shape and reshape it. We see that Ibadan is not only rust and gold trapped between seven hills but also a running splash. There is structure/stability, but motion/disruptive forces

---

[5]For the study of the novel in this respect, see Toyin Falola, *In Praise of Greatness: The Poetics of African Adulation* (Durham, NC: Carolina Academic Press, 2019), 353–87 and Rasheed Ademola Adebiyi, "Communicating Indigenous Knowledge through Exogenous Channel: A Comparative Content Analysis of Adelakun's *Under the Brown Rusted Roofs* and Achebe's *Things Fall Apart*," *Journal of Culture, Society, and Development* 12 (2015): 1–12.

[6]For more on these ideas, see Nimi Wariboko, *Economics in Spirit and Truth: A Moral Philosophy of Finance* (New York: Palgrave Macmillan, 2014), 123–58 and Nimi Wariboko, *The Charismatic City and the Resurgence of Religion: A Pentecostal Social Ethics of Cosmopolitan Urban Life* (New York: Palgrave Macmillan, 2014), 203–5.

[7]See, for instance, the work of Mark C. Taylor, *Altarity* (Chicago: University of Chicago Press, 1987).

are captured in the metaphor of "running splash."[8] The scattered pieces of china are connected in a complex adaptive network fueled by some supreme energy (sun, relationality, or mutuality) that allows each one of them the space and time to breathe, *conspire* (breathe together), or cooperate on their own.

Let us return to the three paradigms: house/structuralism; roof/ poststructuralism; relationship between house and roof/event, complex adaptive network. The spiral narrative structure of the novel supports, highlights, and accents this evental nature of life in the *agboole*/city; it signifies the complex adaptive network of the triune forces Adelakun is deploying to tell her story. A fixed, singular, linear structure would have contradicted the deep structure or philosophical intent of her narrative. In all these, the reader comes to see polygyny (polygamy) as a *name* that harbors an *event* (a possibility that disrupts the fixed order of being).[9] Adelakun demonstrates that polygamy is both an entity and event—structuring, disruptive, and a complexly adaptative force in the *agboole*. Channeling the ideas of the American philosopher John Caputo, I see her novel, in a sense, as a hermeneutics of the *event* that is harbored in the *name* polygamy in Yoruba culture.[10]

Temporality and Desire under the Brown Roofs

As described above, as a young man, Arigbabuwo rejected Western education at the beginning of *Under the Brown Rusted Roofs*. But by the end of the novel, as he walked with his son, he clearly was in love with education. There are two ways to read this temporal delay. I could argue that when Arigbabuwo's father offered to send him to school and Arigbabuwo rejected the idea, he also stored it in some virtual coexistence or eternal substance

---

[8]These words came from the popular poem, "Ibadan," by the J. P. Clark quoted in *Under the Brown Rusted Roof* (5): "Ibadan— / Running splash of rust and gold / Flung and scattered among the seven hills / Like broken china in the sun."

[9]For a discussion of a name that is more than a linguistic object but a locus of event, see John D. Caputo, *The Weakness of God: A Theology of the Event* (Bloomington: Indiana University Press, 2006), 2–9. As Caputo explains, "Names contains events and give them a kind of temporary shelter by housing them within a relative stable nominal unity. Events, on the other hand, are uncontainable, and they make names restless with promise and the future, with memory and the past, with result that names contain what they cannot contain. Names belong to natural languages and are historically constituted or constructed, whereas events are a little unnatural, eerie, ghostly things that haunt names and see to it that they never rest in peace" (*Weakness of God*, 2).

[10]Caputo, *Weakness of God*, 2–7.

with all that is past but not lost or destroyed. The idea awaited being reborn like an *emere* (or *abiku*, a child who dies and only to be reborn by the same woman and dies again).[11] This is precisely what the novel rejects: desire or time cannot do anything by itself. Time or desire needs the spatial, material, and cultural support to persist—to remain and mutate. As Hägglund puts it,

> *Time is nothing in itself*; it is nothing but the negativity that is intrinsic to succession. It follows that time cannot be a virtual existence, since it does not have the power to *be* anything or *do* anything on its own. Indeed, time cannot be anything or do anything without a spatialization that constrains the power of the virtual in making it dependent on material conditions.[12]

The genius of Adelakun (who was an early-twenty-something-year-old when she wrote the novel) is displayed precisely in the beehive life of an *agboole* that gives substance and space to time and desire to live and prosper. The *agboole* enables the desire of the past to be both retained in the present and carried forward into the future. Desire is inscribed as a trace in the *agboole*, in the life of survival as it takes place in the *agboole*. Similarly,

> given that every temporal moment immediately ceases to be, it must be inscribed as a trace in order to be at all. The trace is necessarily spatial, since spatiality is characterized by the ability to remain in spite of temporal succession. The spatiality of the trace is thus the condition for the duration of time, since it enables the past to be retained for the future.[13]

Agbooles exist because they must resist the negativity of time while still subject to the succession of time segments.

The logical implication of time, desire, and *agboole* is the philosophical density of Adelakun's novel. The novel addresses the fundamental questions of life and philosophy and gives the reader clues from which to derive theory and insights in order to respond to the questions, especially as they relate to the connections between time, space, and desire. In all this, we must resist a teleological reading of the novel. It does not portray everything in the *agboole* as oriented toward the realization of the desire for (of) modernity or the final revelation or coming to fullness of the desire expressed in the prologue. Prologue is not epilogue. The sense or fear that the desire could be lost was always there. Neither Arigbabuwo himself nor his first wife,

---

[11]This is one way the traditional Yoruba society explains high infant mortality rate. People believe that it is the same dead child who keeps coming back through the same woman.

[12]Hägglund, *Dying for Time*, 15.

[13]Hägglund, *Dying for Time*, 15–16.

Motara, pursued Western education before Afusa came to the polygamous home. The fact that it could be lost but was not is only contingent. Afusa picked it up and sustained it because of her overarching desire for survival and human flourishing. The long-term desire we see in the novel is really just a series of short-term desires—repetition of an identical sensation to improve one's well-being, to initiate something new amid ongoing social processes as one engages life more abundantly. There is no deity or deus ex machina providentially directing the "word" in the beginning to become the "word" at the end. No automatic, inexorable movement exists between prologue (opening word) and epilogue (closing word). Only retrospectively can one see the contingencies of life transubstantiated into necessity.

Under the Brown Rusted Roofs has no plot leading slowly to its closing pages. Rather, the reader receives fragments, a disarticulation of plot and narratives that only underscores the author's philosophical point. Human beings live their lives in fragments and contingencies; only the retrospective gaze imposes a coherent meaning framework on the running splash of rust and gold, scattered among seven hills.[14] The plot of the novel follows through with Samuel Beckett's stubborn persistence: "I can't go on, I will go on."[15] The plot, like desire in the *agboole*, is induced by the possibilities for higher levels of flourishing or actualization to move ahead. And in this follow-through the plot is not an agent of changes in narration standing apart from the changes themselves. Both in the plot and the content changes, fragmentation or spiral narrative is at work through their co-unfolding.

Desire is repeated or sustained not because it is a timeless telos, but because it is a sign of life, an excess zeal for life, an attachment for mortal life (and not an attachment to bliss repose or immortal life in some eternal realm) that is the hallmark of the *agboole*. *Agboole* daily repeats, re-enacts its attachment to mortal life, a life that is marked by temporal finitude. Repetition is the sign of life and a source of the new in the *agboole*.

The emergence of the New, the proper Deleuzian paradox is that something truly New can ONLY emerge through repetition.... Recall the old example provided by Walter Benjamin: the October Revolution repeated the French Revolution, redeeming its failure, unearthing and repeating the same impulse. Already for Kierkegaard, repetition is "inverted memory," a movement forward, the production of the New, and not the reproduction of the Old. "There is nothing new under the

---

[14]Pardon the allusion to J. P. Clark, "Ibadan," in *Collected Poems: J. P. Clark-Bekederemo, 1958–1988* (Washington, DC: Howard University Press, 1991), 14.
[15]Quoted in Peter Hallward, *Badiou: A Subject to Truth* (Minneapolis: University of Minnesota Press, 2003), 265.

sun" is the strongest contrast to the movement of repetition. So, it is not only that repetition is (one of the modes of) emergence of the New—*the New can ONLY emerge through repetition*.[16]

Adelakun spatializes desire by describing it as a gap, a distention that is inscribed in the body of the *agboole*. The fibers of the unfulfillment of desire, the logics of incompletable desire, inhabit the body of the *agboole*. Desire is also temporalized since the place it occupies in the *agboole* is shown to be indwelled by birth and death, marked by traces of time. *Agboole* allows desire to extend its place in time. In fact, desire is shown to be indwelled by the negativity of time. This desire is not an external metaphysical force that imposes itself on the *agboole* or acts as the impersonal eros that moves the *agboole* and its world. Rather, desire is only embodied in people, their lives, and their movements—desire has its being in human beings. It is operative in their struggles for both survival and human flourishing. And it is always haunted by fear of loss insofar as both the *agboole* and desire are temporal phenomena. Besides, the human struggle for survival is everywhere marked by desire and fear. Hägglund states,

> If one removes the fear of what may happen to a temporal being (chronophobia) one removes the attachment to the same temporal being (chronophilia) since one no longer cares if what happens to it is vital or lethal, beneficial or devastating. Indeed, attachment to a temporal being means that every affirmation is inhabited by negation from the start and even the most active embrace of life cannot be immune from the reactive mourning of death.[17]

Under the Brown Rusted Roofs clearly articulates this condition of human existence and deftly situates the fundamental drama of desire in this interplay of chronophobia and chronophilia. The *agboole* is "perforated" by time, temporal finitude. This logic of incompleteness, of a split, is reflected in the novel's nonlinear narration. Fragments of plots or plots are juxtaposed to demonstrate that even life or desire does not obey "the chronology of *linear* time, this does not mean that it can be exempt from the *succession* of time."[18]

Thus, the 241 pages that separate desire as expressed in the prologue (7–8) and the end of the novel (249) display the bonds of libidinal and temporal life—exigencies of survival, the shiva-dance of chronophobia and

---

[16]Slavoj Žižek, *Organs without Bodies: On Deleuze and Consequences* (New York: Routledge, 2012), 12.

[17]Hägglund, *Dying for Time*, 111.

[18]Hägglund, *Dying for Time*, 113.

chronophilia—that contextualize, engender, transform, and sustain desire. Put differently, Adelakun takes the reader into the nature of the struggles and ethos of individual families that undergirds the now legendary Yoruba quest for Western education. What the outside world celebrates as legendary is produced through the sweat and tears of ordinary families doing their best to survive, cohere, and move forward in time. The Yoruba family or *agboole* does not automatically predispose people to preserve or destroy the desire for modernity, Western education. The *agboole* is a condition for every positive and every negative response to the quest. The *agboole* is necessary but not sufficient for educational success. Individuals—and in this case, women like Afusa—must work out their temporal and spatial paths to the acquisition of Western-styled education. And they must do so within an institution bound by temporal finitude. An *agboole* is never indifferent to its survival as a temporal entity. The fundamental drama of the *agboole* is about continuity of life—survival—and is the condition for the desire of education, Fuji music, thuggery, and party politics. In *Under the Brown Rusted Roofs*, we see various dramas of desire as they are conceived, staged, and eventually live or die in the *agboole*. The *agboole* provides the spatial, temporal, and material support for desire to be born, remain, thrive, or die. The *agboole* is life. Desires are born amid, and transpire, as energies in the life of the *agboole*. In the novel, the desires for (of) life—supremely metonymized as quest for modernity, but never exhausting it—are situated in the complexities of the temporal experience of the *agboole*.

The pursuit of (for the actualization of) desire is always bound by the fear of actual or prospective loss. Jimoh (Afusa's first son) was taken away from the family by a rogue soldier's bullets three months to his graduation from university, "'Why did they have to do this to me? A child that will finish school in three months' time? A child we have already believed will take care of us…' Alhaji [Arigbabuwo] stopped so that he would not betray his manliness by shedding tears in everybody's presence" (190). Rafiu (Arigbabuwo's first son) wanted and rejected his desire, his wife, Mulika, the woman with "one and half legs" (98). Once, he brutally beat Mulika to unconsciousness and everyone was very concerned she would die, but she eventually regained consciousness (113–14). Sikira (one of Alhaji Arigbabuwo's wives) wanted a new husband, so she divorced him but came back after many years as *alalobo*, the one who keeps going and coming back.

Understanding the fear of the loss of what members of the *agboole* care for is a key to understanding how desires and life in the *agboole* work. The possibility that cherished family members could be lost because they are beings bound by temporal finitude explains why members of the *agboole* care about their desires and are not indifferent to the survival of the *agboole*. It is because whatever they are "bound to or aspire for… can be lost that

[they] care about it, that [they] care about what happens."[19] The key point here is that desire in the *agboole* is wrapped up with investment in survival and is not a wish for transcendental object beyond history. Desire is desire for survival (human flourishing) in the immanent earthly realm.

Agboole and Care for Road-Bound Knowledge

Under the Brown Rusted Roofs is an earthy book. Its language is homely, the characters seem almost as "real," flesh and blood, as your next-door neighbor, and its sociology is marked by gravity and solidity. Nothing about it is ungrounded, ghostly, or belong to philosophical bestiary. No abstract, rarified thought. No utopia. Adelakun uses this earthy style of narration to characteristically ground the desire for knowledge. Every quest for knowledge generally presupposes a sociology. From page 10 to page 249, her novel offers an explicit analysis of the sociology of the *agboole*, the relationship of its members to their "reasons, motives, intentions, and actions, and in so doing," according to Alistair McIntyre, demonstrates that moral concepts not only are embodied, but also claim that individual conceptions, grasping, gripping, or formulation of desire is solidly set in a "vision of collective ethical substance," as Frederic Jameson calls it.[20] This novel could rightly be viewed as a work in moral philosophy, explicating the social basis of Yoruba ethos, the materialist foundation of ethos, and moral imagination that is moored to the inner rhythm and relationality, preservation and progress of the well-being of the *agboole*. These are the theoretical hints and hesitations of the *agboole*'s brown rusted roofs, whose eaves revive desires across generations. *Agboole* is the ground from which desire for Western education stands out and stands in.

What then does it mean for the novel to begin and end on the road outside the *agboole*? What does it mean that the structural hints of the persistence and flowering of desire for Western education across three generations are anchored by the road? What does it mean for desire to come full circle on the road? And for the repetition of father's saying about the strength of the houses under the rusted roofs to appear and reappear on the road? A couple of answers come to mind.

First, the desire for Western education signifies (or will come to signify) some distance from the (traditional, existing) values of the *agboole*. The road represents the vantage point beyond the values of the *agboole* and thus

---

[19]Hägglund, *Dying for Time*, 14.
[20]Quotations are from Alasdair MacIntyre, *After Virtue: A Study in Moral Theology*, 2nd ed. (Notre Dame, IN: University of Notre Dame Press, 1984), 23 and Frederic Jameson, *The Ideologies of Theory* (London: Verso, 2008), 189, respectively.

permits the potential "transvaluation" of all values. The path the father and son take is capable of destroying all the existent values of the *agboole*. What they seek will turn out to be a clash of their will-to-power with the forces outside in the struggles to keep the ethical substance of the *agboole*.

All this reminds me of the symbolic role of the road in Nobel laureate Wole Soyinka's play, *The Road*.[21] The road in Soyinka's work is predatory; it is a metaphor for Ogun, who waits when famished to take human or animal lives for food. But the road in Adelakun's novel is not predatory; rather, it is a place for casting vision, for moving into higher dimensions of human flourishing. Now, I can almost hear some scholars objecting that Adelakun is ultimately riffing on the mythology of Ogun, the "Lord of the road" and quintessential explorer who leads people to the essence of wisdom, to press toward creativity?[22] While this is a plausible way of locating the signification of road in her novel, her philosophizing of road is different from that of Soyinka, at least when one compares her novel with his play.

Adelakun's and Soyinka's conceptions of the road are ultimately different because of their different ontologies. The ontology operative in Soyinka's *The Road* is about the fundamental structures of being that are independent of the historically conditioned political and social organizations of life. This is in keeping with his vast knowledge of the "deep structures" of Yoruba worldview (ontology). Adelakun cannot match the muse of Nigerian literature in this respect but she admirably makes up for this "lack" with a bodily ontology that undergirds the *agboole*. Her work shows how bodies weigh against one another in the *agboole*, their "precariousness, vulnerability, injurability, interdependency, exposure, bodily persistence, desire, work and the claim of language and social belonging," as feminist philosopher Judith Butler would say.[23] Adelakun's social ontology of bodies is primarily about the *ex-position* of self to other selves and not some framework of premodern organic harmony, unity, or essence. French philosopher Jean-Luc Nancy argues in his book *Inoperative Community*, a community entails the exposition, the presence of each self to all. The presence of self to self precludes thinking of the community as an essence or effectuating its own essence as something beyond the exposition of self to self. A community is an exposition: the coappearing of finite selves and ensembles of selves, and each self is exposed to an outside. This outside is only an outside of another ensemble of selves. The "being" of community is the exposure, exposition of selves, which "are themselves constituted by sharing, they are distributed

---

[21]Wole Soyinka, *The Road in Collected Plays* (London: Oxford University Press, 1973).

[22]Wole Soyinka, *Myth, Literature, and the African World* (Cambridge: Cambridge University Press, 1976); Jeanne Dingome, "Soyinka's The Road as Ritual," *Kunapipi* 2, no. 1 (1980): 30–41; and William S. Haney II, "Soyinka's Ritual Drama: Unity, Postmodernism, and the Mistake of Intellect," *Research in African Literatures* 21, no. 4 (1990): 33–54.

[23]Judith Butler, *Frames of War: When Is Life Grievable?* (London: Verso, 2016), 2.

and placed, or rather *spaced*, by the sharing that makes them *others*: other for one another," and "whose relationship—the sharing itself—is not a communion."[24]

Nancy argues that there is no common substance that characterizes a community. Members of community only share of themselves, share in their exposure to each other. Each member is an other to others because of the sharing; each singular being shares in the sharing of others. This sharing constitutes the community and the members as singularities and resists their fusion into one subject or communion. "Community is the community of *others*, which does not mean that several individuals possess some common nature in spite of their difference, but rather that they partake only in their otherness.... They are together, but togetherness is otherness."[25]

This is the nature of bodily ontology that Adelakun crafts in her novel. And as Butler argues:

> To refer to "ontology" in this regard is not to lay claim to a description of fundamental structures of being that are distinct from any and all social and political organization. On the contrary, none of these terms exist outside of their political organization and interpretation. The "being" of the body to which this ontology refers is one that is always given over to others, to norms, to social and political organizations.... It is not possible first to define the ontology of the body and then to refer to the social organizations the body assumes. Rather, to be a body is to be exposed to social crafting and form, and that is what makes the ontology of body a social ontology. In other words, the body is exposed to socially and politically articulated forces as well as to claims of sociality—including language, work, and desire—that makes possible the body's persisting and flourishing.[26]

Adelakun thus offers a certain dislocation of Soyinka's philosophy necessary for the reinterpretation of the road. The road is not driven by the horrors of existence or blood sacrifice; it is not always a crossroad of undecidability, or an opening to another realm or the "Fourth Stage" or the "abyss of transition,"[27] but a path, canal to *natality*. Desire is linked with movement, with reaching out to that which completes the self. For Adelakun, this movement is tied to natality, a new beginning. Natality is about birth and

---

[24]Jean-Luc Nancy, *The Inoperative Community*, trans. Peter Connor, Lisa Garbus, Michael Holland, and Simona Sawhney, foreword Christopher Fynsk (Minneapolis: University of Minnesota Press, 1991), 25.

[25]Jean-Luc Nancy, *Birth to Presence*, trans. Brian Holmes et al. (Stanford: Stanford University Press, 1993), 155.

[26]Butler, *Frames of War*, 2–3.

[27]Soyinka, *Myth, Literature, and the African World*, 140–60.

rebirth, the originality of each new human being entering into ongoing social processes. Insofar as each human being entered into this world in utter originality and uniqueness—as a new beginning—he or she has the capacity to act and to start something new, to enact new beginnings. To exercise the capacity to begin is, according to Hannah Arendt,

> the miracle that saves the world, the realm of human affairs from the normal, "natural" ruin is ultimately the fact of natality.... It is in other words, the birth of new men and the new beginning, the action they are capable of by virtue of being born [and born again]. Only the full experience of this capacity can bestow upon human affairs faith and hope, those two essential characteristics of human existence which Greek antiquity ignored altogether, discounting the keeping of faith as a very uncommon and not too important virtue and counting hope among the evils of illusion in Pandora's box. It is this faith in and hope for the world that found perhaps its most glorious and most succinct expression in few words with which the Gospels announced the "glad tidings": "A child has been born unto us."[28]

I earlier stated that desire is the center of the entire symbolic order of the *agboole*—or should I say the novel, even though it is not frontally (didactically) engaged? The symbolic device that enables me to note this about the novel is natality. Desire is symbolically linked with father and son, with the *agboole*'s mastery of new birth, the capacity to begin. A question arises at this point: How much longer will the *agboole* continue to play the role of master of its destiny? Will its care for road-bound knowledge result in a loss of its culture—at least, some important aspects of it?

Agboole as a Vanishing Mediator

The sociological solidity of the *agboole* acts as a bulwark for family members as they negotiate their everyday existence and engagement with modernity (here, represented by the Western educational system, court system, and recent urbanism in the new Ibadan). But this appearance of a bulwark is deceptive, an illusion. The *agboole* seen from a position of parallax view is a "vanishing mediator." Vanishing mediator is a lifestyle, a concept that negotiates and settles the transition between the traditional and modern— two opposing lifestyles or concepts—and eventually disappears.[29]

---

[28]Hannah Arendt, *The Human Condition* (Chicago: University of Chicago Press, 1958), 247.
[29]For both terms see Slavoj Žižek, *The Parallax View* (Cambridge, MA: MIT Press, 2006).

The extant *agboole* that Adelakun describes in its splendor and power is, indeed, a vanishing mediator. Its form lags behind its content. The content of *agboole* is changing: Afusa is pressing for education; Ramoni (one of Alhaji Arigbabuwo's sons) is singing to his banana (penis) about eating "bearded snail" (vagina) to the disgust of his father, Alhaji Arigbabuwo, and the other elders in the *agboole* (215–16); Rafiu is a thug for one of the most corrupt and violent politicians in Ibadan; some of the children of the *agboole* are involved in *alufansa* (dirty talk about genitalia in front of their parents, 216[30]); and the children of the *agboole* are looking for a new way of life outside the traditional career paths, outside the context and parameters of the ethos of the age-old *agboole*. The logic of the changing content will work its ways until it bursts the form of the *agboole*, breaks its husk to reveal a new form in place of the old. Adelakun's placement of the inauguration and revival of a desire for Western education (and the comment about the strong houses under rusted roofs) both times on the road outside the *agboole* calls for this interpretation of the Alabeni *agboole* as a vanishing mediator.

In my opinion, the placement tells us that the appetite or longing for Western education was changing the content of the *agboole* within the form of the *agboole* itself. And by the second father-son walk on the road, the logic of the changing content has worked its way out to the form and is throwing the form off. Listen to Arigbabuwo's praise song (*oriki*, so to speak) for education and you get the sense that the new has come into the *agboole* and it cannot continue as before. Things will soon fall apart—soon the falcon might not hear the falconer. The paean for education probably started forming in his "insides" the day he went to the court to press his divorce against Sikira, his third wife. He saw how a young man "turned around the judgement of three old men because he was more educated" (248).

> My son, that day I swore that if I have to sell my father's grave to make sure my sons finish their schooling, I would…. Congratulations. You're a lawyer? *Alihamdulilahi*! The work you will do with your certificate will be that of abundance. The world will collect it from you and favour you because of it. Your brother too will finish in peace. Those of them that come after you will do well also.
>
> (248)

---

[30]Much of adult talk involves *alufansa*, but when Idaya, a small girl, openly decoded the meaning of "bearded snail" as vagina when the members of the *agboole* were gathered to listen to Ramoni's first juju music album, they were shocked. The reaction of the elders to Idaya's decoding of "bearded snail" means the use of sexual and bodily tropes is somewhat marked by age differences. For young boys and girls to cross this line and begin to talk about "the matter of penis and vagina in," the manner Idaya did before her elders is something they took to be an upturning of their world, including the end of music (216).

Yes, the brown rusted roofs may not collapse into the dust as Alhaji Arigbabuwo stated (249), but they are certainly not the same corrugated iron sheets year in year out. The color of the roofs is also changing as modern architecture dominates the skyline. Ibadan city's roofs are constantly falling off and being replaced. Lest we forget, the *agboole* as a socio-ontological entity is not a transhistorical way of being.

The passage of desire, the transfer of the intergenerational relay baton for modernity, from the first father to son Arigbabuwo and its transit from Arigbabuwo to Kazeem is not the same. It appears to me that young Arigbabuwo's rejection of his father's offer of education indicates the preservation of form, strengthening the cultural form of the *agboole* by not disturbing or disrupting its contents, by not tampering with its ethical substance or way of being. Arigbabuwo grew up to be a sturdy support of the way of life of the *agboole*. The second father-son walk is different in two respects.

First, the talk (or *oriki*) about education happened in the evening before the final father-son (Arigbabuwo–Kazeem) walk the next morning, as Arigbabuwo met his son on the way to the *agboole* (247). Perhaps, this is to indicate that the pursuit of education is a settled matter—already baked into the ethos of the *agboole*. But questions remain about Ibadan's rusted brown roofs, and both fathers must reassure themselves and their sons that all is well. The brown rusted roofs are still a matter for ideological justification.

Let not the reassurance by Arigbabuwo deceive anyone to believe that the rusted roofs and the houses under them have not changed between when Arigbabuwo was a child and the coming of age of his son, Kazeem. To believe this is to repeat a common mistake Western anthropologists make in their interpretations of what African elders say to them about African traditions, practices, and institutions. When anthropologists asked them why they do the things they did, the stock answer is "that is the way our forefathers had it," suggesting that the preferences, practices, artifacts, and institutions are all ancient. But any discerning scholar can see that Africans today are not doing exactly what their parents did. Africans have a culture that is always in the frame of core-periphery. The core is what their fathers and mothers did in response to the challenges they faced; when those responses produced positive outcomes, the next generation retained that knowledge. Only that which has proved valuable to the environment is retained and carried forward. If someone learned a lesson in 1921 and they are dealing with the same environment or issue in 2021, they will apply what was valuable in 1921 to the 2021 situation to see if it continues to be valid. However, the ingenuity of the African order is that alongside the transfer (the core) is the periphery of the individuals identifying and making decisions; how much of this 1921 element is pertinent to our solution? This is how Africans have been flexible enough to survive in a wide variety of environments. They bring to a given situation only those things to the present situation that have proven valuable in the past. When they check out their heritage solutions vis-à-vis their present situation, they discard those that are not pertinent and start looking for what they perceive, through their own intelligence, is applicable to the current situation. At any given moment, they may tell you what the fathers or mothers did—doing so lends legitimacy to the current decision. It does not in any way interfere with them also making their own decisions in how best to address the moment.

Second, Arigbabuwo and Kazeem's walk is purely a formal act, the *agboole* is assuming a new form, becoming an instantiation of modernity, a cultural tool for the appropriation of Western civilization—a sociological order for *reactualizing* Western civilization in Africa. The *agboole* is making "actual" some possibilities of the Western way of life in distinction to the way it is mostly or currently realized in Nigeria.[31] In its own way, the *agboole* is bringing along what has proven valuable in its past to its present encounter with Western education to actualize (re-actualize) the possibilities in Western modernity that the *agboole* can now use to suit its particular logic and dynamics.

If we consider the quest for Western education as the stand-in for the life of the mind (without implying that intellectual life did not exist in the *agboole* before the arrival of Western schooling), then we can read the novel as taking us through the Aristotelean tripartite division of human experience in three generations of the *agboole*. According to Aristotle, human experience can be divided "into labor (*poiesis*), intellect (life of the mind). And political action (*praxis*)."[32] Arigbabuwo's mother was the representation of *poiesis*, passing its rewards to her son and his brother Alhaji Kareem Elelubo. Her son Arigbabuwo became the representation of the *praxis*. Her grandson (Kazeem) is the face of intellect, life of the mind.

What is remarkable is that in the story that mainly spans three generations, Adelakun works through the desires that both background and foreground these three dimensions of human experience in the *agboole*. The movement from one dimension to another does not involve the abandonment of the stages before it. Arigbabuwo kept his feet in his inherited business, even as he sallied forth into party politics. Many of the *values* of an earlier phase or phases are preserved and transcended in the new form. As the *agboole* transitions from one level (space, dimension) of desire to the other, the precariousness of its economic existence seemingly worsens. Party politics left Alhaji Arigbabuwo financially ruined. Political and civic life in the city has turned precarious with the arbitrariness of the military government and

---

[31]This way of expressing my thought is indebted to "Slavoj Žižek: Key Ideas," *Cultural and Critical Theory Library*, accessed July 16, 2021, http://criticaltheorylibrary.blogspot.com/2011/02/slavoj-zizek-key-ideas.html?m=1

[32]Quoted in Isabel Lorey, *State of Insecurity: Government of the Precarious* (London: Verso, 2015), 75–6.

its War against Indiscipline (WAI; 119–22). Future college graduates of the *agboole* face bleak employment prospects as the economy under the military regime collapses. As desires materialized—as if to live into modernity in its triune face of *poiesis*, *praxis*, and intellect—their "usefulness" tends to deteriorate. These details in Adelakun's novel point to her astute understanding of modernity (late capitalism) as a precarious society.[33]

Under the Brown Rusted Roofs offers a sociologically nuanced understanding of how new forms of desire converge in the Yoruba *agboole* for a new push into Western education. And in this adventure, the road, the outside, is not a threat but a path to a revised conception of the *agboole* as it forms subjects. On this path, the (almost) self-governing *agboole* will be subject to a new form of desire, governmentality, and mechanisms of discipline at the same time, even as it forms subjects. The simultaneity of freedom (empowerment) and obedience (subjugation) will be its "essence," which will be tested, contested, and reworked as the *agboole* subjects itself to the dominating knowledge systems of the West in the name of living into modernity.

University Discourse and the *Agboole*'s Desire for Knowledge Acquisition

The search for knowledge—or rather, for Western-derived know-how—is regulated by foreign experts or those who have mastered what Jacques Lacan called the "university discourse" (the agent of social link in the symbolic order is scientific and expert knowledge).[34] Knowledge occupies the space of the master in society and through its claim to be the only source of truth enacts domination of people via its "experts and carriers." The agent of knowledge is no longer located in the *agboole* or the enclave of the traditional Ibadan city. The post-*agboole* knowledge legitimizes the colonizing and postcolonizing master whose presence guarantees it (the new knowledge system). The master's position is also the master signifier that organizes, anchors the meanings of all other signifiers. The new knowledge is placed at the position of truth in every discourse. Traditional (African) knowledge is not given meaning and value because it is not generated within the discourse of the master signifier or the (foreign) expert-scientific knowledge, which is always in the position of "truth" in the university discourse.

This new agent dominates the knowledge system in both the *agboole* and wider Nigeria, and the domination produces a new subject (the colonized or

---

[33]Lorey, *State of Insecurity.*
[34]Jacques Lacan, *The Seminar of Jacques Lacan Book XVII: The Other Side of Psychoanalysis,* trans. Russell Grigg (New York: W. W. Norton, 2007).

postcolonized subject, who, among other things, needs emancipation from mental slavery). This new subject is incomplete, split—decentered from the ethical substance of the *agboole* by the new knowledge and symbolic order of the agent. The subject is split from within, (always) already tending toward surplus-enjoyment of the scientific knowledge, political ideas, thought-patterns, or other products of the globalizing (imperialistic Western) agent. The local person thus subjectivized—the alienated subject—comes under the grip of insatiable desire for the new knowledge and what it represents. The knowledge system (in Lacanian term, S_2) does not want to tolerate any surplus, unassimilated local knowledge, or doubt about its validity (*a*, the object cause of desire, *objet petit a*). Thus, any such unassimilated, unappropriated knowledge must be rejected or declared useless, or subsumed under the category of S_2. The dominant Western knowledge system will not surrender its hegemony or mastery of the universal space of knowledge to local, "nonexpert" knowledge. Modernity is therefore control and domination through knowledge.[35]

The main point is that by throwing itself into the university discourse because of its quest for Western education or modernity defined as Westernization, the *agboole* produces split subjects. The *agboole* now bears a wound (an other-within itself, a bone in its throat, a disturbing sand that might be transformed into a pearl of power/knowledge network). In keeping with my focus on form in this chapter, I now examine how the text of the novel captures the split form of the new *agboole*'s subjects. The text of the novel imitates the split subject. The narration is not one joined thinking—not sequential and not beholden to a linear thought pattern. It is deliberatively disruptive. Fragments irrupt into one another. It soon becomes evident that these irruptions are representations of the new coming into being, of becoming and emergence—of new characters, dialogues, and situations in all of their jouissance of joy, pain, sexuality, fluidity, metamorphosis, and the *agboolean* life, which is deathless. As feminist philosopher and theologian Grace Jantzen put it,

> The split in the text can also be read as the split that constitutes the [body of the *agboole*], the wound that is also a womb, from which come forth [death and birth, old and new, mortality and natality, chronophobia and chronophilia], the disruptive possibilities of new life. It is the source of creativity, even while its other side is [fighting for survival].[36]

[35]Slavoj Žižek, *Incontinence of the Void: Economico-Philosophical Spandrels* (Cambridge, MA: MIT Press, 2017), 200–11.
[36]Grace M. Jantzen, "' Death, Then, How Could I Yield to It?': Kristeva's Mortal Visions," in *Religion in French Feminist Thought: Critical Perspectives*, ed. Morny Joy, Kathleen O'Grady, and Judith L. Poxon (London: Routledge, 2003), 118.

Languaging Characters, Sexing Language, and Nothing

"You don't stop a young girl from growing a large vagina, as far as she can grow enough hair to cover it."

—SIKIRA

"What are you afraid of? ... We cannot fear the vagina so much that we fuck it at the sides. Say it!"

—BABA N'SALE

"Rashidi, did I hear right," he asked between hard breaths, "that you have been using knife to eat your brother's yam behind his back?"

—BABA N'SALE

"In other words—for the moment, I am not fucking, I am talking to you. Well! I can have exactly the same satisfaction as if I were fucking. That's what it means. Indeed, it raises the question of whether in fact I am not fucking at this moment."

—JACQUES LACAN[37]

The dialogues in *Under the Brown Rusted Roofs* are one of its greatest features; Adelakun uses English not only to "speak" Yoruba but also to inhabit the worldview/social imaginary of the Yoruba people. In this particular way, Adelakun's style reminds me of Achebe's, and I agree with poet laureate Niyi Osundare's comment on the book's jacket that "Not since [Chinua] Achebe's *Arrow of God* have I encountered a narrative so proverb-laden and so rhetorically endowed." Osundare also noted that the novel is "frequently funny, invariably serious and wondrously wise"—an accurate description. Indeed, I laughed, laughed, and laughed as I read *Under the Brown Rusted Roofs* for the first time in March 2017 and again in July 2021.[38] The characters are funny, not in a deliberate or direct way but in their speech patterns, which are hilarious, earthy, and incisive. Almost every sentence is full of imagery, imagination, and symbols. The novel's characters

---

[37]Jacques Lacan, *The Four Fundamental Concepts of Psychoanalysis*, trans. Alan Sheridan (New York: Norton, 1981), 165–6. I am aware of the distinction Lacan was trying to make between Sigmund Freud's concept of sublimation and his notion of drive. But the location of his partially decontextualized words here will help focus attention on the theme of this section of the chapter.

[38]I wrote down the idea and outline for this chapter on March 14, 2017, and did not write the full chapter until July 19–21, 2021.

utter sentences that appear to explain, predict, and control their social circumstances, problems, and hopes—in short, their world. Their style of speaking is a form of *worlding* in the Heideggerian sense—sentences not only gesture to the essences of things but also mediate differences among things, among utterances, and among ideas that precede them in ways that *world* (that is reference, define, shape, transform) their world, their being-in-the-Yoruba-world. The characters' language folds, unfolds, and enfolds how they are experiencing their everyday world. Their speech patterns show how the forces of structuralism, poststructuralism, and generative/emergent powers are worked in Yorubaland. Adelakun uses language, specifically Yoruba-English, not only to tell a story but also to enable the reader to "really see beneath the underneath of the sea of rusty dusty roofs, rusty dusty thousands of roofs below" (Lere Laditan, epigraph; 5). Language takes—almost, interpellates—the reader into the depths of the "ocean," the abyss, the watery *profundis* of Yoruba language.

This language is also intensely sexual. Biodun Jeyifo is certainly right when he writes that the novel's language is "deeply steeped in sexual and bodily tropes to evoke character, to probe motivations, to express raw emotions" (page 4 of cover). One particular character, Baba n'sale, is almost incapable of expressing his thought without using colorful sexual language. He employs sexual tropes as a means of effecting a construction or theorization of the female body in and by linguistic practices. His embodied and earthy language buoyed by patriarchal logic devalues women, placing them below men but above children and commodities. His language seems to assign women to some kind of Fanonian zone of nonbeing.[39]

The earthiness, the phenomenological density of language in the novel, makes an utterance, speech to come across as some special unity of sound and meaning. When you hear (read) the words they create images that stand before you as if they are living entities, not as "beings" dispersed in a long Saussurean chain of signifiers in an endless search for meaning or wholeness.[40] They stand firmly rooted in the ground of Yoruba culture, philosophy, linguistic style, and history. Though they (the words, their sounds) are born "in" your very before ("in" front of your eyes and "in" side your ears), they strut, dance, and spin as ancient beings. The words seem to state assuredly that "in the beginning we were, and we were with Yoruba, and we were Yoruba. We were Yoruba before Yoruba." They do not just stand in the airy medium of communication between them and their hearers as if they are *stupid sounds, foolish spirits* such that they do not

---

[39]"There is a zone of nonbeing, an extraordinary sterile and arid region, an incline stripped bare of every essential from which a genuine new departure can emerge. In most cases, the black man cannot take advantage of this descent into a veritable hell" (Frantz Fanon, *Black Skin, White Masks* [1952; repr., New York: Grove, 2007], xii).

[40]Haney II, "Soyinka's Ritual Drama," 39.

know how they ought to enter the inner being of their hearers. They seem to intercede for themselves through wordless groans to be transported into the hearers' inner consciousness. The words are filled with energy, spirit, life, and bravado. This is the magic of Adelakun's competence in forcing English through the Yoruba tongue as Achebe did with the Igbo tongue in both *Things Fall Apart* and *Arrow of God*.

Though Adelakun writes in English, the ultimate source of words is Yoruba reality in its daily pumping rhythm of expansion and contraction of life and its dynamic permanency of reality flashing through the transitory body of the words. In *Under the Brown Rusted Roofs*, the invisible, intangible, ineffable anima, spirit of *agboole*'s reality and the collective self-interpretation of its people—both rolled into a pulsating mass—make its appearance, at once audible, visible, and solid, through spoken words. It appears the people, their culture, geography, and reality breathe themselves "into words, and [find] some provisional survival there."[41] This provisional site is very sensual and sexual.

This brings me to a question: Why do the characters in the novel talk with intense sexual tropes but provide much less vivid descriptions of sexual acts? It is almost as if sexually laden talk is the way the characters pay their tributes to the obscene superego, and the writer spares all the dirty acts of sex. Having gotten rid of dirty, disgusting sex through conversation, they can now have sex in a nice, polite way. Language bears the full burden of sexual openness or exploration, while real sexual encounters are portrayed as clean and uninteresting.

Baba n'sale, who uses the most sexual tropes in the novel, has his sex life almost hidden away in the narrative. His wives go into his bedroom, and the reader gets only the bare minimum: he did it, he rolled away, and he fell asleep (91–3). The reader hears about his sagging, worn-out mattress, which, perhaps, carried the weights and records of his sexual encounters with his eight wives. Much of his sexual prowess seems to have been sublimated into his colorful sex talks. Everyone knows the fellow who boasts about his sexual prowess before his female friends but underperforms when a woman gives him the opportunity. (Remember one of the episodes of the sitcom, *Seinfeld*, aired in 1993, where Jerry boasted that in sex he could bring any woman to orgasm, but Elaine said she faked orgasm the entire time they were dating. He continued to boast and ended up begging her to give him another chance to prove his manliness to her. When Elaine gives in, Jerry again fails to make her climax. Later, when Elaine asks to eat some mango, Jerry thinks that eating the special mango George told him improved sexual performance would be the solution to his predicament and sexual disgrace).

---

[41]Butler, *Frames of War*, 60.

But is this not the classic binary (or antagonism) between sex act and sex talk? Although they are two parts of the same whole, sexual relationship, a third part bridges them. This third part is their difference as such. Sex talk is what prevents the sex act from being fully itself and vice versa. The difference between them is nothing more than "the difference in the very way difference is perceived."[42]

The entire sexual relationship (encounter) appears differently experienced or structured if we look at it from the perspective of sex talk or sex act. There is no neutral way for either sex talk or sex act to enjoy sex, to have full sexual satisfaction. (*Drive* shapes them.) The difference is their constitutive antagonism and precedes them. If the division in sexual relationship into talk and act is complete, that is, without each part having to deal with this excessive, impossible third element that eludes them, there will not be any struggle between the two parts in our symbolic order, and the two will exist as clearly divided parts of the sexual whole. The existence of the third disturbs their harmony as a historically contingent object. In the midst of an out-of-this-world sexual encounter, for example, when the man is saying all the right sweet nothings, the third element intrudes in the guise of the name of an ex-lover irrupting from the mouth of the woman amid her moans. (Is the sexual act not really about endlessly circling around a piece of flesh/hole/void and getting satisfaction by not reaching the goal, but from the persistence of circling around the obstacle that forever postpones full satisfaction? There is a Kalabari-Ijo—in the Niger Delta of Nigeria—joke about a mother teaching her grown son, still a virgin, about sex. She says, "When you climb onto the woman you shall enter into her, then almost pull out, and enter again and almost pull out, enter…" "Why can't you," he interrupted her in annoyance, "make up your mind, mum?")[43] While the sex talk or the sex act is an object of desire, this excessive surplus—the third element—is the object cause of desire, *objet petit a*. It is that which ensures that the best combination of sex talk and sex act does not bring the couple to the stasis of perfect harmony of their sexual relationship. There will always be something missing that eludes them, something will need to supplement—either the talk or the act.

I now return to Adelakun's handling of the connection between sex talk (as in the intense sexual tropes in the language of the characters in *Under the Brown Rusted Roofs*) and the sexual act. I earlier stated that there is an unexpected gap: the talk does not match the act, the connection is broken. Her characters engage in more sex talk than sex acts. Rather than undermine her characterization or indicate any prudishness in her descriptions of the actions *dan le boudoir*, the gap stands for the *difference as such* between

---

[42]Slavoj Žižek, "The Sexual Is Political," accessed July 16, 2021, https://thephilosophicalsalon. com/the-sexual-is-political/

[43]Slavoj Žižek reports a similar joke in his native Slovenia. Indeed, it is my reading of his joke years ago that reminded me of the Kalabari version.

the sex talk and the sex act, the irreducible antagonism between them, the excessive element that eludes them or disturbs their harmony. She does not eliminate the agonistic tension of the difference between the sex act and the sex talk. Trying to resolve it would make her like the Alaafin's wife (in a popular Yoruba legend that informs Arigbabuwo's attitude toward intimacy with his wives) who tried to reconcile, harmonize the difference between the size of the king's penis and his imperial power as a ruler of the Yoruba people. "So you are not even more than this, yet the whole Oyo fears you" (40). The awe of his phallus in her estimation did not stand up to the awe of his royal power. The gap exists between the king as a man and his position as a ruler.[44] The gap between Kantorowiczian material and sublime bodies of the Alaafin surprised her. To speak jokingly, she saw the Lacanian *Real*, which was embodied in the gap. The horror of (that is) the *Real* stared back at her. She tried to close, to domesticate the gap (that which is not fully captured in the symbolic system, that which her language will always fail to master) with her enunciation and was forced to peer into a calabash containing her father's decapitated head.

> She knelt reverently and the Alaafin pointed to a large calabash in the midst of the room. He asked her to open it and she, excited at that singular honour, moved towards the calabash and opened it. To her horror, she found the head of her father inside the calabash, freshly decapitated…. Alaafin explained the previous day to his chiefs and told them he had to show her he was more than what she saw in the bathroom (40).

Is the disconnect between sex talk and sex act in *Under the Brown Rusted Roofs* not raising the age-old debate in philosophy between signifiers and signifieds, the connection between subjectivity and signification? As Todd McGowan, an American professor of film studies and a philosopher, states, "Language creates a significant world to which we can relate, but it also makes evident the division of this world from itself. The signifier is not

---

[44]It appears that the wife "succumbed to the illusion indicated, among others, by Marx in a note in Chapter 1 of *Capital*… 'to be a king' is not an immediate natural property of the person of a king but a 'determination-of-reflection'—that king is a king because his subjects treat him like one, and not the reverse. The proper way to get rid of this illusion is thus not the murder [or mocking] of the king but the dissolution of the network of social relations within which a certain person acquires the status of a king—as soon as this symbolic network loses its performative power, we suddenly see how the person who previously provoked such fascination is really an individual like the others; we are confronted with the material remainder which was stuck on the symbolic… The point is not simply that his transient material body serves as a support, symbol, incarnation of his sublime body; it consists rather in the curious fact that as soon as a certain person functions as 'king', his everyday, ordinary properties undergo a kind of 'transubstantiation' and become an object of fascination" (Žižek, *For They Know Not*, 254–5).

identical with the signified. Isolated instances that suggest an equivalence, such as onomatopoeia, are not primary but rather secondary attempts to bridge a fundamental chasm."[45]

Having said all this, one must be careful not to assert that Adelakun consciously created the gap between sex talk and sex act. (Though the tale about the Alaafin's wife and the well-established queue of Arigbabuwo's wives having sex with him do offer some insight into why sex is nearly bureaucratic in the polygamous bedroom; why it is consigned to an ineffable, apophatic zone of the narration.) Thus, whatever I have written in the previous paragraphs about the psychoanalytical-philosophical connotations of the gap between sex talk and sex act in the novel should be chalked down in a space beyond her work. I believe that any rigorous interpretation of a serious work goes beyond it.

In engaging Adelakun's novel, I have followed the trail of her thinking as it folds, unfolds, and enfolds implicitly through the *Under the Brown Rusted Roofs*. The goal is to regain or uncover the creative impulse that she missed in the actualization of her thought, to connect to "what was already in [Adelakun] more than [Adelakun herself], more than [her] explicit system, its excessive core."[46] This is to say I am reading Adelakun to isolate the key breakthrough of her thought in her novel as they relate to psychoanalysis-philosophy (African and Continental); then show how she necessarily missed the key dimension of her own discovery; and "finally, showing how, in order to do justice to [her] key breakthrough, one has to move beyond [Adelakun]," in the words of Žižek.[47] This going beyond means betraying the *text-flesh* of her thought in order to grasp its *text-soul*. In this section of the chapter, more than any other section, I have situated my analysis of

---

[45]Todd McGowan, *Capitalism and Desire: The Psychic Cost of Free Markets* (New York: Columbia University Press, 2016), 25. Elsewhere, he states that eating an apple is not just eating an apple. "Rather than simply feeling hunger and eating the nearest apple in the manner of a human animal, the subject will seek a satisfaction that transcends the apple through the apple. For the subject of the signifier, unlike for the human animal, an apple is never enough. Once the world of signification exists, the apple's noncoincidence with itself becomes apparent, and the empirical apple ceases to prove satisfying. As an object of need, the apple is just an apple and can satisfy the need. But after the introduction of the signifier, the apple's self-division enables it to signify something beyond itself. A supplement attached itself to the apple in the form of the signifier and this excess remains irreducible to the object. The subject in the world of signification can never just eat an apple but easts what 'keeps the doctor away,' what is juicy and delicious, or what connotes original sin. The apple will embody something more as a result of the division introduced by signification, and the excess attached to the apple produces a satisfaction for the subject that an apple by itself—an apple that isn't an 'apple'—can never provide for an animal that eats it" (McGowan, *Capitalism and Desire*, 23).
[46]Slavoj Žižek, *In Defense of Lost Causes* (London: Verso, 2009), 140.
[47]Slavoj Žižek, *Absolute Recoil: Towards a New Foundation of Dialectical Materialism* (London: Verso, 2014), 33. Žižek adds, "What characterizes a really great thinker is that they misrecognize the basic dimension of their own breakthrough" (Žižek, *Absolute Recoil*, 34).

the novel in that space that is beyond her explicit thought. Doing so enables me to capture the dimensions of psychoanalysis and philosophy that shine through in the explosion of her thought on the African situation (language and reality, incompleteness of desire, gender relations, sex, and subjectivity) and its concrete actualization in her novel but slip into the virtual state and haunt any close reading of *Under the Brown Rusted Roofs*.

Space always exists between authors and their interpreters.[48] This in-between space is manned by the trickster, prankster god of Esu/Hermes who uses *esunectics*/hermeneutics to fit a giant into a groundnut shell.[49] To interpret (to engage in *esunectics*) a work is to enter this space—the place of a cross in a circle, invoking the intersection of temporality, spatiality, and infinity—and engage with the universe of interpretative possibilities and make a selection of which path of meaningfulness to highlight for scholarly discourse.[50]

There is another way to explain the disparity between the intense sexual tropes and the actual bedroom performance/language. The disconnect is also discernible in the form and content of the majority of the dialogues in the novel. A high proportion of the characters express themselves in ways that mobilize a forest of metaphors, divagations, and allusions, whose force far surpasses the actual contents that they bear or transport. Once again, form exceeds content. Why are these observations important? Three reasons: First, they shed light on the disparity I have observed between sex talk and sex act. Second, the logic of the dialogues is not always temporal—as I have already noted, not that of a sequentially unfolding narrative. It is often a spatial one; the oral narrative is a map in which relations and meanings are tied together by their placement in both the performance and the virtual landscape that

---

[48]"No [book] is complete and perfectly self-identical. Rather than being self-contained and thus impervious to critical analysis, every [book] opens up a space outside itself from which we can analyze it and make a judgment on it" (McGowan, *Capitalism and Desire*, 1).

[49]Obododima Oha, "The Esu Paradigm in the Semiotics of Identity and Community," unpublished essay; Awo Falokun Fatunmbi, "Esu-Elegba: Ifa and the Spirit of the Divine Messenger," unpublished essay, July 2021; John Pemberton, "Eshu-Elegba: The Yoruba Trickster God," *African Arts* 9, no. 1 (1975): 20–7, 66–70, 79, 92; Bibi Bakare-Yusuf and Jeremy Weate, "Ojuelegba: The Sacred Profanities of a West African Crossroad," in *Urbanization and African Cultures*, ed. Toyin Falola and Steven J. Salm (Durham, NC: Carolina Academic Press, 2005), 323–40; and Oluwatoyin Vincent Adepoju, "Spatial Navigation as a Hermeneutic Paradigm: Ifa, Heidegger and Calvino," in *The Palgrave Handbook of Africa and Changing Global Order*, ed. S. O. Oloruntoba and Toyin Falola (Cham, Switzerland: Palgrave Macmillan, 2022), 987–1024.

[50]*Esuneutics*: This is named after the Yoruba god of Esu/Eshu. Let me provide my understanding of esuneutics as I garnered from the works of Obodinmma Oha and Oluwatosin Vincent Adepoju and other writers on Esu that I have already cited. Esunectics is about not only the possibilities of interpretation but also a "privileged intellectual tool to reactualize" any extant body of interpretation or ideas. The key term here is *reactualizing*, which is nothing but to make "actual one of the infinite possibilities of interpretation that has not been realized or to restage (rethink) a possibility as is currently realized." The words in quotation come from "Slavoj Žižek: Key Ideas."

the characters "talk" into being. In this mixing of logics, time and history, and space and lateral connections, are made to flow together, without any one of them occupying a privileged position. These kinds of oral dialogues resist attempts to classify them along any schema such as space-time logic, stylistic criteria, or character of speech act as its performance refuses easy conformity to a single type. What anthropologist Karin Barber says about the Yoruba oral literature is aptly relevant here: "Yoruba oral literature in general appears like a vast stock of verbal materials—themes, formulas, stories, poetic idioms—which can float through the permeable boundaries of all the genres and be incorporated into them to fulfill different functions. Genres freely incorporate parts of other genres, with much sharing and borrowing of material."[51]

Third, and more importantly, the disconnect between form and content in the dialogues shows how the dialogues in the novel resemble everyday communications. Sometimes, novelists write as if their characters are in the theater speaking like actors with precise, clean, clinical lines.[52] So, in a sense, the disparity we observe in *Under the Brown Rusted Roofs* confirms that Adelakun was very careful in reproducing the everyday communication style of typical *agboole* members and did not polish or compress their dialogues for theatrical effect. This is one of the most impressive strengths of her novel.

Another Disparity: Infinity, Nothingness, and Spatiality

The spiral narrative structure of the novel invites us to reflect on Adelakun's understanding of space. The notion of space in this novel—that is, the spacing/pacing of events, actions, objects, pericopes, and fragments in the narrative—is like the concept of space in modern physics. In today's physics, space is neither a totality nor a container but the network of objects, the presence of objects and events that creates space. In other words, there is no a priori empty space waiting to contain objects, events, actions, or beings.

---

[51]Karin Barber, "Yoruba *Oriki* and Deconstructive Criticism," *Research in African Literatures* 13, no. 4 (1984): 510–1, quoted in Andrew Apter, *Black Critics and Kings: The Hermeneutics of Power in Yoruba Society* (Chicago: University of Chicago Press, 1992), 118.

[52]The language of theater is about compression. "Compression consists of removing everything that is not strictly necessary and intensifying what is there, such as putting a strong adjective in the place of a bland one, whilst preserving the impression of spontaneity. If this impression is maintained, we reach the point where if in life it takes two people three hours to say something, on stage it should take three minutes. We can see this result clearly in the limpid styles of Beckett, Pinter or Chekhov" (Peter Brook, *The Open Door: Thoughts on Acting and Theatre* [New York: Random House, 2005], 11–12).

Space in *Under the Brown Rusted Roofs* is the network, the conglomeration of objects (stand-in for the others—events, actions, and beings). It is a system of relation among objects, fragments (this is in line with the social/body ontology of the novel, which I have already described). Space is not a preexisting fundamental out there in the literary imagination like pre-Einstein theory of physical space; rather, Adelakun creates space by relating fragments and the gaps between fragments in her narrative.

Adelakun's handling of space is more akin to theater than to film. Instead of presenting things as a logically coherent whole as a film is likely to do (with some notable exceptions), there are gaps, cuts, and discontinuities in the space that the reader is invited to fill with his or her imagination.[53] Reality in this novel is not a tight system of causal continuity. It is never whole. Reality is not identical to itself. Just as there are cuts and gaps between objects that constitute space, there are also cuts and discontinuities between the fragments (pericopes) of stories that form the "body" of the novel. These gaps, these minimal distances between fragments, are disruptive, have creative potentials, and are sites for the emergence of the new.

Like the modern theory of physics, the implicit notion of space in Adelakun's narrative style is infinite. Space in the novel is not pregiven, the narrative creates the space into which it expands. This is made all the more so not because novels create their own worlds but because of Adelakun's dexterity in manipulating the spiral narrative form. The creation and movement into the new space is simultaneous, in the same way the universe expands by creating its own space and expanding into it. Each new fragment added to the collection creates new tension in the narrative and opens new vistas; these, in turn, create new focus, amend our thinking, and move us forward into a space beyond the collection into a new horizon. With what creativity does an expanding narrative space in the novel unfurl the subsequent space it will inhabit? It is the quantum mechanics of the waves and particles of the disarticulated plots. It is the being and power-momentum, "matter and energy" of the fragments; they come together to create and sustain spaces of life, actions, and events. This created space, ever moving, is infinite.

Another structuring of the novel might help us decide what kind of infinity of space we are dealing with here—and what kind of philosophy it espouses. The repetition of the same conversation at the beginning of the novel (7–8) and at the end (248–9)—set within a nonlinear, disruptive structure of plot—informs me about the novel's implicit theorization of infinity. The image of the story is that of the circle; the narrative makes its

---

[53]Peter Brook, "Does Nothing Come from Nothing?" (paper originally presented June 13, 1994, and published in *British Psycho-Analytical Society Bulletin* 34, no. 1 [1998]), reprinted at Centre de International Recherches Etudes Transdisciplinaires, https://ciret-transdisciplinarity.org/bulletin/b15c1.php and Peter Brook, *The Empty Space* (New York: Penguin, 1990), 136–7.

limit constitutive of and internal to itself. The clue is that the story bent back upon itself. This is where Georg Hegel's notion of *bad infinite* and *true infinite* comes in handy. A bad infinite has no external limit. A true infinite, however, makes its limit constitutive of itself; its limits are not external but internal. As Hegel describes it,

> The image of progression in infinity is the straight *line*; the infinite is only at the two limits of this line, and always only where the latter (which is existence) is not but *transcends itself*, and in its non-existence, that is, in the indeterminate. As true infinite, bent back upon itself, its image becomes the circle, the line that has reached itself, closed and wholly present, without *beginning* and *end*.[54]

The crux of the conceptual issue here is that this idea of limit within limit (that is, *limitness*) enables us to envision an alternative to the logic and oppressive system of the *university discourse* that McGowan says, "nonetheless remains within the spirit of modernity."[55] Where does this kind of internal limit exist in the relationship between the *agboole* and Western-inflected modernity? Where is the internal limit of the subject themselves (members of the *agboole*) as they integrate into the logic of Western domination and disregard for Africa's knowledge systems and ethos? To quote McGowan again,

> The limit that [the imperialistic Western university discourse] cannot integrate is that of the true infinite. This limit is internal, a self-limitation of the [subjects themselves]. A self-limiting system, precisely what Hegel theorizes with his concept of the true infinite, is the only tenable alternative to [the imperialistic Western university discourse]. It does not pose an arbitrary limit that the [imperialistic Western university discourse] can quickly subsume but clings to the limit as constitutive of the system itself. To subsume the limit thus becomes unthinkable.[56]

Through fragments one can examine the "nothingness" of space in the novel, traverse from infinity to the fecund nothingness of creativeness. Fragments, the collection of fragments in a spiral narrative structure—by definition—create pockets of silences, voids, and nothingness. These are spaces of creativity from which the new emerge. The splits in the narrative as a result of the deliberate disarticulation of the plot are like the silence, the spaces between words in a spoken sentence that enable us to understand

---

[54]G. W. F. Hegel, *The Science of Logic*, trans. George Di Giovanni (Cambridge: Cambridge University Press, 2010), 119, quoted in McGowan, *Capitalism and Desire*, 137.
[55]McGowan, *Capitalism and Desire*, 137.
[56]McGowan, *Capitalism and Desire*, 140.

the meaning of a sentence. There is a silence that inhabits all that has been spoken or written, and every new word or sentence speaks from the silence that follows the full stop (period). Creativity or innovation usually springs from the dwelling place of silence. Every act of renewal, innovation, or fresh perspective wells up from the silence of the last achievement (understanding) and the ones before it and allows for (craves) emptiness. The void, the no-thing-ness, the silence, the margin is the source of the new. It is the place where the artist, the painter, the scholar, the dancer, the musician, the priest, the scientist can touch the *prima materia* of the eros of creativity. The splits in the narrative and the attendant silent spaces in *Under the Brown Rusted Roofs* enable me to fruitfully engage with the literary and moral imaginations of the author. The silence, it seems, is the fecund void from which additional meanings float out of the narrative—at least, we have seen how they speak to the nature of oral literature in Yoruba.

Together, both the silence and sounds of the fragments speak to another aspect of Yoruba culture: spatiality; space as an immanent power of life. Spatiality here is about the co-presence of the members of the *agboole* with one another and with God (Allah and/or Yoruba local deities). The spatiality of the *agboole* is realized and made visible in the mutuality of the members that is open to Allah's (the gods') active presence, transformative action, and surprises. Spatiality is always and everywhere in Yorubaland and in other traditional African communities a crucial dimension of social relations.

Elizabeth Jarrell Callender interprets spatiality in her dissertation (which explores Karl Barth's doctrine of the divine perfection of omnipresence) in a way that is insightful for interpreting the ethics of the *agboole*. According to Callender,

> Barth claims that God is spatial, thereby rejecting the common belief that God is a-spatial. Spatiality, defined as "proximity at a distance," describes the way in which one is present to another in the most intimate and personal fellowship possible yet without becoming the other. Individual distinction ("distance") is not merely upheld but is real only in the union of a rightly ordered fellowship ("proximity"). Barth also asserts that God has His own space and even is His own space. Furthermore, God makes space for others to have their own place.[57]

This sense of spatiality is discernible in *Under the Brown Rusted Roofs*. Spatiality in this novel is never limited to human beings transforming spaces into places to live. Its portrayal of how life hangs together in the *agboole*

---

[57]Elizabeth Jarrell Callender, "A Theology of Spatiality: The Divine Perfection of Omnipresence in the Theology of Karl Barth" (PhD dissertation, University of Otago, Dunedin, New Zealand, 2011), 241.

captures the true meaning of spatiality as referring to human beings' co-presence with one another and with their God or gods. It captures the connection-making power of spatiality in the *agboole*. One may argue that even the form of the novel's narrative aligns with the form of spatiality as I have defined it here: spatiality as the immanent presence of members of the *agboole* to one another in a network of connections of places and people. The novel—as I have stated for the umpteenth time—is a network of fragments and pericopes, their co-presence with one another and with the creative spiral narrative (or the *agboole*'s "investment in survival") representing the spatiality of the *agboole*.

The dynamics of both movement and continuity in spatiality (in the *agboole* and in the spiral narrative structure of the novel) are not about closure, but a *recapitulatio*. It is to begin, to open up (*be-ginnan*) the iterative dynamic of becoming itself, to stir up the matrix of possibilities again. Each new relation or repetition guarantees this beginning. A relation is a (productive, rhythmic) repetition, *recapitulatio*.[58] Relation is the supreme capacity of humans. In the unfurling of their humanity and their making places out of space, they open relation up, cut it open again and again, redesign, redirect, or repair its fluid dynamics as it carries them deeper and deeper into its depth. Every fresh relation comes from an initial relation that maps upon the new alternative pathways of excluded possibilities and novel immediacy.

Concluding Remarks: The Nature of Desire in *Under the Brown Rusted Roofs*

The novel opens, after the prologue, with an almost "empty *agboole*." It is a site of emptiness, absence; yet, we see a pregnant woman, the wise Afusa in labor pains, who eventually gives birth to a male child (10–16; additionally, a female pregnant goat is bleating, perhaps because of its own birth pangs). It appears Afusa was groaning and travailing for the fullness of the *agboole*, eagerly waiting for the signs of the future, for the transformation of the body (content) of the *agboole*. This scene reminds me of other stories of genesis or primordial creation—of the emptiness, of the female figure hovering, groaning, hatching, and life breaking forth out of water. This scene of birth and pregnancy speaks to the prospects for the continuity of life, the *agboole* bound up with or animated by its primary "investment in survival," the

---

[58]"A repetition is by definition never the 'same' as that which it repeats. It is always already other. In its iterations it becomes readable, a code" (Catherine Keller, *Face of the Deep: A Theology of Becoming* [New York: Routledge, 2003], 186).

capacity, desire to live on. As Hägglund expresses it, "To survive is to live on in a temporal process of alteration, where one is always becoming other than oneself. In contrast, to be immortal is to repose in a state of being that is eternally the same."[59]

As she labored in pain in the empty *agboole* (a symbol of an incomplete-being-in-the-world), Afusa threw things out of her doors and windows to catch the attention of a hawker passing by. The hawker helped her find a traditional midwife for the baby's birth. Not long after, the home was full of people. The incomplete is now complete, the empty *agboole* has become full, so to speak. The force of being as expressed in the form of a woman in labor forcefully reaching for help, in the mutuality of relations, and in the birth of a child, has brought about the "completeness" or "fullness." A son was given to them—a strong and healthy "male with nine bones" (9), a symbol of human flourishing and, in this particular case, the first one in the *agboole* that would go on to attend university. The son, Jimoh, was not only the first to actualize the existential ideal of going to school but also the first to pursue it to the tertiary level owing to the force of his mother's desire, grit, and determination.

This opening scene, indeed, speaks to how Adelakun philosophizes desire in *Under the Brown Rusted Roofs* as the space for the motion between existential ideal and achieved human flourishing, between fullness and emptiness as a force of being, the power of an incomplete being-in-the-world. This form of desire is not defined by its circulatory motion around (transcendental, eternal) lack, but operates as an opening through which a person might realize her ideal, step back into it, or reconstruct it to actualize her potentialities or critically comprehend her becoming and identity. Desire as a force of being, as the power of an incomplete being-in-the-world, draws its form and content from women's and men's lived experiences and lived endurances.

Desire here is not merely an affective activity but responsiveness to concerns that are conducive to well-being. It is about accountability to things that *matter* to the person. Desire is not some kind of heteronomous weight, a form of alien gravity that determines a person's behavior but a shared autonomy and shared commitment in the matrix of the *agboole*. By desire the individual (like Afusa) or the *agboole* as a whole is open to destiny, to filling the existing gaps in actualization of destiny (hers and her children's). In the exercise of shared autonomy and shared commitments to the collective well-being of the *agboole*, the individual *performs* desire.

In *Under the Brown Rusted Roofs*, Adelakun presents desire as the immanent present/not-yet relation between people and their creativity or ideal, between potentiality and actualization, between form and content

---

[59]Hägglund, *Dying for Time*, 8.

in the movements of personal and group development. In her creative imagination, we see the *agboole* as a *plural agency* constituted and driven by not only the desires of individuals specific to their own well-being but also the desires of the relationship of *us-ness* that unites and preserves their joint autonomy.[60] In this nuanced description and hermeneutics of the *agboole* and its rhythms, rhymes, and dance of life, Adelakun's novel is a subtle and insightful "theorization" of the philosophy of agonistic communitarianism among the Yoruba of Nigeria.[61]

---

[60]Jean-Luc Nancy, *Being Singular Plural*, trans. Robert D. Richardson and Anne E. O' Byrne (Stanford, CA: Stanford University Press, 2000).

[61]Nimi Wariboko, "Between Community and My Mother: A Theory of Agonistic Communitarianism," in *The Palgrave Handbook of African Social Ethics*, ed. Nimi Wariboko and Toyin Falola (Cham, Switzerland: Palgrave Macmillan, 2020), 147–63.

2

The Black Moon on the White Surface: A Philosophical Analysis of A. Igoni Barrett's *Blackass*

Furo Wariboko awoke this morning to find that dreams can lose their way and turn up on the wrong side of sleep.

—A. IGONI BARRETT, *BLACKASS*, 3

Furo Wariboko wakes on the morning of a job interview to discover he's turned into a white man: red hair, green eyes, pale skin. In this condition he plunges into the bustle of Lagos to make his fortune. Pursued from the streets to the boardroom by those who would use him, Furo hides the evidence of his former life—his family, his name [changed it to Frank Whyte], his black ass—as he reinvents himself. In this wicked satire, Furo's search for an identity deeper than his skin leads to the unraveling of his own precariously constructed story.

—A. IGONI BARRETT, *BLACKASS*, PAGE 4 OF COVER

Introduction

Igoni Barrett's *Blackass* is a performance matrix of perception, movement, and meaning.[1] It is a story of how we perceive our own bodies and those of others. It is about the movement and circulation of bodies in Lagos, Nigeria. It is a fast-paced narrative of people in motion crafting meanings for what their bodies have done to them and what they are doing to their own bodies. Bodies take strange colors; bodies copulate, dance, and eat; bodies seek other bodies for pleasure, profit, and oppression. Lagos itself—a body of bodies—is simultaneously a sublime and abjected body, both fascinating and repellant. In bodies, the story lives, moves, and has its being. Dream is the mode of existence in which bodies most freely perform and in which they are caught in performativity (in the Judith Butler sense).[2] In performance, persons act as if they enter into their actions as preexisting subjects with preexisting bodies. But in the freedom and constraint of performativity, their subjectivity is constituted by their acts, their aspirations, and the drama and dramatization of their bodies. Their bodies are made and remade in "the reiteration of norms which precede, constrain, and exceed the performer," without foreclosing possibilities of transformation.[3] Performing and performative bodies bring into being what they dream about. Bodies in *Blackass* are always becoming. Bodies change their skin color. Male chests grow female breasts; fetuses grow within female bodies. They acquire identities that are split—new bodies carry with them the indivisible remainders of their old selves.[4] Black butt cheeks tarry on white skin surface. Penis occupies or conceals the void of the vagina. Bleached skin on the face leaves a lingering trail of putrefaction. In *Blackass*, Barrett combines the act *of* saying something, the act *in* saying something, and the act *by* saying something to probe how human beings, bodies, perform their identities or the mutability of identity. Identity is like a totipotent stem cell that can be molded into different organs and shapes.

What is the philosophical implication or importance of Barrett's novel? What does his reading or mythologization of bodies performing incompletable identities say about the African postcolony or the philosophy (psychoanalysis) of identities or human existence? *Blackass* is an ideological

---

[1] A. Igoni Barrett, *Blackass* (Minneapolis, MN: Gray Wolf, 2015). Throughout this article and at times in the notes, I use parenthetical citations for Barrett's quotations; I use footnotes for other references.

[2] Judith Butler, *Bodies That Matter: On the Discursive Limits of "Sex"* (New York: Routledge, 1993), 234.

[3] Butler, *Bodies That Matter*, 234.

[4] "He knew that so long as the vestiges of his old self remained with him, his new self would never be safe from ridicule and incomprehension" (111).

critique of the Nigerian postcolony and its underlying racism, colorism, identity crisis, sexism, sexuality, and classism. The ideological critique is not in the form of clearing the illusions (false ideas) that capitalist and postcolonial ideologies inflict on Nigerians to legitimize sociopolitical domination. It is not about exposing the hidden truths of hegemonic class. The novel does not take us behind any smoke screens to reveal the "real" of reality that the dominant class or social order has hidden from us. Rather, *Blackass* is in the form of an exposition of the "fantasy-construction which serves as support for the [incredible postcolonial] 'reality' itself," as Slavoj Žižek is wont to put it.[5]

Barrett brilliantly shows how ordinary Nigerians, the so-called dupes of ideology, are complicit in the construction of the postcolonial reality or the ideological fantasy that sustains it. The characters Furo (Frank Whyte, the main protagonist); Syreeta; Tosin; Obata, Headstrong (Victor), Igoni (not the author), Arinze, Alhaji Yuguda; and Baby and her friends are constitutive of the postcolonial reality: the meaning each person attributes to it, their drives, their fantasy that all things are possible in Nigeria, their enjoyments, and energies are all embedded in the cultural processes, the socio-symbolic universe of meaning making in the postcolony. Arinze, Furo's boss, on hearing that one of his company's drivers (Victor) has realized his dream of migrating to Poland says to Furo, "'One of the reasons I will never leave Nigeria is because, in this country, anything can happen.' Cocking his head at Furo, he smiled into his eyes. 'And you, Mr. Whyte, are a perfect example of that'" (247). Each of these men and women contributes to the frustratingly inescapable fantasy that interpellates them. Ideology is motivated in each person from within via desires that are complicit with the postcolonial status quo. The characters like the rest of their fellow citizens use desire-driven fantasy to avoid staring into the void, abyss, and chaos that is Nigeria. This Nigeria that *Blackass*'s characters fail to look at or recognize is not some naked reality out there, but rather the fantasy that structures each of their realities. In fact, Nigeria is not separate from such fantasy. As Žižek put it, "fantasy constitutes our desires, provides its coordinates; that is; it is literally 'teaches us how to desire.'"[6]

Barrett displays this (Žižekian) critique of ideology in his conveying of the experiences, dialogues, practices, and behaviors of the novel's characters. Their illusion or their acceptance of the hegemonic ideology is never portrayed as a matter of false knowledge, but always as rooted in the fantasies and ideological dreams they constructed for themselves and then try to live into them. Žižek captures this point well when he states,

[5]Slavoj Žižek, *The Sublime Object of Ideology* (London: Verso, 2008), 45.
[6]Slavoj Žižek, *The Plague of Fantasies* (London: Verso, 1997), 7.

If our concept of ideology remains the classic one in which the illusion is located in knowledge, then today's society must appear post-ideological: the prevailing ideology is that of cynicism; people no longer believe in ideological truth [no longer believe in the truth of their nation state]; they do not take ideological proposition seriously. The fundamental level of ideology, however, is not that of an illusion masking the real state of things but that of an (unconscious) fantasy structuring our social reality. And at this level, we are of course far from being a post-ideological society....[Ideology is the belief] which is radically exterior, embedded in the practical, effective procedure of people.[7]

In this study, I explore the philosophical trappings of *Blackass* to harvest Barrett's ideas and understandings about ontology, personhood, dream, philosophy of the body, and theories of identity—and present them with a technical precision required for philosophical writing. Of course, in bringing Barrett into philosophical discussions, I may misread both the novel and the philosophies I bring to it, but I believe uncovering and interrogating the philosophical worldview that frames or undergirds *Blackass* is necessary to following Barrett's philosophical scent into the worlds of some of the major thinkers in human history. The central purpose of this chapter is to identify the political, psychoanalytic, and theoretical questions that *Blackass* raises, not least as they resonate with the themes of split identity, ontological incompleteness, and the fantasies structuring the Nigerian postcolony.

The Split African: *Blackass* and Critical Theory

Identities are, as it were, the positions which the subject is obliged to take up while always "knowing"... that they are representations, that representation is always constructed across a "lack," across division, from the place of the Other, and thus can never be adequate—identical— to the subject processes which are invested in them.

—STUART HALL[8]

There is a dimension of *Blackass* more than *Blackass*.[9] *Blackass* is a multidimensional, deeply layered work that evokes more than just a

---

[7]Žižek, *Sublime Object*, 30–1.
[8]Stuart Hall, "Who Needs 'Identity'?" in *Questions of Cultural Identity*, ed. Paul Du Gay and Stuart Hall (London: Sage, 1990), 6.
[9]This way of expressing my thought was inspired by Slavoj Žižek, *For They Know Not What They Do: Enjoyment as a Political Factor* (London: Verso, 1991), xxiv.

common perception. Barrett's *Blackass* offers a scintillating meditation on subjectivity and identity. He draws attention to the special relationship between subjectivity (identity) and the gap within any identity (subjectivity). The gap is not between the subject and what he or she claims, or between the person's identity/subjectivity and any external interpretative position of it. The gap is located in the identity or subjectivity itself. Every identity or subjectivity is split from within. There is always a leftover, a remainder in it, meaning self-identity is impossible. The identity of something cannot be self-identical. Furo was transformed into white man, but his ass is black, pointing to us that the limit of whiteness is inscribed with it in the guise of the stubborn "moon" on a white surface. His whiteness is cleft from within, between the errant white skin and the void of its place.[10] The black patch resists the whiteness from within. The black buttocks give body to the void—in other words, materializes the body—and by extension, gives body to the emptiness of the imposturing of whiteness. It externalizes the completeness of whiteness, whiteness is the whole, the *All* of humanity. The completeness of whiteness cannot be found in whiteness itself, just as the meaning of a word is found in other words. In *Blackass*, Barrett thus deftly gestures to the ontological incompleteness of reality itself.

The notion of incompleteness also applies to blackness. Furo is a dialectical identity of these two sides. Much like the famous ambiguous duck-rabbit drawing by American Gestalt psychologist, Joseph Jastrow, whether one views Furo from a whiteness or blackness perspective, one sees the same phenomenon. From one point of view, Furo is all about whiteness; from another, he is blackness. Perspective simply shifts on one and the same person, not two persons brought together in the form of cojoined twins. The whiteness is the embodiment of blackness, and the blackness is whiteness in process. Personhood is unchanged, but one sees two different takes from two angles of vision. The blackness and whiteness are not two halves that add up to a greater whole. Rather, there is only one personhood. For each of them (whiteness or blackness, split from within), "the ultimate split is not between two halves, but between Something and Nothing, between the One and the Void of its Place ....[It] is the *same* element which encounters itself in its 'oppositional determination'—or, in other words, the opposition between the One and its Outside is reflected back into the very identity of the One."[11]

Postcolonial Subjectivity and Postcolonialism

All this opens up new perspective into Barrett's thought. The novel *Blackass* is blackness without blackness. It is about a form of Black life deprived of its positive content. There is something fundamental going on here. The

[10]Žižek, *For They Know Not*, xxvi.
[11]Žižek, *For They Know Not*, xxvi.

postcolonial subject is often conceived as the effect of postcolonialism and its brutal effect on consciousness or identity. In this novel, causality is reversed: far from causing the postcolonial subjectivity, postcolonialism is its effect. As Žižek explains,

> The logic of this reversal is ultimately the same as the passage from the special to the general theory of relativity in Einstein. While the special theory already introduces the notion of curved space, it conceives of this curvature as the effect of matter: it is the presence of matter which curves space—that is, only an empty space would have been non-curved. With passage to the general theory, the causality is reversed: far from causing the curvature of space, matter is its effect.[12]

Postcolonialism is transposed from the external to the internal. There is postcolonialism insofar as the Nigerian subject is inconsistent, does not coincide with her Nigerianness. Postcolonialism is the embodiment of this inconsistency. The negativity assumes in Furo a positive existence. Postcolonialism is not an external reality out there. It emerges when the Nigerian gets caught in her inconsistency. Postcolonialism is what happens when One becomes Two—one person becomes a twosome. The one is split from within. The person does not become two persons or two opposing forces but is split between an identity and the void of its place.[13]

Postcolonialism is the rupture/gap itself that makes the African not fully African. The postcolonial subject is the thin wedge between African and not-African (European). He is both the old and the new at the same time. Furo is both black and white at the same time. His old self and new self are caught in a self-relating exchange in which the Africans who did not wish to be white but became white for those Africans who wish to be white, and thus throw those who long to be white into debt by their passing from the old to the new.[14] (This is one way to interpret the forceful seizure of Furo's skin and its branding with whiteness. So, the innocent scapegoat went into the pit of sacrifice on the behalf of others, thus putting them in his debt.[15])

Blackass is an attempt to symbolize/domesticate the traumatic event of Africans becoming other-than-themselves—dealing with texture of reality

---

[12]Žižek, *For They Know Not*, xxx.

[13]Žižek, *For They Know Not*, xxvi.

[14]The dialectical relationship is reinforced by Barrett inscribing himself into the narrative.

[15]The theme of sacrifice is abundant in this novel. Furo's determination to "pass" into the white world is couched by him as a personal sacrifice. His desire to perform into white privilege and be a child lost to his family—becoming dead to his mother, in particular—is rendered in the religious language of sacrifice. He sees his going away from his family as something that is best for them (38). "A child was a mistake he couldn't make. For many reasons, but above

that have been damaged—making sense of a noncontinuous texture of reality, of a violent cut into their symbolic order by invading and marauding whiteness, European imperial powers. Furo is synecdoche and his violent transformation is the metonym of the colonial trauma event. On the fateful morning of his job interview, Furo woke up into nonexistence. This is not like René Descartes who sat by his fireside and, in long process of annihilating thought, gradually eliminated the extended world around him, put it into nonexistence, declared it not real, fictional, and eventually told himself that he alone undoubtedly exists. Descartes' *cogito* is the empty space that results after a person has eliminated the rest of the world from the self. The resulting Cartesian "I," emanating out of the void, is transparent, fully conscious of itself, and in complete command of its destiny. The "I" can with deliberate and self-assured steps fill in the void of the subject. But Furo the black man was violently captured by whiteness—not too dissimilar from the capture of Africans and transportation to the white world during slavery— and found himself a "fiction," nonexistent, with everything around him marked with solidity and gravity. He had a feeling of free-falling, of being sucked into a world other than blackness. Unlike Descartes, his thought could no longer sustain his existence as a black person; black pigmentation has to be abjected. Furo cannot say "*Cogito, ergo sum*" (I think, therefore I am). "The mere thought of a reversion to his former stasis was anathema to him" (40). Here is an inversion of the Cartesian logic.[16] Perhaps, a black body completely transformed into a white body does not need to engage in anti-Cartesian logic and could succeed as a great adventurer, but not in a world in which there are white bodies.

---

all for the same reason he had left his family behind. Suffer alone and die alone" (253). This effusive religious rhetoric is coming after he descended into hell (the dark night he spent in the abandoned Golgotha of a building where he was tortured by mosquitoes, the massacring heroes of anti-colonial resistance (38, 40)) and rose again. After this passage through suffering and hell, he became in his mind another white deity to save black bodies and souls. Furo's cant about sacrifice and dying alone to spare people some trouble is only a thinly disguised attempt to sacralize his *passing* into the privilege of white hue, to veil the fact that his physical transformation is not accompanied by psychological transformation, to soften the thrownness of his "mulatto-being," hybridity, or "inter" life into the psychic violence of his new black-white chaosmos. The disguises are all staged for the ease of inter-lifer Furo's *passing*, crossing over into white world or living into the telos of the white life as African American history of mixed-race children taught us. See Brian Bantum, *Redeemed Mulatto: A Theology of Race and Christian Hybridity* (Waco, TX: Baylor University Press, 2010), 41–83, for a brilliant analysis of passing in America. Days after I completed the writing of this chapter and its point about racial "passing" in African American life and literature, I came across Julie Iromuanya's brilliant essay on *Blackass* on July 12, 2021, which confirmed my intuition of using "passing" as a critical framework to interpret Barrett's work. See Julie Iromuanya, "'White Man Magic': A. Igoni Barrett's *Blackass*, Afropolitanism, and (Post) Racial Anxieties," in *Afropolitan Literature as World Literature*, ed. James Hodapp (New York: Bloomsbury Academic, 2020), 71–84.

[16] Žižek, *For They Know Not*, xxiii–xxxiv.

Through the character of Furo, Barrett builds a complex relationship between blackness and whiteness in the postcolony and the psyche of the subject, ever more subtly exploring how postcolonial subjectivity creates postcolonialism. Unlike the precise prohibition of movements like Black Power ("Thou shall not covet whiteness"), the ethical injunction of *Blackass* is "Thou shall not." The prohibition is truncated—just as the subject is divided or split. The mere "Thou shall not" further *divides* the subject and highlights the logic of postcoloniality. As I have demonstrated with my analysis of the logic of ideological critique in the novel, postcolonial subjective destitution is not some invasion of the self by an external agency but rather a split within the self—the subject is torn between her fantasies for whiteness and her black life. The subject is split, de-completed by the other within. Thus, the prohibition is not simply "Thou shall not covet whiteness" given the confusion in desires. It simply says, "Thou shall not covet." Do not desire... what? Without knowing exactly what is proscribed or prohibited with just the formal, empty form of obligation, the ethical injunction takes the form of, as Giorgio Agamben explains, "a trial in the Kafkaesque sense of the term, perpetual self-accusation without a precept."[17] "Do not covet" is like the abstract *Sollen* ("ought to be") of the Kantian categorical imperative in its formal indeterminacy.[18] "Do not covet" is a split in ethics between form and determinate moral duties. I demonstrate later that this split majorly affected Furo's ethical character, especially in his inability to tell the truth of his situation to his family and in his drive to exploit others for his needs. *Blackass* shows us how postcolonial subjectivity ruins the norms and morality of African communities.

Often in popular discourses and literature, the relation between black and white is set up as a binary. The white world is set up as an "imaginary supplement," as compensatory consolation to the misery of black existence. In the imaginary dyad, the blissful white world cancels the terrifying excesses of the Nigerian black world. Implicit in this binary is a third term that "mediates" the two poles of the dyad and precipitates a horrifying reverse of the blissful white world. This fear of the misery of displacement in the white world retroactively cancels out all other miseries. The white world is already operating within the black world, and the black man is already displaced. Those in the black world live in constant fear of missing out on the presumed enjoyment of the white world. They fear being convinced by one's peers or others that one is not living the white man's dream. They fear being rejected by *white ideal*. We see Furo, thoroughly a "white man," being

---

[17]Giorgio Agamben, *The Time That Remains: A Commentary on the Letter to the Romans* (Stanford, CA: Stanford University Press, 2005), 108.
[18]Immanuel Kant, *The Metaphysics of Morals* (Cambridge: Cambridge University Press, 1996).

constantly displaced from whitehood.[19] He could not completely enjoy the white world; though he was *in* it, he was not *of* it.[20] His accent, his native name, anxiety over being discovered as a fraud, and the fear of his progeny being born with black skin are obstacles before him that ignite a gnawing fear of displacement. The fear is always retroactively canceling the horrors of black people abducting themselves into the hostile white world. The only way to endure the horrors of black-skin-white-masks is to remember "the infinitely more frightening horror" of being left out of the white world, so that the "horrors undergo a kind of 'transubstantiation' and become so many manifestations" of the wrath of displacement.[21] Barrett's exploration of the subjectivity of the postcolonial subject excavates the mediating fear between the dyad of black misery and excess white enjoyment in the African postcolony. And this is one part of the parallax view that permeates the novel at even its deepest structural level. The parallax view "is the apparent displacement of an object (the shift of his position against a background), caused by a change in an observational position that provides a new line of sight."[22]

The Parallax View of the *Blackass*

Blackass is a novel that compels the reader to see things as they emerge, shift, and disappear between two opposing poles. That is to say, it urges one to adopt the parallax view of reality. The transformation of Furo from black man to white man represents a shift in observation position that enables the reader to gain new perspective on ontological reality as we interpret

---

[19]Examples of Furo's fear of not being accepted by the white world are on pages 49, 111, 118–19. Is Furo's fear about not being accepted by other whites not remind us of the mixed-race son in Langston Hughes's 1927 poem, "Mulatto," that has the constant haunting refrain, "I am your son, white man!"? Hughes's poem brings an interesting perspective to *Blackass*; in his hybridity of epidermal whiteness and psychological blackness, Furo could be likened to a mulatto/a existence. His existence is a dialogue between transgression, hybridity, and contestation. Furo has transgressed into the white world. He is a hybrid of "black blood in white face," and his traffic with the white world carries the potentials of serious contestations (see Bantum, *Redeemed Mulatto*, 13–14, 21). But Furo's hybridity also speaks to the intermixture of identities. His "inter" life "indicates the depth to which all lives, stories, and cultures are bound up into one another in complicated webs of desire and loathing" (Bantum, *Redeemed Mulatto*, 81). Furo—which in Kalabari means, among other things, lineage, bloodline, genealogy, womb, stomach—points to the fact that the line of every lineage of identity started from or is articulated in a womb abounding in grown-ass subtleties and genealogical niceties—or from a stomach "polluted" with differences and transgressions.

[20]Žižek, *For They Know Not*, 17, 21, inspired this analysis.

[21]Quotation is from Žižek, *For They Know Not*, 21.

[22]Slavoj Žižek, *Living in the End Times* (London: Verso, 2010), 244.

ourselves as cultural subjects in the African postcolony. Through this way of seeing, Barrett draws his readers into seeing the negativity inherent in reality and in our constructed identities. Furo as white man is a negativity, the very gap that separates a person from his cherished identity. Furo's body is his cherished enemy. Barrett opens up this negativity in Furo's identity and does not easily let it sublate into a synthesis between black and white—he instead lets the reader tarry with the negative. Furo's identity—or more precisely, his subjectivity—is the absolute negativity of his substance.

In *Blackass*, identity is split from the idea of substance, which is mutable, labile, and constructible. Thus, identity (or subjectivity) is the gap that separates the person from his or her substance, the person from the *thing*. Subjectivity is the abyss of possibilities that lies beyond the tangible, visible person; the gap beyond the person and the *thing* conceived in the negative mode. Identity, subjectivity is not what lies within you, the positive content you tightly hold on to, but is the negative space beyond the limit the subject is trying to fill out with positive content.[23] A person and her identity are "'inherently mediated,' so that an 'epistemological shift' in the subject's point of view always reflects an 'ontological' shift in the object [identity] itself."[24] Barrett represents this epistemological shift in the subject's point of view as a dream that results in an ontological transformation; a black person becomes a white person, and man becomes woman.

The subject making this epistemological shift is always inscribed into her own image of the ontological shift in the guise of a stain, blind spot, a splinter of the old self in the new constituted by the subject. Furo's black ass is such a stain. Igoni's woman's penis (261) is an objectivized splinter of the abjected male self. In the words of Žižek, identity or subjectivity in Barrett's novel speaks to a "reflexive short circuit, this necessary redoubling of myself as standing both outside and inside my picture, that bears witness to my 'material existence.' Materialism means that the reality I see is never 'whole'—not because a large part of it eludes me, but because it contains a stain, a blind spot, which indicates my inclusion in it."[25]

Barrett's point that identity is not substance but a negativity speaks to the issue of how Furo lives out his new life. He never tries to overcome the negativity. He lives as a black man whose life is one of loss in relation to the white world, his other.[26] This way of developing Furo's character

[23]Slavoj Žižek, *Tarrying with the Negative: Kant, Hegel, and the Critique of Ideology* (Durham, NC: Duke University Press, 1993), 21.

[24]Slavoj Žižek, *The Parallax View* (Cambridge, MA: MIT Press, 2006), 17.

[25]Žižek, *Parallax View*, 17.

[26]Alex Mangold, "Introduction: Performing Žižek: Hegel, Lacan, Marx and the Parallax View," *Žižek and Performance*, ed. Broderick Chow and Alex Mangold (New York: Palgrave Macmillan, 2014), 1–12, quotation on 8.

makes a subtle and profound Hegelian point "that the subject does *not* survive the ordeal of negativity: he *effectively* loses his very essence and passes into his Other."[27] Furo, with his black ass—his black *yansh*—cannot overcome the negativity of what has happened to him and passes into his white other.

The Unchangeable Black *Yansh*

The black ass, the stubborn *yansh* (patch) of blackness on Furo's buttocks, represents the leftover that totalizing whiteness could not seize. The *yansh* is a reminder of the traumatic loss, violent takeover, capture of the body, brutal erasure, and cancellation of Furo's *indigenous* somatic features. It is a stand-in for the cut into the flesh of being. The novel ends without healing this wound of scission. There is apparently no reconciliation. And yet, a reconciliation has been before us all along: the cut itself is the reconciliation. To overcome whiteness or blackness, which already exists within the postcolonial subject, is to adopt a shift in perspective. We reinterpret the black ass as a whole that is always split from within itself; whiteness can never fully become itself, cannot reach its own place. There is always an impediment, an obstacle within it, which refuses complete identity that sets identity in motion. The black ass is what refuses whiteness from "encompassing all differences." The black ass here represents not only "the radical negativity which forever blocks the fulfilment of every positive [white] identity" but also that of any identity.[28]

Barrett's message here is that all identity is ontologically incomplete (always decentered from within). The black ass is the particular that disavows and subverts the universalizing whiteness, so Furo's whiteness cannot achieve identity with itself. The nonidentity between the ass and the rest of the body, between black and white, also speaks to the inherent nonidentity of whiteness with itself. The other is always within the self. Every claim of identity is a failed totalization masquerading as truth, an attempt to domesticate an internal antagonism and integrate it into a harmonious rational whole. In the *Phenomenology of the Spirit*, Georg Wilhelm Friedrich Hegel wrote about the nonidentity of substance and split, the split of substance, and that the subject is not his or her substance—rather, a gap always separates subject (identity) from substance, whatever that may be.

---

[27]Slavoj Žižek, "The Eclipse of Meaning: On Lacan and Deconstruction," in *Interrogating the Real*, ed. Rex Butler and Scotts Stephen (London: Continuum, 2006), 217.
[28]Žižek, *For They Know Not*, 69.

The disparity which exists in consciousness between the "I" [Furo's I of a black man] and the Substance [whiteness, white skin] which is its object is the distinction between them, the negative in general. This can be regarded as the defect of both, though it is their soul, or that which moves them…. Now, although this negative appears at first as a disparity between the "I" and its object, it is just as much the disparity of the Substance with itself. Thus what seems to happen outside of it, to be an activity directed against it, is really its own doing, and Substance shows itself to be existentially Subject.[29]

The admixture of black and white sheds another perspective on the split nature of Furo's subjectivity. In his hybridity, Furo is an individual incarnation of the masculine kingdom, the figure of man. This is precisely the person that does not exist (perhaps only in dream, fantasy, and novelists' heads). No man, no person embodies the different qualities of Man, no person has them all; no one is structured as the *All*. So, as we can see, Furo is split between black (black ass) and white (white skin). In the capitalist world where almost everything is commoditized, where we see Furo commoditizing his whiteness (or is it his split-ness?) to climb his way to prosperity, it is the logic of the capitalist commodity world that offers profound insights to his patchwork of a body. His body is split into "use value" and "exchange value." The black ass is the "exchange value" insofar as "it is of no particular use, [it] exhibits and [represents] 'exchange value' of all" bodies.[30] As per the logic of the novel, the black body can be exchanged for another body, which incarnates "usefulness," "profitability," or dignity and respect in the white gaze. The visible, publicly accessible whiteness of Furo's body exhibits and personifies "use value." The split of Furo's flesh into black ass and white body; the split of his *sarx/soma* into exchange value (the symbolic equivalent of all bodies degraded insofar as they are catalogued as commodities, enslave-able flesh, and *homines sacri* in the postcolonial capitalist regime) and use value (the property bodies must have to satisfy corporations' quest for profit or to induce quick promotion in the Nigerian corporate world. Whiteness is associated with supreme enjoyment) demonstrates the coexistence of the of "use value" and exchange value" in one body. Yet we should not forget that in the postcolonial world, whiteness as "use value" is only a form of appearance. The paradox of whitewashed postcoloniality in Nigeria as conveyed by Barrett's novel is that the notion of white man arrives at its being-for-itself by reflecting itself in its opposite, the black man, the embodiment of which negates white body's notional

[29]G. W. F. Hegel, *Phenomenology of Spirit*, trans. A. V. Miller (Oxford: Oxford University Press, 1977), 21.
[30]Žižek, *For They Know Not*, 114.

universality and appears as (stands for) Human in general by nature of its exchangeability and being the *part of no-part*.[31] The black body in its "expanded" form as the bearer of excess social weight of suffering passes into the "general" form when it is excluded—when it is the *part of no-part*, exempted from the collection of bodies with access to enjoyment—and thus appears as the general equivalent of all human bodies, as the immediate incarnation of the Human (the entire human race) as such. The black body is the universality of Human Body, incarnated in individual racialized (race-d) bodies.[32]

I can now say in a certain sense that in *Blackass*, Barrett offers us a proposition: *The white human being is a black person.* This means that the black person's identity cannot be identical with itself. Whiteness is "none other than the 'force of negativity' which prevents [black person] from fully 'becoming itself.'"[33] This point is relevant to emphasize because it is not enough to say that there is no identity between Furo's white body and black ass. To think this way is to implicitly presuppose that Furo is "two persons" with no identity between them. But the point I am making here is that there is only a single self that is internally split, which cannot come to identity with itself. The black ass is none other than the nonidentity of whiteness with itself. And white body is none other than the nonidentity of blackness with itself.[34] This is the *blackassness* that is hidden under every skin, and it is written by the hieroglyphics of dreams (227).

Theory of Dream

Dream is the organizing metaphor of *Blackass*. In order to adequately interpret the special role dreams play in this novel, we must distinguish between what I see as two types of dream: constative and performative.

---

[31]Žižek, *For They Know Not*, 124, inspired this analysis. See also Jacques Rancière, *Disagreement: Politics and Philosophy*, trans. Julie Rose (Minneapolis: University of Minnesota Press, 1998) for the concept of *part of no-part*. Rancière conceptualizes the *demos* as both a part of the community and is the whole community. Rancière believes that a society is internally split between the part that counts and the part that does not count, the *part of no-part*, which is identified with the whole community. A fundamental difference, antagonism exists between the parts of the community: while the part that does not count wants to undermine the order of distribution of bodies and places, the part that dominates aspires to maintain the harmony of specific human-being together, the way of being, the consensual practices that reject the political logic of the egalitarian act.

[32]Žižek, *For They Know Not*, 124. His analysis of the commodity form, following Karl Marx, inspired this discourse of the black body.

[33]Žižek, *For They Know Not*, 119.

[34]Žižek, *For They Know Not*, 119.

Constative dream describes a state of affairs according to the criteria of the dreamworld, the world of sleep. Performative dream does something to and alters the status (being, ontology) of the dreamer (sleeper) at the impossible point of intersection between the real world and the dreamworld. Such a dream has the capacity to alter the reality to which it refers. Performative dream happens twice: first, when it transgresses the boundary between reality and dream; second, when it misfires, transforming the inner (supposed) substantial identity of the dreamer and constructing it in the form of its opposite for either the subject's transgressive enjoyment or disavowal. The misfire can produce a potentially incestuous object. Black-male Furo in his performative dream became a white man and, in the very impossible point of intersection of dream and reality, also confronted his femaleness in the form of Igoni, the transgender woman. "Pity the man who never becomes the woman he could be" (58). The novelist implies that there is a woman in every man—a being that can irrupt into the open in a performative dreamworld. This is the subject thrown before himself as his own, potentially incestuous object.

In Barrett's novel, the Kafkian dream not only erases an external division between the dreamworld and the real world but also transforms internal distinction or repressed sexuality within each dreamer and ejects them into the real world to shadow (haunt) the enjoyment of the erased external division. All these lead us to the third form of the Barrettian dream, a kind of surplus beyond the effect produced by the performative dream: the split performative dream. The performative dream, which can bring about its own reality, suffers an inherent imbalance that can force it to engage a "new reality" in the form of its opposite. It seems a performative dream that transforms reality outside the dreamworld also transforms the "inside" essence of the dreamer, which the dreamer must face as his shadow, mirror self in the real world. The dreamworld, which can take a fantasy inside the "head" and make it real, is also capable of taking an inner ontological opposite and making a full object, a double in the real world in its dramaturgical process of the "shock of the real," in its carnivalesque reversal of reality. Put differently, such a dream necessarily misfires, splitting the subject (dreamer) into its at once sublime and abject selves, its fascinating and repellant selves. Faced with this choice between the fascinating and repellant selves, the subject must make the choice of acceptance or abjection. Furo must choose his fascinating white self (Frank Whyte) and his "repellant" black-transgender-woman self (Igoni). "At sunrise, I discovered his black ass. And when he awoke, after he called me [Igoni] back to bed and slipped his hand between my legs, he, too, found my secret. It is easier to be than to become. Frank should have known that. His shocked reaction to my [woman's] penis proved that he didn't" (261).

I am not done with the "conceptualization" of dream that is implicit in *Blackass*. Dreams like identity have contradiction (other) as their internal condition. The same dream can be seen from two different points of view. Dreams are often characterized by *paraconsistent logic*, which rejects the classical law of noncontradiction. In the dreamworld, two contradictory events (or attributes possessed by an entity or person) can be true both at the same time and in the same way. This "incoherency" may well represent the noncoincidence of a thing (dream) with itself, the minimal difference between a thing and itself.[35] This minimal difference "is the point at which a thing has the potential to unravel into a multitude, or split into antagonistic oppositions."[36]

Barrett sets his story within this (minimal) gap between the two segments (dimensions) of Furo's dream that inaugurated the narrative of the novel. One part—Furo's angle—happens instantaneously. Igoni's part began to come into focus, realization on the second day. This minimal gap cannot be removed. Once you remove it, the novel disappears. The novel is the very form of this gap itself and speaks to an ontology that considers reality itself as incomplete and split from within.

The Character Igoni

The character Igoni (the author's middle name) was born in 1979 as the author. He is Kalabari like Barrett, and so on. The male Igoni character became a transgender woman, but Barrett is still a man. Why Barrett chose to name a character after himself remains unclear. Is this another parallax view of the dreamworld, of dreams that burst forth from their world and drag the writer into it? It appears Igoni Barrett opened a wardrobe door, fell into a fairytale, saw the story of Furo being played out, watched it, and brought it back to us in his more self-conscious moment or release (return) from the fairy world. In the novel, the Igoni character drops several hints that he/she is eavesdropping on the story of Furo (261). I am also aware of Kalabari-Ijo legends of how creative minds generated great stories in ancient times. Often, creators of art in the form of masquerade displays or dancing society will say they learned everything from *owu amawa'pu* (water spirits). They secretly watched the gods play or were captured and taken into the water spirits' secret sacred world.[37]

---

[35]Žižek, *Parallax View*, 17.
[36]Simon Ellis and Collin Poole, "Collaboration, Violence, and Difference," in Chow and Magold, *Žižek and Performance*, 213.
[37]Robin Horton, "Ekineba: A Forgotten Myth," *Oduma* 2 (1975): 33–6 and Robin Horton, "The Kalabari Ekine Society: A Borderline of Religion and Art," *Africa* 33 (1963): 94–114.

Another explanation for Barrett inscribing his name into the novel as a character's name might be to offer literary critics a glimpse of his personal idiosyncrasies to enable them to get to the "truth" of his work. But this transformation of the male character into a transgender woman belies any suggestion that the writer's inner conflicts or intimate individual psyche are the basis of the public expression of Igoni as a character. The reader needs to take a parallax view of Igoni to clearly see what Barrett is doing with this character.

Transgender woman Igoni's identity is ultimately her place in the symbolic order. Igoni (which means stranger, visitor, foreigner, sojourner in Kalabari) disturbs the notion of harmony, consistency, or wholeness of the symbolic order. Igoni represents the excess that the prevailing socio-symbolic order of male-female cannot capture. Igoni marks the point in the social order that says no order can completely totalize human experience or capture the variety of expressions of human experiences. So Igoni's place in the symbolic order "is the point of eruption of the otherwise hidden truth of an existing social order."[38] The point of eruption represents a space, a gap that refuses closure of systems of identity. This is the very gap Furo, the white man, has to confront: the antagonism between his dream-transformed white heterosexuality and his dream-created opposite, transgender (black) woman. Earlier, I made the argument that both transformations (Furo's and Igoni's) are the results of the same dreamwork. Where there is (new) subjectivization, there is an excessive surplus, a supplement to the subject itself, which the subject must disavow to perform or affirm its existence.[39] In the novel, we see Furo (Frank Whyte) rejecting, disavowing Igoni (or the obscene supplement of the black ass, the black moon on the white surface). When Furo is with transgender woman Igoni, he confronts the latter's "woman's penis" as an obstacle to his sexual jouissance. He fails to recognize the "negativity" of Igoni or Igoni's woman's penis as the condition of possibility of his own emergence as a white man, the positive ground of his transfiguration. More importantly, he fails to recognize Igoni (the "foreigner") as his own substance because he fails to recognize that there is no pure positivity in the subjectivization process. An otherness always threatens, haunts, or undermines self-identity. For Furo to see the abjected, disavowed "substance" as his own requires a parallax shift of perspective.

---

[38]Slavoj Žižek, *Looking Awry: An Introduction to Jacques Lacan through Popular Culture* (Cambridge, MA: MIT Press, 1991), 40.

[39]This way of expressing myself was inspired by Peter M. Boenisch, "Who's Watching? Me!: Theatrality, Spectatorship, and Žižekian Subject," in Chow and Mangold, *Žižek and Performance*, 51.

Furo as a Synthetic Ideal

Furo is a synthesis of black and white. As Sakiru Adebayo argues in his study of *Blackass*, he is two in one. "Furo Wariboko, the main character, seems to be the most elusive figure. Is he really a white man? Or, for analytical ease, is it useful to read him as a black man? But what if he is really two in one? Being an allegory and an absurdist narrative, the novel opens these possibilities of reading Furo in various dimensions."[40] In my estimation, Adebayo was too quick to move away from this observation. He did not explore why the idea of the composite—what I have called elsewhere the "synthetic ideal"—is a key to interpreting African culture and worldview.[41] As Wole Soyinka would have explained it, Adebayo did not examine the code on which the composite or synthesis is based, the code that accents the elastic nature of knowledge.[42]

What if Barrett presented Furo as a composite to signify that such a possibility of existence gives harried African youth the best chance of navigating postcolonial Nigeria wherein whiteness is privileged while also contested and resisted? Furo as an admixture reflects this ideal. In the Kalabari culture in which Furo is situated (and from which Barrett also comes), the synthetic ideal (the other-within, the space beyond binary opposition) is the best way to navigate reality, accessing the aesthetic value of phenomena. From men to gods, from aesthetics to art, from textile design to ancestral screens, from the living to the dead, the Kalabari idea of perfection is the collage, the composite, the blend. In Kalabari culture, the provocative, the excitable, the lovable, the acceptable, and the ideal neither stand apart at the hilltop nor dwell in the valley but adhere at the conjunction of the extremes. This concept of the ideal type principally derives from predilection to borrowing, transformation, and reinterpretation of "foreign elements." In Kalabari social practices they locate the beautiful, the dangerous, the powerful, and the exceptional at points of admixture. The position in their value system that indicates excellence, danger, or power is often points that are embodiments of differing categories. The admixture category, not the pure, is what is held up to be the high point. What kind of artifact, ideology, or ideas often show up as the ideal type in Kalabari? The ideal type is often

---

[40]Sakiru Adebayo, "The Black Soul Is (Still) a White Man's Artefact? Postcoloniality, Post-Fanonism, and the Tenacity of Race(ism) in A. Igoni Barrett's *Blackass*," *African Studies* 79, no. 1 (2020): 143–59, quotation on 147.

[41]Nimi Wariboko, "Kalabari: A Study of Synthetic Ideal," *Nordic Journal of African Studies* 8, no. 1 (1999): 80–93.

[42]Wole Soyinka, *Myth, Literature, and the African World* (Cambridge: Cambridge University Press, 1976), 53–4.

a composite of many types. Kalabari show a bias for the composite or prefer to create their identity by drawing elements from many sources.[43]

It is important to mention that the synthetic ideal, which aims to create composites, is not totalizing. Nor is it the logic of erasing or swallowing differences. The notion of ideal in Kalabari culture does not correlate with anything like Platonic essentialism. It is not geared toward reaching or appropriating the Intelligent Form of any existing thing. The concept of ideal does not mean that any existent thing is automatically adjudged to be an imperfect copy or imitation of the Intelligent Form. The synthetic ideal is not the Ideal from which every physical manifestation is deemed inferior and considered to have fallen short of the glory of the eternal form. The ideal is always the combination of attributes of whatever is brought to existence or socially constructed to advance human flourishing. In this sense, the ideal subverts the binary logic that decides whether a thing/existent belongs to the Ideal or not. The ideal is not a mere subversion of the logic of binarism. It is an open recognition of the split character, incompleteness of identity or ontology, and a willingness to confront or "traverse" the split. Thus, the notion of the ideal presses toward inclusion rather than exclusion, or what Soyinka called "a non-doctrinaire mould of constant awareness."[44] Harry Garuba has argued that this way of understanding reality—what he referred to as "animist materialism"—is fundamental to many traditional (non-Western) African communities. Garuba noted that many major writers in Africa, Latin America, and India have poached the "possibilities of narrative presentations inherent" in this kind of worldview.[45] "Writers such as Ben Okri, García Márquez, and Rushdie [used] the techniques and strategies to construct a narrative universe in which transpositions and transgressions of boundaries and identities predominate."[46]

Barrett's transformation of Furo into a synthetic ideal, a white man amid blacks, raises a number of questions. Is whiteness cultural or substantial (hypostasis, *ousia*)? How does the transformation of the substance of pigmentation induce cultural whiteness? Questions also arise about the qualitative distinction between the (skin-deep) "substance" of whiteness in Furo and that of all other white persons in the world. Furo, indeed, was concerned that his progeny would be black (254). So, there are two *ousiai* in whiteness: real and dreamed (acquired).

Furo definitely has the dreamed *ousia*, the one that is not transmissible. But his mind, the locus of his cultural self-interpretation, is black ("I'm a

---

[43]Wariboko, "Kalabari," 80.
[44]Soyinka, *Myth*, 54.
[45]Harry Garuba, "Explorations in Animist Materialism: Notes on Reading/Writing African Literature, Culture, and Society," *Public Culture* 15, no. 3 (2003): 261–85, quotation on 271.
[46]Garuba, "Explorations," 271.

Nigerian"), at least, for most of the twenty-seven days of his ordeal. The point here is that Furo's mind was not immediately assumed by the pigmentation of whiteness. This is not to say that Furo is divided into two *prosopa*. He is a single human being, one person, though he possesses "two natures." Furo in the deep conception of the novel is a perfect white man with a perfect *black mind* (the totality of a person's creative self-interpretation of the self or moral life—the soul, which is often preformatted by Eurocentric values and the white gaze).[47]

Thus, a union of whiteness and blackness exists in Furo's transformation. To use a theological language, Barrett presents the two "natures" as "undergoing no confusion, no change, no division, and no separation... the property of both natures is preserved and comes together into a single person and a single subsistent being."[48] Barrett does not really present the reader with Furo's inner struggles as he became a new man. Whatever we get by way of inner psychological deliberations (conflicts) goes no further than the initial meditation and apprehension of any migrant to a new country (town). Furo slipped into his skin almost perfectly. He is perfect white man, perfect black man. This is the description or the stuff of the salvific beings. This is Nicene logic. And its metaphysical insight and aesthetic are part of the sense and sensibility of Nigeria, of the deep structure of the country's ethos. Novels can lose their way and turn up on the right side of theology.

No wonder Syreeta, Arinze, Umukoro, and Yuguda see Furo as a savior for their various projects. They all hasten to worship the salvific, aesthetic, and economic-strategic value of whiteness. To Syreeta, Arinze, Umukoro, and Yuguda, white skin is the symbol of progress, the light that will translate Nigerian into the marvelous light of European civilization. Syreeta wants Furo for the social mobility she will gain in the postcolony for having a mixed-race child. She exemplifies the behavior many black women exhibited toward their white lovers that Frantz Fanon excoriated in 1952. For any of such women her white partner whom she loves conditionally is "her lord. She asks for nothing, demands nothing, except for a little whiteness in her life. And when she asks herself whether he is handsome or ugly, she writes: 'All I know is that he had blue eyes, blond hair, a pale complexion and I loved him.'"[49]

Rather than offering Furo the position of salesperson for which he applied, Arinze gave him an executive position as public relations officer of Haba! Alhaji Yuguda offered Furo the position of head of his construction

---

[47]For a discussion on the soul as a social construct, see Nimi Wariboko, *Economics in Spirit and Truth: A Moral Philosophy of Finance* (New York: Palgrave Macmillan, 2014), xii–xiii, 6–8, 10–11, 161, 178.

[48]"Council of Chalcedon—451," in *Decrees of the Ecumenical Councils*, Vol. 1, *Nicaea 1—Lateran V*, ed. Norman P. Tanner (London: Sheed and Ward, 1990), 86–7.

[49]Frantz Fanon, *Black Skin, White Masks* (1952; repr., New York: Grove, 2007), 25.

firm. In making the offer he said, "'I need a leader who can command respect and inspire fear. That person is you…. You'll get respect because you're white. They'll fear you because you're Nigerian. You know the tricks, you understand the thinking, you speak the language'" (243–4). Is the description of Furo by Alhaji Yuguda not that of a salvific being, a perfect man for the Nigerian postcolony as conceived and sustained by the elites? If not already a salvific being, Furo was quickly becoming one.

Being and Becoming in the Annals of *Blackass*

Becoming is an attribute of existence that is "better to possess than not to possess."[50] To exist means to be subject to transformation, to be caught up in ongoing process of "becoming." To exist means "to be sustained by elements of stability that prevent annihilation, but it also means being subject to the transforming creativity that empowers this process of becoming."[51]

The tension between being and becoming is a major theme of the novel. "It is easier to be than to become" (261). Barrett repeats this statement several times in the book (see also 148, 166), accenting an ethos of immutability while continuously pursuing a storyline of mutability. Is this orientation not part of the paraconsistent logic or the Nicene logic of the novel? Yes, but there is something more. In the deep structure of the novel—more precisely, the novel's argument—there is a Pseudo-Dionysian pattern of thought. This is when Barrett affirms immutability as the true nature of existence (being) and then denies its literal application to human phenomenal existence. In this apophatic style of thought, Barrett both affirms and denies the applicability of immutability to human existence, while somehow situating his narrative in the gap between that affirmation and denial to resolve the tension between mutability and immutability.[52]

Consider the character Igoni. In one breath he is both the fictional version of the author (51–2, 54, 77, 78) and a character like the rest in the book. Some of the character's words are "nearly identical to ones from

---

[50]Rebecca L. Copeland, *Created Being: Expanding Creedal Christology* (Waco, TX: Baylor University Press, 2020), 4.

[51]Copeland, *Created Being*, 48.

[52]Apophaticism: This is a form of negative theology and practice: some philosophers believing that God is indescribable, unknowable, and inconceivable speak about the attributes of God in negative terms and sentences. The accent of conception of God falls on what God is not. The opposite of apophaticism is cataphatic: speaks directly about the positive attributes of God, claiming that human beings can have positive knowledge of God. Thus, to speak about something through denial of its attributes is an apophatic practice. The opposite is true of cataphaticism.

an interview Barrett did with Granta."[53] Yet, Barrett denies that Igoni the character bearing his first (middle) name is a fictional version of himself. Is Barrett trying to play God here? First, as the presumed narrator with a God's eye view of reality, he is as omniscient as narrators go in novels. The character Igoni tells Tekena, Furo's sister, to call him Morpheus (94), the Greek god of sleep and dreams who appears in human form to dreamers in their sleep. His brother, Phobetor, appears in dreams of people as animal forms. One of Morpheus's sons is Metamorphosis. Barrett names one of the chapters of Blackass, "Metamorphosis" (257), and it comes after the chapter "Morpheus" (159). Now, wait for it: Blackass is a riff on Franz Kafka's The Metamorphosis, which is a story about Gregor Samsa, a traveling salesman who awakes one day an insect. So, Barrett or Igoni is the father, the precursor of Kafka and Kafka is brother Phobetor, who turns Gregor into an insect. Barrett can say to Kafka, "Before Abraham I was." He can also say Kafka is my father, and as his son, I do whatever the father does.

In Furo's story, Barrett starts by making "becoming" easy; then he affirms becoming; then he denies that becoming is easy; then he tells us that becoming what you are not originally involves a lot of hard work; and finally, he negates the contradiction between these two positions. In Blackass, identity or existence is the becoming of being, being is becoming. This is a key ontological insight of the novel that plays out in the story and the use of language.[54] But overall, neither language nor literature is capable of relentlessly conveying positive knowledge of existence in the African postcolony. Life in the postcolony is full of contradictions and illusions, and to understand it we must think in paraconsistent logic and in the complex procedure of Pseudo-Dionysian apophaticism. Barrett uses the illusion of dreams to warn Nigerians not to succumb to the illusion of language and literature, or, as I stated earlier, to remind his readers not to buy into the argument of ideological illusion. Although Barrett's overall style seems to deftly portray the existential conditions of the African postcolony through apophatic denials of its positive attributes, this kind of storytelling functions cataphatically in the race debates in the novel. It works cataphatically with regard to asserting positive claims about blacks' self-understanding and (unconscious) fantasy and the privileges of whiteness (Western civilization)

---

[53]Michael Schaub, "An Audacious Transformation Bogs Down in Blackass," March 6, 2016, https://www.npr.org/2016/03/06/468941255/an-audacious-transformation-bogs-down-in-blackass

[54]"To be *actual* is to be a process. Anything that is not a process is an abstraction from process, not full-fledged actuality.... Since the world as we experience it is a place of process, of change, of becoming, of growth and decay, the contrary notion that what is actual or fully real is beyond change leads to a devaluation of life in the world" (John B. Cobb Jr. and David Ray Griffin, *Process Theology: An Introductory Exposition* [Louisville, KY: Westminster John Knox, 1976], 14).

that are in turn used to define the destiny of black as white in the Nigeria postcolony. In a sense, the novel is written to authenticate the applicability of Fanon's insight made at the height of colonialism to present-day postcolony with its psychopolitics and necropolitics of race. Fanon wrote in 1952 that "as painful as it is for us to have to say it this: there is but one destiny for the black man. And it is white."[55] In a 2016 interview with *Farabale Africa*, Barrett stated,

> For most people that's a controversial statement, especially if you are black. That quote resonates elsewhere in the book and in Nigeria in general…. The world we engage with today is based on a western model. In the end, the destiny of the black man so far has been to become white…. I felt [the citation from Fanon] was painful but honest.[56]

Blackass is a cataphatic claim about the destiny of black people in a world dominated by whiteness. It affirms Fanon's thesis, and insists that subservient attitude of blacks toward whites is knowable in some sense, if not in the soul/mind, at least in behaviors, practices, and actions.

If what I have argued so far about this novel is accurate—that it rejects substantive ontologies—then what is the substance of whiteness that could possibly be the destiny of black people? Neither Fanon nor Barrett views whiteness as a universal shared substance. Their preferred ontology is relational; relationships are what is fundamental to being. What is shared universally is mutually transformative interdependence. Thus, whiteness as a destination-identity means that blacks entering into this "interdependence" abject their particularity into the particularity of whites without transforming whiteness. Such is the destiny of subjective destitution or the logic of kenotic destiny (nadir of emptiness and captivity).

I have resorted here to the notion of relational ontology to save Barrett and his novel from the criticism that if there is no substance (as the novel ceaselessly demonstrates by its accent on peripety and nimiety of bodily transformations), then what is the substance of whiteness that blacks are trying to grasp. The power of relational ontology as a possible solution to the conundrum of absence of destination-substance that serves as destination-substance for blacks weakens once you seriously consider the statement: whiteness is the destiny of blacks. If blacks all "pour" into whiteness, then relational ontology as applied in this context collapses. Relational ontology cannot exist if there is only one solitary being. Relationship is about irreducible interdependence of beings, particulars—none existing entirely alone. If whiteness is the only "entity," the only destiny, then there is no

---

[55]Fanon, *Black Skin, White Masks*, xiv.
[56]Quoted in Adebayo, "The Black Soul," 144.

existence as we know it today. At least, whiteness needs the existence of blackness as an other to know itself. But if Fanon is right that blackness is a zone of nonbeing, then ultimately all the fine points of substance or relational ontologies do not matter.[57] The black person has to first find his or her being.

Given the context of the Nigerian postcolony in a world dominated by whiteness, there needs to a third space beyond substance and relational ontologies or beyond subjugated, degraded blackness and white supremacism. This brings me to one shortcoming of *Blackass*—or at least, a shortcoming of its underlying philosophy that I have been unraveling in this chapter. The novel does not offer a space for an alternative dream; at best, it offers a space that was not fulfilled.

The Nonconcluding Ending of the Novel

Barrett ends *Blackass* by giving the impression that Igoni, who has befriended Furo's sister, Tekena, would expose Furo, make him confront his mother and sister, and bring him out of hiding. This ending assumes that his family members would see him, recognize him as their own flesh and blood, and not think that of the prospect of meeting Furo as a cruel joke played on them by Igoni, the transgender woman. Let us not forget Furo's reaction when he read the missing person announcement about him in the newspaper. He knew even his parents would not recognize him in his new, transmogrified person:

> His face had sloughed off immaturity. Then again, the unexpectedness of his skin shade, eye colour, and hair texture was the octopus ink that would confuse his hunters, as even he wouldn't have recognized himself in a photo of his new face, and so neither would his parents nor anyone who based their looking on his old image. He knew at last that he had nothing to fear. He was a different person, and right here, right now, right in his face, he could see he looked nothing like the former Furo.
>
> (156)

Yes, Barrett presents Furo as waiting at the door of Igoni's apartment, waiting for sixty-six minutes for his mother to knock and call out, "'Furo—are you there? Come and open the door'" (262, the last line of the novel).

---

[57]"There is a zone of nonbeing, an extraordinary sterile and arid region, an incline stripped bare of every essential from which a genuine new departure can emerge. In most cases, the black man cannot take advantage of this descent into a veritable hell" (Fanon, *Black Skin, White Masks*, xii).

Let us assume that he opened the door—what did his mother see? Frank Whyte, the white man, is visible to her and her daughter, but Furo, the black man, is invisible to her. White-man Furo ($Furo_2$) is the only person who recognizes black-man Furo ($Furo_1$) and $Furo_2$ and to whom all persons (mother and daughter) are visible. White man Furo can see all persons, but to all persons, Furo the black man is invisible. This creates, replays, or displays an age-old power dynamic. In this novel, $Furo_2$ represents the white imperial powers that subjugate the Nigerian postcolony.

Powerful rulers have the means to remain invisible to their weak subjects while overcoming ordinary persons' authority to be invisible to them. They want the other to be visible even as they remain invisible. If the other cannot see them, then the other cannot accuse or condition them even if the powerful leaders exercise dominating, unquestionable authority over them. But powerful rulers can freely accuse, condition, or ignore the other. This is a political-ethical dimension of the invisibility of the powerful.

Decades ago, Emmanuel Levinas clearly made this connection between invisibility and ethical responsibility with his use of the myth of Gyges. As Plato related the myth in *The Republic* (359d–360b), after an earthquake, a shepherd of the king of Gyges found a ring in a tomb that could make him invisible to others by turning it toward himself. While he remained invisible to them, they were visible to him. When the ring was turned away from him, he became visible to them, and he continued to see them. Having this power of invisibility at will, he seduced the queen, killed the king, and assumed the throne himself. Levinas interpreted the myth as "the very myth of the I... which exist non-recognized.... [When one sees] without being seen... [it is] a determination of the other by the same, without the same being determined by the other."[58]

For Levinas, the asymmetrical cognition of the other that the power of invisibility provides speaks of the evasion of the ethical responsibility. This is a key for interpreting the ethics of the potential interplay of $Furo_1$ and $Furo_2$ at Igoni's door. The effect of "invisibility to others is ethical immunity to the command of the Other," to be held accountable to the other, to respond to the call that social coexistence demands.[59] As philosopher Corey Beals puts it, "The condition of Gyges is the 'eventuality of all unpunished crimes,' and this impunity is related to being 'non-recognized'.... This myth captures the very ontological structure... that Levinas seeks to overthrow."[60]

---

[58]Emmanuel Levinas, *Totality and Infinity*, trans. Alphonso Lingis (Pittsburgh, PA: Duquesne University Press, 1961), 61, 170.
[59]Corey Beals, *Levinas and the Wisdom of Love: The Question of Invisibility* (Waco, TX: Baylor University Press, 2007), 77.
[60]Beals, *Levinas*, 77–8.

The power or myth of the invisibility of Furo$_2$ in Nigerian society captures the very ontological and political structures of foreign sovereignty that must be overthrown. Nigerians who want to transform their country must seek out all methods by which invisibility is practiced in the country. Religion, politics, academia, and business must begin to take their responsibility to the other seriously. The other must become truly visible to all of us, and we must be visible to the other.

Now the reader may question my speculation about possible endings for this speculative novel. She might ask why I don't just accept the conclusion of Furo's story as Barrett has in *Blackass*. But I see in *Blackass* something more than the novel itself. Barrett relentlessly points out to his reader the fervent struggle or burning desire of Furo to live into his new self, the Oyibo man; in doing so, Barrett makes a very Hegelian point. The Hegelian subject does not overcome the ordeal of negativity, the split in substance that created and sustain subjectivity.[61] More importantly, the novel demonstrates that identity is not substance to be taken at face value. Substance is no real unchanging, eternal *thing* that shores up identity; it is appearance qua appearance. "In the opposition between the corporeal-material and the pure 'sterile' appearance, subject is appearance itself, brought to its self-reflection; it is *something that exists only insofar as it is appears to itself.*"[62] So, overcoming the ordeal of negativity by dual, error-free co-recognition at Igoni's door undermines the basic philosophical underpinning of the novel. Putting basic philosophy aside, questions remain about the possibility of mutual recognition.

I have argued that the meeting between Furo and his mother and sister might not produce a recognition of him on their part. There can be no recognition (re-cognition, a knowing-again) without identity. Furo's body is recognizably not itself. In the magical realist world of the novel the body was sown (in the dream) in blackness and rose through its own internal power into the bloom of whiteness in the waking hour. Is the seed that was sown the same (identical) with the "wheat" that sprouted? Is Furo's family, which did not sow the seed, likely to recognize the tree or fruit that came forth from the seed that fell to the ground and rotted to give new life? Where is the material continuity between the seed and the fruit apart from memory or mental capacity of the age-old Furo that is stored in the cranium of the new Furo? (We have so far not asked the question, if the transmogrification of Furo is mind-transplant or pigmentation change? Did Furo's brain get a new body?)

Do all these questions not remind you of early Christians' debate about the resurrection body? Or about God, who makes people die and

---

[61]Žižek, "Eclipse of Meaning," 217.
[62]Žižek, *Parallax View*, 206.

puts them back together in resurrection, and the risen body that has been radically transformed—sown in natural body, raised as spiritual body (1 Cor 15:44)—but which can still be recognized as belonging to the same person. Is Barrett here not God who tries to resurrect the dead (Furo) with his ending of *Blackass*? Didn't painter Henri Matisse and writer James Joyce, independently, say that they were God? The works of great minds point us to an alien infinity—the potentialities of humans that are always inexhaustible. There is a sense in which a person's excellent achievements express and even point beyond his or her current historical being, to their potential New Being as a historical reality, as Paul Tillich put it.[63]

George Steiner also noted the spiritual nature of human creativity but approached it from a different angle. For him, the creativity, the excellence of human *poiesis*, is not about their new being (not just about the transformation of humanity) but something bigger. The so-far inexhaustible deployment of forms by humans is in sheer competition with the "other Craftsman," the "other Shaper." He posited the hypothesis of alternative divinity as the motive behind the drive to excellence. Humans are not imitating God in excellence. Excellence or creativity "is radically agonistic," Steiner explained. "In all substantive art-acts there beats an angry gaiety. The source is that of loving rage. The human maker rages at his coming *after*, at being, forever, second to the original and originating mystery of the forming of form."[64] After completing a painting at Venice's Chapel of Rosary, Matisse declared to Sister Jacques-Marie, "I did it for myself." Sister Jacques-Marie then objected, "But you told me you were doing it for God," to which Matisse then uttered his famous reply, "Yes, but I am God."[65] Indeed, one does not need to be Matisse to play the role of creator. In a substantive work, the human being, "the artist, like the God of creation, remains within or behind or beyond or above his handiwork," intoned James Joyce, and when we encounter it, we meet its creator—or at least the image of the creator.[66]

I will not argue with the reader if she says Barrett is not playing God or beating an angry gaiety. If he is not playing God, then I say there would not be any recognition of Furo by his mother and sister. This brings me to another possible ending of the novel. Furo's mother's knock at Igoni's door (Saturday, July 14, 2012; the twenty-seventh day of his transformation into a white man) is actually a transposition of the mother's knock on the fateful

---

[63]Cited in Nimi Wariboko, *The Principle of Excellence: A Framework for Social Ethics* (Lanham, MD: Rowman and Littlefield, 2009), 99.

[64]George Steiner, *Real Presences* (Chicago: University of Chicago Press, 1989), 204.

[65]Steiner, *Real Presences*, 209.

[66]Steiner (*Real Presences* 209) is quoting from James Joyce's *A Portrait of the Artist as a Young Man*.

Monday morning of Furo's transformation, June 18, 2012, when he had his job interview and began his transformation (5).[67] One could interpret his mother's second knock as the one that woke Furo from the dream. On June 18, when Furo's mother knocked three times to wake him up, he built the sound of her knocking and his response to them into his dream and continued to sleep. Now at the end of the novel, her knocking is what finally woke him as the knocking could no longer be incorporated into his dream. Didn't Sigmund Freud in his *The Interpretation of Dreams* already teach us about this trick of dreams?[68] A father has just lost his son and was grieving by the son's coffin. He fell asleep. In his dream he saw his son standing by his bed which was in flames, and he cried out to him: "Father, can't you see I'm burning?" The father soon woke up and saw that the room was on fire caused by a candle that fell on the dead son's shroud. He had simply smelled the smoke of the burning shroud and dead son and built it into his dream to continue his sleep. He prolonged the sleep and only woke up when the dream became unbearable. Žižek once quipped that "reality is for those who cannot sustain the dream." In interpreting the meaning of the father's dream, Žižek wondered,

> He had smelled the smoke while asleep, and incorporated the image of his burning son into his dream to prolong his sleep. Had the father woken up because the external stimulus became too strong to be contained within the dream-scenario? Or was it the obverse, that the father constructed the dream in order to prolong his sleep, but what he encountered in the dream was much more unbearable even than external reality, so that he woke up to escape into that reality.[69]

The reader could still argue that my proposed ending does not account for the total twenty-seven days of events the novel portrays. Tongue in cheek, let me remind the reader that artists are like God in whose sight a

---

[67]I worked out the actual days and calendar year, given the clues provided in the story. Furo was born on May 6, 1979. His life in the novel began thirty-three years after his birth. June 18, 2012, was both the day of the job interview and his transformation. On June 19 he met both Igoni and Syreeta for the first time. The newspaper belonging to Bola (Syreeta's sugar daddy) that he read in Syreeta's house was dated Tuesday, June 26. He read this newspaper on June 28 and saw in it the missing-person announcement that his family put out (155). Furo started his job at Haba! on Monday, July 2, 2012. On Sunday, July 1, 2012—the day of biblical first day of creation and the day of resurrection of Jesus Christ—he adopted a new name, Frank Whyte (158). Alhaji Yaguda offered him a new job on July 11, 2012, to start on Monday, July 16, 2012. On Friday, July 13, 2012, he went to Igoni's apartment and spent the night there (260–1).
[68]Sigmund Freud, *The Interpretation of Dream* (New York: Macmillan, 1913), 403.
[69]Slavoj Žižek, "Freud Lives!," *London Review of Books* 28, no. 10, May 25, 2006, http://www.lrb.co.uk/v28/n10/slavoj-zizek/freud-lives

single day is like a thousand years (Ps 90:4). On a more serious note, let me remind the reader about how time is compressed in the genre of magical realism. To make my case about the extreme condensation of time, I turn to the tale of Jorge Luis Borges (1899–1986), the famous Argentine short-story writer. In his novella, "The Secret Miracle," Borges tells the story of Jaromir Hladik, a Jewish writer in Prague sentenced to death by the occupying Nazi forces in 1939. Scheduled to be executed on March 29, 1939, Hladik's most important preoccupation during the ten days before his demise was to finish a three-act tragedy he was working on before his arrest. "He had already completed the first act and a scene or two of the third. The metrical nature of the work allowed him to go over it continually, rectifying the hexameters, without recourse to the manuscript. He thought of the two acts still to do, and of his coming death."[70] He prayed to God in the night before his scheduled execution to grant him just one more year to finish the drama, which he hoped would bring glory to God, who owns all centuries and all time, and to himself. Then came the morning of the day of execution and at 9:00 a.m., Hladik stood before the firing squad, expecting an answer to his prayer.

The firing squad fell in and was brought to attention. Hladik, standing against the barracks wall, waited for the volley. Someone expressed fear the wall would be splashed with blood. The condemned man was ordered to step forward a few paces. Hladik recalled, absurdly, the preliminary maneuvers of a photographer. A heavy drop of rain grazed one of Hladik's temples and slowly rolled down his cheek. The sergeant barked the final command.

The physical universe stood still.

The rifles converged upon on Hladik, but the men assigned to pull the triggers were immobile. The sergeant's arm eternalized an inconclusive gesture. Upon a courtyard flagstone a bee cast a stationary shadow. The wind had halted, as in a painted picture. Hladik began a shriek, a syllable, a twist of the hand. He realized he was paralyzed. Not a sound reached him from the stricken world.

He thought: I am in hell, I am dead.

He thought: *I've gone mad.*

He thought: *Time has come to a halt.*

Then he reflected that in that case, his thought, too, would have come to a halt. He was anxious to test this possibility: he repeated (without moving his lips) the mysterious Fourth Ecologue of Virgil. He imagined that the already remote soldiers shared his anxiety; he longed

[70]Jorge Luis Borges, "The Secret Miracle," in *Ficciones*, trans. Anthony Kerrigan (New York: Grove, 1962), 147.

to communicate with them. He was astonished that he felt no fatigue, no vertigo from his protracted immobility. After an indeterminate length of time he fell asleep. On waking he found the world still motionless and dumb. The drop of water still clung to his cheek; the shadow of the bee still did not shift in the courtyard; the smoke from the cigarette he had thrown down did not blow away. Another "day" passed before Hladik understood.

He had asked God for an entire year in which to finish his work: His omnipotence had granted him the time. For his sake, God projected a secret miracle: German lead would kill him, at the determined hour, but in his mind a year would elapse between the command to fire and its execution. From perplexity he passed to stupor, from stupor to resignation, from resignation to sudden gratitude.

He disposed of no document but his own memory; the mastering of each hexameter as he added it, had imposed upon him a kind of fortunate discipline not imagined by those amateurs who forget their vague, ephemeral paragraphs. He did not work for posterity, nor even for God, of whose literary preferences he possessed scant knowledge. Meticulous, unmoving, secretive, he wove his lofty invisible labyrinth in time. He worked the third act over twice. He eliminated some rather too-obvious symbols.... There were no circumstances to constrain him. He omitted, condensed, amplified; occasionally, he chose the primitive version. He grew to love the courtyard, the barracks.... He found it: the drop of water slid down his cheek. He began a wild cry, moved his face aside. A quadruple blast brought him down.

Jaromir Hladik died on March 29, at 9:02 in the morning.[71]

Hladik thought he had a miracle. God stopped time for him, giving him an entire year to finish his drama. He thought he had finished his tragedy, but he left behind an incomplete literary work. In the interval of seconds between when the sergeant gave the order to shoot and the time he fell dead, time had apparently condensed into one infinite segment, and he was working, writing at incredible suprahuman speed. But all this was in his mind; objective time did not change for him. His experience of time as condensed was only subjective, a mental one. His

mind was cut off for a moment from external reality and the instruments that measure it and withdraws completely into itself: a suspension of physical time whose counterpart is an extraordinary intensification of mental time. To speak here of a contraction of physical time or an extension of mental time amounts to the same thing. For the few seconds that separate the order to fire and the arrival of the discharge, Hladik's consciousness is exacerbated to the point of accomplishing in a few brief moments the work of an entire year. But in this mind, it is the lived content of an entire year that is condensed in the lightning speed of a moment. "For his sake, God projected a secret miracle."[72]

Let us return to the *Blackass*. Given what I have explained about dreams and the genre of magical realism, we can say that the events of the novel's twenty-seven days are part of prolonged sleep, a long dream from which he wakes to the knock of his mother saying he is late for the interview slated for 11:00 a.m. on June 18. The novel provides ample hints to consider the transmogrification and everything that happened thereafter as a dream. Remember that Furo "awoke… to find that dreams can lose their way and turn up on the wrong side of sleep" (3). At a point when Furo became worried about his epidermal whiteness, we read that he "was alone in his lingering dream" (4).

The other scenario for the ending of the novel, which will continue the magical realism, phantasmatic realism, or animist realism of the narrative, is that of the m(other)'s gaze, which turns his skin color back to normal, its original pigmentation.[73] In his dreamworld or scenario, he was captured and transformed by the negrophobic white, (post)colonial gaze, which, as Fanon taught us, has only one destiny for the black person: to become white. But the mother's gaze, the other gaze to the white (supremacist) gaze, also (potentially) has the power (social currency) to transform (re-present), to liberate her son from the prison of corporeal malediction. If the ease of Furo's transmogrification represents the "unbearable lightness of [his] being or crushing weight of Fanonian 'zone of non-being,' his mother's immutable skin color represents the gravity and endurance of that 'eternal power' which can kill and make alive, heal the leprous skin of the 'spectres of whiteness of postcolony.'"[74] The mother's gaze is the revolutionary potential of the zone of nonbeing that counters ontological erasure as Fanon theorized.[75]

Instead of theorizing about the m(other)'s gaze, I could turn to the concept of the parallax gap: the family always sees him as a black man, and others who did not know him before June 18, 2012, the fateful day of his transformation, see him as a white man. This gap brings Barrett's story into another Kafkian tale about the man who finds himself in a gap and has to simultaneously fight an enemy on either side of him. Suspended between (or

---

[72]Stéphane Mosès, *The Angel of History: Rosenzweig, Benjamin, and Scholem*, trans. Barbara Harshav (Stanford, CA: Stanford University Press, 2009), 8.

[73]For "animist realism," see Garuba, "Explorations," 261–85.

[74]Adebayo, "The Black Soul," 143.

[75]Derek Hook, "Death-Bound Subjectivity: Fanon's Zone of Nonbeing and the Lacanian Death Drive," *Subjectivity* 13, no. 28 (2020): 355–75.

subtracted from) the "no more" (or no longer acceptable, blackness) and the "not yet" (pigmentation is white but still learning to be white), Furo faces two antagonists like Kafka's parable of the *He*.

> He has two antagonists: the first presses him from behind, from the origin. The second blocks the road ahead. He gives battle to both. To be sure, the first supports him in his fight with the second, and he wants to push him forward, and in the same way the second supports him in his fight with the first, since he drives him back. But it is only theoretically so. For it is not only the two antagonists who are there, but he himself as well, and who really knows his intentions? His dream, though, is that some time in an unguarded moment—and this would require a night darker than any night has been yet—he will jump out of the fighting line and be promoted, on account of his experience in fighting, to the position of umpire over his antagonists in their fight with each other.[76]

Kafka's *He* has the dream of jumping out of the struggle. But this is not possible for our Furo as a transformed man, for he is forever caught in the gap. The gap never disappears. The gap is resistance itself, the dead struggle between blackness and whiteness in the postcolony. From one perspective, one may say patriotic Nigerians should elude this battle if they want to create a flourishing society for themselves. From another, we may advise them to engage it, to traverse the gap, getting a healthy sense of themselves and their social world; coming to the recognition that all things (including identity, self, the social world) are always incomplete and imperfect; and reaching the unpleasant acceptance that all egos are structured by fantasy and there is no possibility of complete or total jouissance. There is another way for patriotic Nigerians to interpret the Kafkian gap in the parable and traverse it. At a deeper level, the parable is about human beings stepping into the continuum of time to create a gap between the past and future in which they change the meaning of the past and stop or redirect its perceived evil trajectory in order to help life flourish better. These two ways of dealing with the gap might provide the necessary level of human flourishing that could help Nigerian young adults rid themselves of the dream of transforming into white people so as to survive in their own country.

I can see yet another Kafkian way to end the novel. Mama Furo and her daughter open the door, and, shocked by seeing a strange white man standing before them, never enter until it is closed again—waiting for Igoni

---

[76]Franz Kafka, "He: Notes from the Year 1920," in *The Great Wall of China, Stories, and Reflections by Franz Kafka*, trans. Willa Muir and Edwin Muir (New York: Schocken, 1946), 276–7, quoted in Hannah Arendt, *Between Past and Future* (New York: Penguin, 1968), 7. Arendt slightly amended the translation from the German.

to come and lead them to the "real Furo," the black man. Does this not remind you of "Before the Law" in Kafka's 1925 novel, *The Trial*?

> *Before the law stands a doorkeeper. To this doorkeeper there comes a man from the country and prays for admittance to the Law. But the doorkeeper says that he cannot grant admittance at the moment. The man thinks it over and then asks if he will be allowed in later. "It is possible," says the doorkeeper, "but not at the moment." Since the gate stands open, as usual, and the doorkeeper steps to one side, the man stoops to peer through the gateway into the interior. Observing that, the doorkeeper laughs and says: "If you are so drawn to it, just try to go in despite my veto. But take note: I am powerful. And I am only the least of the doorkeepers. From hall to hall there is one doorkeeper after another, each one more powerful that the last."*[77]

The village man sat down beside the gate (the Law) and waited for him to be admitted until decades past. When he was about to die, he used his last breath to ask the doorkeeper,

> *"Every man strives to reach the Law," ... "so how does it happen that for all these many years no one but myself has ever begged for admittance?" The doorkeeper recognizes that the man has reached his end, and to let his failing senses catch the words, roars in his ear: "No one else could ever be admitted here, since this gate was made only for you. I am now going to shut it."*[78]

The hour and six-minute wait at the door before the knocking started may be alluding to this Kafkian story (262). What does Kafka's parable tell us about the plight of Furo's mother and daughter? Their (lost) son is within their grasp but unreachable and incomprehensible because of his whiteness. For what is the signature of the African postcolony if it is not about a continuous inaccessibility, unreachability of human flourishing, or a cycle of dreams and black-skin-white-mask rulers who as doorkeepers to the site of human flourishing bar the people from entering into their mansion of enjoyment? *Blackass* is structured around the presence of human flourishing as a lack, as a void, as human flourishing-as-lack, and the fantasies to overcome it. Performative dreams like the one Furo suffered are a *postivization of lack*, giving it some skin, the fantasy of making a silk purse out of a sow's ear.

Barrett ends his story with a slight adjustment to the way it ended for the countryman. He moves the story from passivity to interactivity. Barrett

---

[77]Franz Kafka, *Collected Stories* (London: Everyman's Library, 1993), 173–4.
[78]Kafka, *Collected Stories*, 175.

gives some agency to Furo's mother. "His mother called out, 'Furo—are you there? Come and open the door'" (262). And the person who waited was Furo, the aspiring doorkeeper. Does this ending suggest that *Blackass* is ultimately about agency to reclaim blackness from the zone of nonbeing or the destiny of whiteness?

Unconscious, Truth, and Human Being as Praxis

Blackass informs, if not convinces, us that a dream has been realized or materialized by turning up on the wrong side of sleep, and that this materialized dream is the stuff of nightmare. When Furo is confronted directly with his fantasy, he wants to run away but cannot do so. The physical confrontation is not merely a case of reality catching up with desire (dream), but the representation of Nigeria as a place where desires for basic human flourishing alienate people from themselves, to abject their selves, to absorb values alien to them. In Kafka's *Metamorphosis*, Gregor woke up an insect (bug, vermin, beetle), and all he could immediately think about is that he would be late for work after which he wondered how he would make money in the capitalist world.[79] Furo woke up as a white man, and all he could think about was being late for his job interview. This is, perhaps, an indication that the transformation is a dream that irrupted into the waking state, the unconscious exceeding its bounds.[80] The unconscious surfaces to disrupt the order of things. A dream come true is a nightmare. When Furo's fantasies refused to remain in the unconscious but became realized, horrible things happened.

I argued earlier in this chapter that there is a certain leeway to interpret the events of the novel as all happening in a dreamworld, as some kind play of the unconscious.

Perhaps Furo's whiteness is only a dream "branded in the underside of his consciousness" (Barrett 2015, 111). His magical transformation may be something "embedded in the perched earth of his subconscious" (Barrett

---

[79]*Ungeziefer*, Kafka's word for the creature Gregor turned into could be translated as vermin, insect, bug, and more importantly, "unfit for sacrifice."

[80]Even Igoni's transformation from male to female arose the subconscious. "While searching for Furo's story, I, too, underwent a transformation. I was more relieved than surprised by this happenstance. The seeds had always been there, embedded in the parched earth of my subconscious. I had heard their muted rattling in the remembered moments of my sleeping life" (83; see also 111). Furo thinks that his dream or black ass is "something branded on the underside of his consciousness" (111).

2015, 83). After all, Fanon (1952) argues in the context of Martinique that it is very commonplace for a black person to dream of a form of salvation that consists of magically turning white. He cites an instance of one of his psychiatric patients who dreamt of himself as a white man in a room full of white people. Fanon regards this as the fulfilment of his patient's unconscious wish, for the unconscious expresses itself freely in dreams. In Freudian psychoanalysis, the unconscious is the most fruitful place to look for explanations of human actions. Through the unconscious, we realise how humans are driven by desires of which they are unaware. Blending fantasy with realism, Blackass delves into the scaffold of its characters' collective unconscious and encodes meaning in allegories and figurations.[81]

The world of the unconscious that burst forth from dream into reality, that took place at the wrong side of sleep, is like Hegel's "Night of the World." The mind of the (post)colonized, tortured with half-truths, an inferiority complex, and a self-deprecating desire for whiteness operates in fragments of wholes. His abjected self is trying to be part of a whole that will not accept him as a whole person. He senses his existence but experiences it as something without a form, as if the light of his existence has been transformed into the formlessness of night. I must impress Fanon's view into service here. "Quietly simple that when Blacks make contact with the white world a certain sensitizing takes place. If the psychic structure is fragile, we observe a collapse of the ego…. His actions are destined for 'the Other' (in the guise of the white man), since only 'the Other' can enhance his status and give him self-esteem at the ethical level."[82]

Indeed, in this Fanonian world of ego collapse and fragmentation, one gets the impression that the very unity of black person's being (body) is magically dissolved. The black body under the pressure of white gaze becomes a desubjectivized multitude of partial objects, not a unified totality. The black body becomes a "kind of vaguely coordinated agglomerate of partial objects": here the black skin, there a collapsed ego, over there the white mask, and close to it the consuming fire of white supremacy.[83] Does this conception of the body subjugated to the white gaze, caught in the widening gyre of colonial hang-ups (169) not surprisingly echo Hegel's conception of the radical negativity of the subject ("Night of the World")? Hegel states in *Janaer Realphilosophie* (1805–6):

[81]Adebayo, "The Black Soul," 148.
[82]Fanon, *Black Skin, White Masks*, 132.
[83]Slavoj Žižek, *Organs without Bodies: On Deleuze and Consequences* (New York: Routledge, 2004), 172.

The human being is this night, this empty nothing, that contains everything in its simplicity—an unending wealth of many representations, images, of which none belongs to him—or which are not present. This night, the interior of nature, that exists here—pure self—in phantasmagorical representations, is night all around it, in which here shoots a bloody head—there another white ghastly apparition, suddenly here before it, and just so disappears. One catches sight of this night when one looks human beings in the eye—into a night that becomes awful.[84]

To deliver himself from the nightmare, free-falling world, and homeless darkness of existence (40), all Furo needs to do is to tell the truth of his situation to his family members and those who knew him before the transformation. Several times, he reached the point of pondering the truth, the truth of "coming out" to his family, especially his mother, and each time, he failed.[85] He repeatedly could not get to the truth and enunciate it. Barrett ends the novel by giving us the impression that Furo will eventually redeem himself and tell the simple truth. I have demonstrated above that this ending is debatable given the overall logic of the narrative. Nonetheless, I can discern a certain Hegelian logic in Barrett trying to get Furo to the point of telling the truth. One could ask why Barrett raised the question of truth, of Furo revealing himself to this family over seventeen pages of (or times in) the novel, and failed that many times, and finally present us with a coquettish possibility of a coming-out-of-the-closet ceremony, self-disclosure. To answer this question, I must resort to Hegel. There is no direct path to the truth. The so-called set of failures is the solid material base that allows fleeting truth to shine through, for the emergence of that coquettish possibility of truth on the last page of the novel.

The "set of failures" is like what Hegel says about the phallus: it is both an instrument of urination and insemination and a conjunction of the high and low, when he is illustrating the two readings of "Spirit is a bone."[86] If we see only failure in the failures, then we are like those in Hegel's reasoning who can only discern the phallus as the male organ of urination. But to see a possible path to success from the failures is to be like those who can also discern the phallus as an organ of insemination, the higher function of generation. Hegel's point is that we do not directly go for the best option or proper result with our first choice, but only through repeated failures. The choice of "insemination" comes only through repeatedly choosing

---

[84]Donald Phillip Verene, *Hegel's Recollections* (Albany: SUNY Press, 1985), 7–8.
[85]*Blackass*, 5, 22, 38–40, 112, 141, 151–6, 182–3, 254, 261; 17 pages in all.
[86]G. W. F. Hegel, *Phenomenology of Spirit*, trans. A. V. Miller (Oxford: Oxford University Press, 1977), 210.

"urination"; we arrive at the true choice via the wrong choice. If Furo tried to directly choose truth, he would infallibly miss it. Truth emerges through repeated failures of nerves as their aftereffect.[87]

But as Furo was failing to get to the truth, we were seeing the construction of his identity and character. I write this not only because fiction is a construction but also to point us to both an underlying conception of freedom and a theory of identity in the novel: that human beings (identities) "are all constructed narratives" (83). There is something between the brutal reality of being transformed into white and "the properly human symbolic universe of normative commitments: the abyss of freedom."[88] At this point of his transmogrification, Furo is a free subject who must not only do his duty but also establish what the duty is. How does a man only recently "ontologically" transformed derive his determinate moral duties from the *formal* character (formal emptiness, a formal character yet to generate any content of *Sittlichkeit*, ethical substance) of his whiteness?[89]

I now turn to the theory of identity. What it means to be a Canadian or a Nigerian and who and what the Nigerian or Canadian is as a human being is narratively constructed: the particular form of humanity or citizenship in any given nation is always a result of human activities, an outcome of contingent processes that are articulated, interpreted, or written as (into) the "body" of the nation (what they experience themselves to be).

On my first reading of "are all constructed narratives," I did not see any important philosophical implication of the sentence, which I considered common in academic discourses. But on my second reading—and reading it alongside with a statement about the debt Furo owed to his family ("Theirs is a debt of semen and milk, of blood and sweat and tears. A debt he could never repay nor escape" [155])—it occurred to me that there is a certain kind of philosophical anthropology, the theory of the human being in *Blackass*. The human is not just a narrative construct but a composite of *bio*, biological debt represented by semen, milk, and other bodily fluids, and *logos*, the narrative. Barrett's philosophical anthropology as I have lifted up from this work is not far from Black feminist scholar Sylvia Wynter's notion of "human being as praxis." According to Wynter, the human being is a praxis rather than a noun, a performative enactment of being a human. Every person is *hybridly* (flesh/mythoi, person/stories, *bios*/narrative coding, historicized unfolding of *being*/political coding of *being*) collective. *Bios* here connotes two senses: the biological life, the flow of natural reproductive life

[87]See also Slavoj Žižek, *The Puppet and the Dwarf: The Perverse Core of Christianity* (Cambridge, MA: MIT Press, 2003), 81–5.
[88]Žižek, *For They Know Not*, xii.
[89]Žižek, *For They Know Not*, xxiv.

of the people, life as bare potentiality, and the political life as Agamben uses it in his notion of the *homo sacer*.[90]

Let me conclude this section of the chapter by asking if Furo is actually a character. How do our examinations of the notions of unconscious, truth, and human-being-as-praxis as they relate to Furo help us theorize him as a fictional character? I posit that Furo is not a character in the traditional sense; there is something in Furo more than Furo himself. He is an "organizational device," a *ficelle*; Barrett has constructed a figure that represents the terrifying excess of postcolonial subjectivity, a subject around which the excessive fantasies of postcoloniality circulate. Furo's transmogrification, his whiteness, allows Barrett to unify different raw materials in one person. His character is supposed to make everything clear about the Fanonian black man whose destiny is white. Furo is Barrett's *point de capiton*, the "quilting point," which organizes the heterogeneous fantasies, hopes, morals, goodness, and evils of the postcolony into in consistent narrative. According to Frederic Jameson, Don Quixote is not really a character at all, but rather an organization device that permits Cervantes to write his book, serving as a thread that holds a number of different types of anecdotes together in a single form. (Thus Hamlet's madness permitted Shakespeare to piece together several heterogeneous plot sources, and Goethe's Faust is an excuse for the dramatization of many different moods.)[91] Similarly, Žižek has noted that "Henry James designated this kind of narrative character whose actual function is to represent within the diegetic space its own process of enunciation—the discursive structure of the work itself—the by the term *ficelle*. (Maria Gostrey in *The Ambassadors*, for example, is a *ficelle*)."[92]

What we have in *Blackass* is the creation of this character, a quilting point of heterogeneous materials through the somnambulistic illusion of dream, all made acceptable through the reader's prior exposure to the genre of magical realism. As I indicated earlier, it is not easy to discern if Furo as a white man is dreaming or if he is awake (dream-bound wakefulness?). Is Furo as a black man dreaming to be white or a white man dreaming to be black? (Is his transmogrification a body transplant or mind transplant?) This reminds me of the story of Chinese philosopher Zhuang Zi, who dreamt he was a butterfly, pleasantly fluttering about. When he awoke, he asked himself, Am I now a butterfly dreaming to be Zhuang Zi? For him, there must have been some distinction, some difference between the two states

---

[90]See Katherine McKittrick, ed., *Sylvia Wynter: On Being Human as Praxis* (Durham, NC: Duke University Press, 2015) and Alexander G. Weheliye, *Habeas Viscus: Racializing Assemblage, Biopolitics, and Black Feminist Theories of the Human* (Durham, NC: Duke University Press, 2014).
[91]Frederic Jameson, *The Ideologies of Theory* (London: Verso, 2008), 9.
[92]Žižek, *For They Know Not*, 18.

of being a man and being a fluttering butterfly. This difference Zhuang Zi chalked up to the transformation of material things.

In line with my earlier discussion that in the postcolony the subject could easily be equated with his or her own fantasy, they become an object of fantasy; and so, when Zhuang Zi was dreaming about being a butterfly, he was in the correct form. Is the butterfly fantasy not correlated with the dream of black person being white? The answer is yes insofar as whiteness or butterfly is the "object which constituted the frame, the backbone of [the] fantasy-identity…. In the symbolic reality he was Zhuang Zi [Furo Wariboko], but in the Real of his desire he was a butterfly [white person]. Being a butterfly [white man] was the whole consistency of his positive being outside the symbolic network."[93]

Concluding Reflections: Sankofa Bird's Eye View

Furo Wariboko awoke this morning to find that dreams can lose their way and turn up on the wrong side of sleep.

The opening line of *Blackass* retroactively posits its own presuppositions. A traumatic kernel of the African postcolony is converted into a body makeover. The first words of the novel reveal an ongoing existential dramatization of the painful psychic content of the black body. Through these words, Barrett brings out the implicit presuppositions of the African postcoloniality. He also reveals social identity as the retroactive effect of contingency. Identity is neither a reflection of any underlying substance nor the visible manifestation of a deeper necessity.

First, we must dispose of the sense that the first line offers us the beginning of the story and a key to the form of the story. Only from the whole story can we retroactively understand or reconstruct the genesis, the first lines, even in its most literal sense. Karl Marx once said that "human anatomy contains a key to the anatomy of the ape."[94] Marx clearly understood that the human being came after the monkey in the evolution tree. His point was that we can only effectively reconstruct the evolutionary process of the monkey knowing the finished product of the human being. Not until the reader is in the thick of *Blackass* do they realize that a "miracle" of pigment transformation is possible. (Nigeria is already a "whitewashed" society, overdetermined by countless black-skin-white-masks, too many

---

[93]Žižek, *Sublime Object*, 46.
[94]Karl Marx, *Grundrisse*, trans. Martin Nicolaus (New York: Penguin Classics, 1973), 38.

of its citizens have white envy, and whiteness is both their phantasmatic supplement and unconscious. Furo's transformation is thus an eruption of the unconscious into the conscious.)

It is only after the reader has taken a synchronous cut of the universe of the narration that one can adequately comprehend the historical conditions out of which the first line emerged or is justified. The first sentence becomes not a reported speech but retroactive performativity—that which retroactively produces, defines its own presupposition, and explains its historical genesis. The first sentence presupposes what it ought to explain. Re-seeing the first sentence transforms it from an imaginary register into a symbolic register.[95]

With the passage from the imaginary to the symbolic, the real question is no longer the (Kafkian) absurdity of the transformation but instead, the "efficacy" of the narration in exposing the unconscious of the African postcolony. The symbolic reveals the mystical preserve of the *colonial undead*, the spectral evil, monstrosities of colonialism haunting the postcolony. This preserve is the space between the formal death of colonialism and the death of its specter, the colonialism that endures beyond death and must be killed. Furo is this monstrosity, haunting specter as such, a manifestation of this space. He embodies it. He is biologically (imaginatively) a life force, but symbolically the undead.

Once you have read the entirety of *Blackass*—grasped its logic and dynamic—you realize that its opening line is not the "beginning" of the novel but the tip of the iceberg of a postcolonial world. The first words of the novel presume a world with a logic of emotion that only takes up an acute affectivity with Furo's transmogrification. The novel proceeds as if the reader is supposed to know without any particular details that the "pre-world" of Furo or all the characters in the novel is one in which blacks want to be white and consider, in Fanonian terms, their desired destiny to be whiteness. This disposition seems not to deeply affect the reader and the world she imaginatively steps into. Suddenly, everything comes crashing down for the Nigerian resident and the spectating reader alike when Furo emerges as the concrete detail of such longing, as if the inner wishes of the resident of the pre-world are handed over to them on a platter of gold and asked to enjoy it. This realization turns out to be a terrifying excess of their secret hearts. The passage from the universal (universe of everyone longing to enjoy the pleasures of whiteness) to its existential particularity (the image of transfigured Furo) is the key tension that drives the narration. The ultimate driving force of Furo as an organizational device is not his passion (hustle) to succeed but the constant passage to the particular. We are not seeing a generalized phantasmatic image of a white man who has it all but the unique

---

[95]Žižek, *For They Know Not*, 210, inspired this analysis.

struggles of one white man. So, precisely, the ultimate driving force of the novel is the imbalance, disconnect, and scission between particular existence and universality.[96] In *Blackass*, Igoni Barrett does not merely, cheaply oppose whiteness to blackness, the negative to the positive. Blackness as a positive being tarries with whiteness (negativity) and materializes itself as the negativity—the negativity of black persons who assume their ultimate destiny is whiteness. It is this kind of philosophical subtlety that recommends Igoni Barrett's *Blackass* as a genuine breakthrough in Nigerian novels and a critical partner in academic philosophical dialogues.

---

[96]Žižek, *For They Know Not*, 122, inspired this analysis.

3

Bad Governance and Postcoloniality: Literature as Cultural Criticism

Introduction

Unbearable poverty. Excruciating suffering. Unyielding trauma. Postcolonial incredible.[1] Power vulgarity. These are some of the morbid symptoms or effects of governance in Nigeria, the choking string of unutterable treason of the nation's depraved ruling class. In the front, Nigerians see only immiseration; in the back, they have experienced sixty years of deprivation; on the right, they face unending corruption; on the left, they witness the all-pervasive anomie; and at the center, Nigerians see nothing but a black hole. Governance in Nigeria is a storm blowing out of the people's patrimony, a destructive wild wind that spreads doom and gloom across the regions, piling ruin upon ruin, wreaking havoc on the ethics and morals of society.

Between 1960 and now (summer 2021) the nature of governance has drastically changed for the worse. In the mid-1960s when the five army majors struck in a coup d'etat and overthrew the civilian government of Prime Minister Tafawa Belewa, governance had, perhaps, three possibilities. Governance somewhat represented an uncomplicated embodiment of the citizens' hope for their socioeconomic uplift, or an uncomplicated embodiment of corruption, or the uncertainty of part good and part corruption. Now we have only two options: sociopathic corruption or the uncertainty of whether corruption is going to treat the citizens with divine or demonic impunity. Chris Abani, in his novel *GraceLand*, captures

---

[1]Tejumola Olaniyan, *Arrest the Music!: Fela and His Rebel Art and Politics* (Bloomington: Indiana University Press, 2004), 90.

something about this shift in the nation's morality in a dialogue between the protagonist Elvis Oke and his friend Redemption.[2] In the 1960s, when the characters were younger, the movies had three archetypes: John Wayne, the *ur*-character for uncomplicated goodness; the Actor, always part villain and part hero; and the Bad Guy, the embodiment of malicious evil. By the early 1980s, things have changed, the movies had changed, mirroring the changes in scale of corruption and anomie in the country. To Elvis this was all confusing until Redemption explained: "Now dere is only Bad Guy and Actor. No more John Wayne."[3]

This novel portrays the nihilism that has settled on Nigerians as the certainties that constitute the "fence" of the ethical domain of a society are gone. The word ethics comes from ethos, which in its etymology means the "fence" that keeps animals within their protective pen or "dwelling," and by extension the "cement" or bonds that hold a society together.[4] Within the limits of the fence a society seeks harmony, the harmony of ethos, the congruence between the character (way of life) of the individuals and the community's moral values. The moral institutions of the community work to translate the fence, the domain of moral values, into the bonds of the community, co-belonging. They transform the law (norms, *nomos*) into its spirit, that is, the individual internalization of the expectations and requirements of the law. In *GraceLand*'s Nigeria there is a break in the ethos, a rupture in the specific mode of being together. The pathway between moral principles of a people and their ensuing concrete mode of existence or way of being has been forgotten. Ethics or the harmony of ethos today amounts to a dissolution of forms of practices and discourses into corruption. A new "ethics" has emerged insofar as we understand ethics as "the kind of thinking in which an identity is established between an environment, a way of being and a principle of action."[5] In *GraceLand*'s Nigeria, wracked by corruption, nihilism, and anomic repercussions of the civil war, the ethical options presented to the sixteen-year-old Elvis for self-formation and socialization as he enters adulthood are severely limited. His possible ethical turns are a series of specific conjunctions of the Colonel (murderous agent or face of the postcolonial state), the King (a corrupt beggar who aspires to transform the system and avenge what was done to him during the civil war, 1967–80), and Redemption (a man with an unbelievable ability to function, to survive

[2]This way of linking the dialogue to the moral situation of Nigeria was inspired by Hugh Hodges, "No, This Is Not Redemption: The Biafra War Legacy in Chris Abani's *GraceLand*," in *Writing the Nigeria-Biafra War*, ed. Toyin Falola and Ogechukwu Ezekwem (New York: James Currey, 2016), 380–99.
[3]Chris Abani, *GraceLand* (New York: Farrar, Straus and Giroux, 2004), 147, 190.
[4]Paul L. Lehman, *Ethics in a Christian Context* (Eugene, OR: Wipf and Stock, 1998), 24–5.
[5]Jacques Rancière, *Dissensus: On Politics and Aesthetics*, ed. and trans. Steven Corcoran (London: Continuum, 2010), 184.

and eke out a living from the deadly jaws of corrupt agents of the state). More importantly, in this novel we see Nigeria as a place in which the hopes for and narratives of national economic development have been abandoned, where grotesque and obscene display of necropower passes for the height of human civilization, and existential nihilism protrudes as the wet blanket spread by what goes for governance over the citizens. Things that happen do not make sense. Ambulances do not carry sick people to hospitals, but carry dead people for a fee as part of elaborate funeral processions. In one of the most moving scenes in the novel, Elvis has gone home after being tortured by the state, the Colonel, to discover that his Maroko ghetto in Lagos megacity has been razed down by the government and in the process his father had died. He raked through the rubble where their house had stood with his bare hands to find the body. A soldier discovered what he was doing and stopped him, threatening to kill him. "If you annoy me I will kill you and add you to your father." The soldier would only let him take the body for a fee, a bribery. When Elvis responded that he had no money, the soldier replied, "No what? Get out of here." He immediately "descended on Elvis and pounding him repeatedly with his rifle butt. Elvis stumbled away. The tears that wouldn't come for his father streamed freely now as he felt worthless in the face of blind, unreasonable power. He could return later, when it was dark, but he knew the body would be gone" (306). This scene broke my heart. Governance is all about humiliating the people and generating confusion all over the country.

Governance in Nigeria is the "pitiless incubus that feeds on their most valuable possession, dreams, which it endlessly defers and derides."[6] The words between the quotation marks were actually used to describe the city of Lagos, the commercial hub of Nigeria. The disposition to see Lagos or parts therein as metonyms for the whole country is an old practice of scholars and artistes of Nigeria. Fela Anikulapo-Kuti in his song "Confusion Break Bone" compares the absolute chaos of Ojuelegba, a street in Lagos, to Nigeria.

I sing about one street for Lagos	I sing about a street in Lagos
Dem call am Ojuelegba	They call it Ojuelegba
I think e compare how Nigeria be	I compare it to Nigeria
One crossroad in the center of town	
Chorus: Larudu repeke	
For Ojuelegba	At Ojuelegba
Moto dey come from east	Vehicles approach from east
Motor come from west	From west

---

[6]Olaniyan, *Arrest the Music*, 90.

Motor come from north	From north
Motor come from south	From south
And policeman no dey for center	And no policeman to direct the traffic
No confusion be that oh-o	The result is utter confusion!
Chorus: Pafuka na quench	It is utter confusion[7]

Governance in Nigeria is like the traffic at Ojuelegba, a permanent state of crisis, anomie that replaces or ruptures normality. Governance is a national terrorism of power and the exercise of this power is very arbitrary. This very arbitrariness defines the present Nigerian postcolonial state. As Achille Mbembe puts it, "What distinguishes our age from the previous ages, the breach over which there is apparently no going back is existence that is contingent, dispersed, but reveals itself in the guise of arbitrariness and the absolute power to give death any time, anywhere, by any means, and for any reason."[8]

The Postcolonial Incredible and Nihilism

Why do the governed accept such confusion and arbitrariness as governance, exercise of power, and sovereignty? From the perspective on Nigeria given to us by Abani's *GraceLand* we infer that there are many forces or factors at work that we cannot fully account for in this chapter. We would like to focus on only two of them: the *postcolonial incredible* and passive nihilism (or the "soteriology of ambiguity"[9]). Governance just like daily existential condition is an incredible phenomenon, a situation of perpetual crisis, crisis-as-norm. Tejumola Olaniyan describes the reign of the incredible in these words:

> The "incredible" inscribes that which cannot be believed; that which is too improbable, astonishing, and extraordinary to be believed. The incredible is not simply a breach but an outlandish infraction of "normality" and its limits. If "belief," as faith, confidence, trust, and conviction, underwrites the certainty and tangibility of institutions and practices of social exchange, the incredible dissolves all props of stability, normality, and intelligibility (and therefore of authority) and engenders social and

---

[7]Olaniyan, *Arrest the Music*, 96.
[8]Achille Mbembe, *On the Postcolony* (Berkeley: University of California Press, 2001), 13.
[9]Karen L. Carr, *The Banalization of Nihilism: Twentieth-Century Responses to Meaninglessness* (Albany, NY: SUNY Press, 1992), 3.

symbolic crisis.... A presupposed interregnum that increasingly threatens to become the norm, a norm with a rapidly consolidating hierarchy of privileges feeding on and dependent on the crisis for reproduction.[10]

The reign of the incredible is not transitional as Fela might have thought when he resisted it with his full vigor; it is a permanent state in Nigeria. It is the form the unfolding of Nigeria's history has taken at the moment. In this condition of the incredible, governance renders and heightens the vulnerability of citizens. The enormity of pain and agony of the incredible scale of social anomie, not unlike torture and trauma, often serves to focus victims' minds on the self, the survival of their bodies and pursuit of daily bread, cutting off connections to larger social relationships and resulting in the production of atomized individuals and the fragmentation of society.[11] It appears that instead of generating the wherewithal to defeat the incredible most of Nigerian citizens have accepted not to challenge it. Elvis finds it irritating that his friends accept the condition of anomie or even finds it funny as some even feed from it or contribute to it in their own small ways. He cries, "That is the trouble with this country. Everything is accepted. No dial tones or telephones. No stamps in post offices. No electricity. No water. We just accept" (58). It is easy to see this hapless acceptance of the reign of the incredible by the citizens as a case of passive nihilism; an acceptance of the dissolution of meaning or sense in the way life hangs together in Nigeria. But we should not yield to such an easy conclusion. There is a certain soteriology of ambiguity, a dialectic, a juxtaposition of opposites to it. On the one hand, there is a definite sense of loss of meaning, a sense that the country has lost something meaningful or desirable, something important for human flourishing. On the other, there is a conviction that it is important for some citizens to pursue and create alternative situations that might redeem the nation from the reign of the postcolonial incredible. The tension is between a realization that all might have been lost and that there is still meaning or credible existence that transcends the chaos and arbitrariness of the postcolonial incredible. Let us take, for instance, the King of Beggars, a figure in *GraceLand* placed outside the order of the law, but in an unexpected way he summons up the courage and active will to confront the state represented by the Colonel. And in the confrontation both of them died. In death, the King is temporarily "deified" by the masses and "turned into a prophet, and advance guard, like John the Baptist, for the arrival of the Messiah" (303). Certainly, the death of the King does not offer any redemption or reprieve from the reign of the incredible and necropower, but it gestures to its possibility, leaning into some sense of transforming or

---

[10]Olaniyan, *Arrest the Music*, 2.
[11]William T. Cavanaugh, *Torture and Eucharist* (Malden, MA: Blackwell, 1998).

transcending the condition. The novel ends with Elvis taking on the name of his friend Redemption at the terminal gate to take his flight to the United States. The flight attendant called him:

> Elvis stepped forward and spoke
> "Yes, this is Redemption."

(321)

The ambiguity here is that the escape from Nigeria might well be the redemption that the sixteen-year-old boy needs in order to refocus his life, or there is hope of redemption for the country as the Elvis character seems to be a metonymy for Nigeria, or that his friend Redemption who offered him his passport to travel has found a "smart" way to reach for redemption even by exploiting the cracks and chaos of the system superintended by the postcolonial incredible. Of course, it may also represent Chris Abani's way of asking the reader difficult questions: Can anyone wrest any redemptive force from the nihilism that is Nigeria? Or, how is it possible to have faith in Nigeria?

Elvis himself is an embodiment of this soteriology of ambiguity. He is at once a voice of hope, resisting nihilism, and at the same time the disposable subject who is involved in the crimes and absurdity of the incredible postcolonial situation. He bears the basic ambiguity, the unbearable tensions of the Nigerian masses: there is the ever-present ineradicable need for transformation, certainty, and hope that is locked in mortal battle with despair rooted in utter emptiness and shattering confusion of life in the country. To be fully human, to be an authentic Nigerian under these circumstances, is to affirm (though not with laughter and dance) this internal agonistic struggle within oneself without literally going mad or being torn into pieces by the unbearable, volcanic tensions. It is to affirm this vexing existential ambiguity without expecting to sublate the juxtaposed opposites into some higher synthesis. In sum, the character of Elvis in Abani's *GraceLand* represents the impossible possibility of faith in Nigeria.

We must explain the ambivalence, the antimony that is Elvis, and for that matter Nigeria, within the context of governance in its postcolonial state. Governance, or rather the experience or impact of it on the people, is the loss of contact with anything explainable, meaningful, or truthful, or patriotic in managing the affairs of a people (multitude). It is an existence of shattering confusion—a void of not-knowing that is characterized by nihilism, inescapable suffering and degradation of life, and in this state of meaninglessness the "eternal length" of every single day bursts forth: a perpetual day that despoils the past and defers the future. To survive or persist in this miasma ordinary citizens like Elvis must become existential hero, self-consciously confronting the void, struggling not to give in to it, not to deny it either, but to find the *courage to be* in it. Oh Tillich, the authentic *courage to be* exists only in Nigeria!

The macabre governance of the grim postcolonial incredible is a temporal extraordinaire. By seizing the time of Nigerian citizens, not allowing them to move forward or to ignite the potentialities of the past but crushing them in the eternal now of crushing, seething excess suffering, governance has become a *temporal cancer*. It causes the segments of time to fight against time in the same way cancerous cells fight against their own body. Governance is an historic process, or more precisely a sign language of the historicity of the postcolonial incredible, an emblem of a congested, debris-filled history that is the uncanniest guest of time. It is a machinery that arrests time, forcing it into a standstill and making it churn endlessly in one place, losing its ambiguity only to spurn and spew out waste, decay, sickness, disease, and death onto Nigerians. Simply, governance is *governmentonoma*, cancer of governmentality. In their encounter with governance or *governmentonoma*, both time and citizens become fatigued. Time, arrested and wrested from its energy-giving wheel of motion, loses its power to birth change. And Nigerians entrapped in motionless time are also fatigued as they are chewed up in the useless churning of immobile time. Within the postcolonial incredible, temporality is an experience of fatigued time and fatigue of time.

The Postcolonial *Différance* and Politics of Not-Knowing

In the daily confrontation with the postcolonial incredible as sustained and orchestrated by governance, Nigerians are stripped free of any pretentions to know, the unfamiliar and unexplained cannot be subsumed under any categories of the known and understood. The utterly strange has been divested of its power to surprise, shock, or fascinate. They know by not knowing, by not making sense, by embracing a grotesque version of the Derridean *différance*. Every new happening, directive, pronouncement, or policy is almost present in and of itself, so different from all that came before it and will come after it that it has to have its own unique context for one to decipher it. Because this suspension of the normal process of understanding cannot (always) be done, the meaning of the new is deferred. Every day of survival in the postcolonial incredible is a day of postponement of meaning and intelligibility. Since meaning and sense are now perpetually deferred then that which is improbable, astonishing, and extraordinary is *believed* in the vortex of an abyss (no foundation, limit, and, strangely, no surface) of uncertainty. Believing here is not about any claim about the reality of truth, but a denial of the possibility of knowledge, a dissolution of standards, or resistance to any claim to distinguish truth from falsehood, warranted from unwarranted belief. What loosely binds "belief" to the daily happenings or pronouncements is the "trace" of the postcolonial incredible. Each of them "being constituted on the basis of the trace [or traces of traces] within it of the other elements of the [incredible] chain or system."[12] In this way, postcolonial *différance* becomes one of the important ways the postcolonial incredible inscribes or negotiates epistemological nihilism on the minds and bodies of Nigerian citizens. This should not be construed to mean that Nigerian citizens are passive recipients of an inexorable working of the postcolonial incredible as orchestrated by the state.

The state is a production of a diffuse chaotic economy of norms in the incredible situation. The state is constituted by the postcolonial incredible; it is a "substantive effect" of the postcolonial incredible, always performatively produced and compelled by the practices that cohere with the harmony of ethos of the incredible situation. This does not mean that there is a doer (named the incredible) that preexists the deeds of the state or its citizens. The postcolonial incredible is always doing and the deeds constitute the phenomenon and also the participants as subjects in multi-directional ways. There is not a metaphysics of an identity of the postcolonial incredible behind the doings of the state, citizens, and external actors; that identity or being or coherence is "performatively constituted by the very 'expressions' that are said to be its results."[13]

The state is caught in the postcolonial incredible and postcolonial *différance* as much as the citizens. In February of 2016, a debate broke out among Nigerians on the *USA African Dialogue Series*, an online discussion forum for African intellectuals and Africanists. The issue was whether or not supporters of the Buhari Administration were defending it without regard to logic or facts as the naira went into a free fall. Moses Ochonu, a professor of African History at Vanderbilt University in the United States, stated that "employing offensive and ineffective logics and tactics, these fanatical supporters of the president are doing more reputational harm than good to their hero, and turning away compatriots who would otherwise be willing to give the president a fair hearing on the mounting disappointments with his administration."[14] The learned professor was particularly ticked off by President Buhari supporters (in both government and the general populace) arguing that the naira-dollar exchange would have gone up to N1,000 to $1 from the N300 to $1 it was in January 2016 if Jonathan Goodluck had won the 2015 presidential election. Criticizing Buhari supporters for their

---

[12]Jacques Derrida, *Positions*, trans. Alan Bass (Chicago: University of Chicago Press, 1981), 26.
[13]Judith Butler, *Gender Trouble: Feminism and the Subversion of Identity* (New York: Routledge, 2007), 34.
[14]Moses Ochonu, "How Not to Defend Buhari," USA Africa Dialogue Series, Wednesday, February 17, 2016, https://groups.google.com/forum/#!topic/usaafricadialogue/P4LqeenuytQ

attitude of not-knowing that is marked by what he called "offensive and ineffective logics and tactics," he ponders:

> Where does one begin on this fanatically blind, impulsive defense of Buhari? First of all, that statement begins from a premise of absence, which is a no-no in logic. Jonathan did not win, so we do not and cannot know what would have happened to the Naira had he won. That belongs in the realm of known unknowns, to paraphrase Donald Rumsfeld.[15]

Before I comment on Ochonu's statement as a continuation on my commentary on governance in Nigeria, I would like to further introduce his public scholarship. He is a public intellectual who regularly comments on debates about the Nigeria socioeconomy. Sometimes Ochonu reminds me of Fela, except that instead of wielding a saxophone against the postcolonial state he wields the pen. Once Tejumola Olaniyan wrote this about Fela's work: "Evident in Fela's body of work is a gargantuan will to articulate, to *name*, the incredibility [the postcolonial incredible] and thereby inscribe its vulnerability .... Fela's expressed objective is the overthrow or at least the amelioration of the reign of the incredible."[16] Ochonu as a public intellectual has, in my opinion, a similar objective.

Now let me return to Ochonu's "How Not to Defend Buhari." I read his essay with keen attention. I almost completely agree with him. Almost, but not entirely, because the mention of Rumsfeld in the above quote opens a path for us to explore the state and not just how its paid and unpaid defenders are caught in the web of the postcolonial incredible. I want to analyze this opening to shed light on the peculiarities and depths of defending or criticizing governments in power in Nigeria within the context of the postcolonial incredible and postcolonial *différance*.

What got me thinking is the remark about Donald Rumsfeld's "known unknowns." I heard Rumsfeld when he said it in February 2002 as the United States was planning to invade Iraq. Rumsfeld mentioned three categories of (potential) information: (a) *known knowns*, (b) *known unknowns*, and (c) *unknown unknowns*. The first category is about things that Rumsfeld and the Bush administration knew that they knew. There were also things about Iraq that they knew that they did not know. Finally, there are things that Rumsfeld and Bush did not know that they did not know.

Rumsfeld's categories of relationship between known and unknown provide an interesting lens, tongue in cheek, to analyze the psychology and psychoanalysis of political production of knowledge in Nigeria's public square. All three of Rumsfeld's categories are shaky in Nigeria. In the

---

[15]Ochonu, "How Not to Defend Buhari."
[16]Olaniyan, *Arrest the Music*, 2.

Nigerian political environment, we are never certain of the *known knowns*. Facts are never sacred; wealth and status authenticate "facts." Those who support or oppose governments spew lies in the public square with straight faces and no one seems to care. It appears nothing is known and nothing can be known. Are there *known knowns* in Nigerian politics? How does anyone debate policies or conduct public relations in this kind of environment?

What is it about the inner workings of government, whether Buhari's, Jonathan's, or Obasanjo's, that we can say as Nigerian citizens *we know that we know*? Didn't President Jonathan lament that members of Boko Haram were in his government and yet he could not readily identify them and flush them out as he should? Tell me, is there anywhere outside of Nigeria where members of the government at the highest level are not a *known known*?

Of course, this means that those of us outside government—and even many inside past and present administrations—*know that we do not know* what is happening in our governments. Commodore Ebitu Ukiwe was next in power to President Ibrahim Babangida and yet he did not know when a decision was made to make Nigeria a full member of the OIC (Organization of Islamic Cooperation). The last minister of defense in Jonathan's government knew that he did not know how many weapons the then National Security Adviser bought in the now infamous disbursement of billions of dollars by bullion vans.

Known unknowns, the second of Rumsfeld's categories, is the state of affairs of those in government and their most ardent supporters. When people are reared and are enmeshed in this sorry state of affairs, the use of "speculative counterfactuals and denial of the present state of affairs" is likely to be commonplace. This is a play of the *known unknowns* that Ochonu is talking about. Didn't we rear generations of Nigerians on this illogic of counterfactuals? Is the whole logic of military coups not ultimately based on a counterfactual reasoning? If we the saintly soldiers did not intervene and overthrow the evil politicians, the economy and polity of Nigeria would have gone to the dogs. I provide this modest historical perspective to nuance our analyses as we castigate present-day Nigerians or Buhari's supporters as trafficking in counterfactual logic.

Let us now shift focus to Rumsfeld's third category: *unknown unknowns*. There are things that our leaders and their supporters do not know that they do not know. What if the opposition possesses some damaging information or groundbreaking analysis about the government about which the head and his henchmen have no knowledge? This haunting question has compelled various governments in Nigeria to peremptorily act in order to forestall bad news. Acting out of fear, they work hard to ruin, before the materialization of the so-called bad news, the reputation of the opposition or anyone who does not agree with their policies.

If crude tactics do not work, you can be sure that such leaders of government will consult religious specialists to "coerce" the omniscient God to translate *unknown unknowns* to *known unknowns* or pray away the *unknown unknowns.* It is common knowledge that governments at state and federal levels award contracts to pastors, imams, and traditional religion specialists to "spiritually solve" pressing social problems or put at bay unseen, not-yet actualized problems in opposition's "spiritual laboratories." Is it not true that what Ochonu has ascribed to President Buhari supporters is characteristic of our public square as a whole? Alas, my Nigeria!

Slavoj Žižek, the radical Slovenian philosopher, added another category in the relationship between known and unknown in his critique of Rumsfeld's "amateur philosophizing." He states that "what Rumsfeld forgot to add was the crucial fourth term: the 'unknown knowns,' the things we don't know that we know—what is precisely the Freudian unconscious, the 'knowledge which does not know itself,' as the French psychoanalyst Jacques Lacan... used to say."[17]

There are beliefs, suppositions, knowledge, theologies, and philosophies that our leaders adhere to without being aware of them. As John Maynard Keynes put it in his 1936 *General Theory of Employment, Interest and Money*, "Practical men, who believe themselves to be quite exempt from any intellectual influences, are usually the slaves of some defunct economist. Madmen in authority, who hear voices in the air are distilling their frenzy from some academic scribbler of a few years back."[18] This attachment or attunement to defunct old ideas often nudges Nigerian leaders to routinely ignore well-articulated present-day ideas that could help the country. There is a certain kind of anti-intellectualism in our top leaders and politicians such that they always pay the closest attention to old ideas, and they are brilliant on old ideas, but disdain current cutting-edge thoughts. This is the knowledge that does not know itself, and in its lack of consciousness and epistemic humility, it poses a great danger to the country. Ochonu pointed out this in his critique of Buhari's defenders.

There is finally the contextual fifth term in Nigerian politics and government: *non-unknown knowns*. The things we know but we consciously handle them as if we don't know them. A leading Nigerian politician related this experience to me in 2010. It is about how politicians lie to one another.

In the rest of the world lies work because one party is duped or cannot distinguish the truth from falsehood. In Nigerian politics truth and lies work differently. One of my political operatives or even a major politician comes to me, asking me for money for a project he has done and I immediately know that he is lying. He also figures out that I know that he is lying. I do not call him out and he does not apologize to me.

---

[17]Slavoj Žižek, *Event: A Philosophical Journey through a Concept* (London: Penguin Books, 2014), 11.
[18]John Maynard Keynes, *General Theory of Employment, Interest, and Money* (San Diego: Harcourt Brace Jovanovich, 1964), 383.

I still give him the money he has asked for. I do it because it is a necessary investment to keep the client-patron network in good working order in order to win election and then recover all my investment plus some return. He also knows this.[19]

There is an important reason why I have named this fifth term *non-unknown knowns*, with the double negation as qualifier. This follows the logic of what Kant called "infinite judgment." *Non-unknown* does not negate a predicate, but affirms a non-predicate. Let us take an example from another place to clarify this point. "The soul is mortal" is a positive judgment. This statement can be negated in two ways: (a) "the soul is not mortal" and (b) "the soul is non-mortal." In the first instance, the predicate ("mortal") is negated, but in the second case, a non-predicate is asserted. "The indefinite judgment opens up a third domain which undermines the underlying distinction," as argued by Žižek.[20]

This occurs in the same vein when we say a "person is inhuman" instead of "he is not human," a new space beyond humanity and its negation is opened up. "'He is not human' means simply that he is external to humanity, animal or divine, while 'he is inhuman' means something thoroughly different, namely that he is neither human nor not-human, but marked by a terrifying excess which, although negating what we understand as 'humanity,' is inherent to being human."[21]

The fifth category of *non-unknown knowns*, this special Nigerian category, is neither known nor unknown, but marked by a horrifying surplus of corruption and ruination of national ethos among the politico-governing classes, although negating what we understand as "government" is inherent to governance in Nigeria. Public administration and the provision of information and debates in the Nigerian public square have opened up a new space beyond government and its negation. The closing of this monstrous space is the best way to defend any government at this crucial phase of our national development.

Governance and Time Gap

Governance has not only created a monstrously new epistemological space, but it has also created a new space, a strange gap in time. No exploration of governance in Nigeria will be deemed adequate without analyzing the

---

[19]Nimi Wariboko, *Nigerian Pentecostalism* (Rochester: Rochester University Press, 2014), 281.
[20]Slavoj Žižek, *Less Than Nothing: Hegel and the Shadow of Dialectical Materialism* (London: Verso, 2012), 166.
[21]Žižek, *Less Than Nothing*, 166.

historically situated phenomenon of what we may name as the *eternal now of perpetual curse*. This arises from the trauma that governance has visited upon the people. One of the definitions of traumatic event is that it is a happening that overwhelms the epistemological ballast, or exceeds the conceptual-linguistic determinations, or surpasses the range of human experience such that it cannot be easily grasped or integrated into a person's or group's knowledge system or identity. Either because the events like the primal ("original") one occur frequently or images and fragments of it keep intruding into the present, the survivors of trauma tend to organize their lives around *this* present period of the pervading intrusions. Trauma alters the time of survivors, or at least their relationships to time. The past stays in the present; the present is a churning of lived and expected traumatic experiences. The past claws the future into the present. The gravitational force of the excessive weight of the traumatic event that lingers into the present bends the future into the present—the future is a reenactment of the invaded, intensified present, a kind of mathematical squaring of the "primal" period. Put differently, the future is only an awakening to an earlier experience. Commenting on Freud's work on trauma on First World War veterans, Shelly Rambo writes that the trauma they experienced "is not located in the past but instead is located in the gap between the occurrence of the traumatic event and a subsequent awakening to it. The suffering does not solely lie in the violence of trauma's impact (in its happening) but in the ways in which that happening, that occurrence, was not known or grasped at that time."[22]

Before we turn the focus to governance as a source of traumatic events or as the prime unyielding traumatic event on Nigerians, let us examine two basic types of trauma: historical and structural. The First World War is an historical trauma, a punctual, monumental event or series of past events that overwhelm the psyche, identity, or interpretative schema of the shell-shocked veterans. Structural trauma, according to Dominick LaCapra, "is not an event but the anxiety-producing condition of possibility related to the potential for historical traumatization."[23] We pivot to the special case of Nigeria by adding a third category that combines both historical and structural traumas into a devilish brew, *micro-trauma*. This trauma is not a result of a single event of magnitude and horror, but relentless micro-daily events that produce anxiety related to the potential for shattering cessation of existence quite possibly from sudden devastating illness, increased poverty, terror, vulgarity of power, or death. This is daily, constant, ongoing exposure

---

[22]Shelly Rambo, *Spirit and Trauma: A Theology of Remaining* (Louisville, KY: Westminster John Knox Press, 2010), 20.
[23]Dominick LaCapra, *Writing History, Writing Trauma* (Baltimore: Johns Hopkins University Press, 2001), 82.

to heightened vulnerability to disable or terminate physical, psychic, or social lives. The vulnerability, contingent, dispersed, all-pervading can suddenly become materialized absolute disaster "anytime, anywhere, by any means, and for any reason."[24] When daily living conditions, the encompassing environment of everyday life is a pressure cooker of arbitrary micro-aggressions and micro-attacks, then the citizens are dying by a thousand cuts that never stop bleeding. This trauma is delivered in the fashion of constant drops of water that crack a rock.

The average Nigerian citizen is plunged into all three types of trauma and these attacks have been going on for over sixty years of the postcolonial state. Under these awful conditions of giving constant battles to historical, structural, and micro-types of trauma, the subjective perception of the victims of bad governance is bound to change. If we are to borrow Hannah Arendt's word from a very different context, I will describe the "present" in which the Nigerian victims of trauma-giving governance live with these words. Ordinarily, time is a flow of uninterrupted succession, a continuum but in Nigeria it is broken in the middle, at the point where the traumatized citizens are imprisoned, at the point where their socioeconomic development is in standstill, and this standpoint "is not the present as we usually understand it but rather a gap in time" which constant bad governance, its abolishing the past and future, keeps in existence.[25] Only because the postcolonial state inserts bad governance into the time of Nigerians and only to the extent that the state stands its ground does time exhaust itself into fatigued time and fatigue of time. The pain of the past is turning and turning in a widening vortex, the present cannot hear the past; things fall apart; the present cannot move and mere anarchy is the center. Now a blues-dimmed, incredible-laced tide is loosed, and everywhere confusion breaks the bone of time and change. Time has lost its forward-propelling motion. This is the traumatizing truth of governance in Nigeria. It is this existential condition in which the past and the future seem to have been erased, in which categories of time are rendered inoperative, that I have named as the *eternal now of perpetual curse*.

The eternal now is precisely neither time nor eternity, and it dwells paradoxically within time and timelessness while belonging to neither. Time no longer governs the rhythm of development; it is a pure manifest and acts as an incubus. Time as having severed the nexus between human activities and transformation of society becomes only the tormenting pure noise of clocks, chronometers, tower bells, and aches, all sounds of the echo chamber of gigantic torture apparatus. In this perverse state, the present deepens

---

[24]Mbembe, *On the Postcolony*, 13.
[25]Hannah Arendt, *Between Past and Future: Eight Exercises in Political Thought* (New York: Penguin Books, 1968), 11.

anomie, ensures futility, and resists redemption. Time itself is an anomic figure. Time is a prime *homo sacer* in Nigeria: it can be killed but never sacrificed to produce justice or socioeconomic transformation.

Chris Abani's *GraceLand* amply demonstrates the endless repetition of suffering of ordinary Nigerians in the vicious grove of wretchedness under conditions in which both human beings and time have become *homines sacri*. The trauma of existence in Nigeria is portrayed through many devices in *GraceLand*. Abani indicates Nigeria's deviation from the linearity of time or shows the collapse of the linear conception or perception of time by use of intertextuality. Each chapter of the novel is framed by ethnographic descriptions of the Igbo kola nut breaking ceremony and recipes for food or pharmacopeia medicinal herbs written by Beatrice, the late mother of Elvis. These intertexts, according to Hugh Hodges, "illuminate nothing about the narrative" or, as Amanda Aycock maintains, debunks the notion of "the idea of a discernible line of progress in history."[26] The events recorded in the ethnographic notes of the past do not flow into the present. The ethnographic descriptions of the kola nut ceremony and recipes from a deceased mother may well be flashbacks that disrupt the present, irrupt into the linear temporality of experiences, and are the past events that frames the present on its sides.

Beatrice's recipes, in a journal that Elvis carried with him, do not gesture to the future of pharmaceutical knowledge or culinary expertise. Ethnographic notes and recipes are parts of fragmented memories and images floating around in a traumatized existence and not well integrated into the present experience. And they do not point to the future—certainly not a future different from traumatic experiences of the past and present. There now appears a disjunction in the linear flow of time. Perhaps, even something more sinister is at play here. The past appears to have been abolished; past events do not lead to present events. The cut between the past and the present in the novel only helps us to distinguish the past from the present and imagine a world in which the past has been *deactivated* and the structure of time does not allow us to anticipate the future. Intertextuality here symbolizes the arrest and scrambling of the time of the postcolonial fabric of existence.

Abani's weaving in and out of texts may well offer not only a deep deconstruction of existence, but also signals how traumatic experiences shatter the coherence of identity. The three unrelated stories (kola nut, recipe, and Elvis's) not only reflect the fragmented narrative structure of trauma victims, but also echo the fragmentation of identity or self. Abani's techniques of intertextuality, repetition, and indirection mimic the

---

[26]Hodges, "No, This Is Not Redemption," 389; Amanda Aycock, "Becoming Black and Elvis: Transnational and Performative Identity in the Novels of Chris Abani," *Safundi* 10, no. 1 (2009): 14.

"forms and symptoms of trauma." In trauma, as Anne Whitehead argues, "temporality and chronology collapse by repetition and indirection."[27]

Abani beautifully records this collapse of temporality and chronology by the speed of the narrative. He narrates "Elvis's time in Lagos at a slower rate than his rural childhood. While the reader notes the passing of earlier years, 1983 moves slowly, suggesting a slowing down of progress and a deceleration in the development of both Elvis and, by extension, Nigeria."[28] "This grinding to a halt of personal and national progress" at the present political moment is the *eternal now* of perpetual curse, the abyss of bad governance in which Nigerians are imprisoned.[29] Do not make the mistake to think that because time has been arrested, activities of citizens and their postcolonial state have also crawled to a stop. On the contrary, the more the people get deeper into the eternal now, into the travail of unending day, the busier they get, spinning their wheels in one place. Abani shows that increased laborious pace of life may well indicate the standstill of national and personal progress and the cessation of progressive temporality.[30] Elvis noted at the beginning of the novel that he wakes up to the "sounds of babies crying, infants yelling for food and people hurrying but getting nowhere" (4). Time, precisely social time, slows down in the eternal now. Of course, it should be in Nigeria. Science tells us that time slows down around any massive object. Governance in the postcolonial state is a massive failure and it is what keeps the external now in existence. The external now is a black hole. Just as dead stars create black holes, massive dead or deadly governance creates the black hole that is the *eternal now of perpetual curse.* At the end of the novel, Elvis, evaluating his place in the world or precisely in the eternal now of suffering, figured himself as "that scar, carved by hate and smallness and fear onto the world's face" (320). The eternal now of perpetual curse is a scar carved by postcolonial incredible, oppression, and corruption onto Chrono's face.

Leadership and Governance

In the preceding discourses, we have offered a stern critique of governance in Nigeria. In this section of the chapter, we want to provide some sense of the political theory of governance and leadership that undergird this chapter as an exercise of cultural criticism.

---

[27]Anne Whitehead, *Trauma Fiction* (Edinburgh: Edinburgh University Press, 2004), 3.
[28]Sarah K. Harrison, "'Suspended City': Personal, Urban, and National Development in Chris Abani's *GraceLand*," *Research in African Literatures* 43, no. 2 (Summer 2012): 100.
[29]Harrison, "Suspended City," 100.
[30]Harrison, "Suspended City," 100.

We learned from Aristotle that the key task of all political and ethical thought is how to enable everyone in the community to live well in the appropriate human ways. The Greek word for leader, *arkhon*, comes from the verb *arkhein*, which means to begin, to rule, to command. The leader begins something new and he or she commands, governs. He or she sets up the institutional framework, ideas, rules, and practices that not only sustained that new beginning, but made room for the new to emerge. All this is done so that all persons in the community can live well in appropriately human ways. Leadership involves taking a person, group, or institution along a path or journey. The leader may not know the final destination but must assuredly know the starting point. The leader explicitly interprets his or her work from the perspective of the elimination of poverty, unfreedoms, and discriminations as necessary for good human functioning of all persons and for *excellence*. Excellence is the actualization of the potentialities of all citizens so each and every one can be all that he or she can be. A leader's concern is to create the ethos, change the orientation of the system or polity so that every human being will have the opportunity to actualize to the highest possible level his or her potentialities.[31]

Thus, in this chapter our primary thinking on leadership and creating spaces for the poor and the youth to flourish should be about how to develop a society that can best release the potentialities of persons and institutions for the common good and for human flourishing. For any person eager to stimulate economic development, the primary challenge is to create and sustain a polity in which every citizen has the opportunity to actualize his or her potential to the highest level possible and is assured of a minimum standard of living.

What is the importance of this focus on leadership? One of the monumentally stark results of the living conditions portrayed in Abani's *GraceLand*, of life in the cauldron of the "eternal now," and surviving amid the surfeit of suffering afflicted on the people by bad governance is that crushing poverty and severe socioeconomic inequality are now "raw and naked, no longer softened by promises of 'not yet.'"[32] Writing "crushing poverty" sadly reminds me of this scene in *GraceLand* where Nigeria's postcolonial rulers literally cracked chests and crushed life out of residents of

---

[31]Elsewhere I have given a description of the meaning of excellence and how it can be made to work in Nigerian political leadership. See Nimi Wariboko, *The Principle of Excellence: A Framework for Social Ethics* (Lanham, MD: Lexington Books, 2009); "Excellence as a Moral Vision for Political Leadership," in *Nigeria: Leadership and Development. Essays in Honor of Governor Rotimi Amaechi*, ed. Eme Ekekwe (Bloomington, IN: Authorhouse, 2011), 61–80.

[32]James Ferguson, *Global Shadows: Africa in the Neoliberal World Order* (Durham, NC: Duke University Press, 2009), 186, quoted in Ashley Dawson, "Surplus City: Structural Adjustment, Self-Fashioning, and Urban Insurrection in Chris Abani's *GraceLand*," *Interventions* 11, no. 1 (2009): 20.

Maroko already crushed by the excess weight of suffering. The government had come with bulldozers, soldiers, and policemen to erase the ghetto, and the residents in a moment of heroism organized a protest. Elvis's father, Sunday, was the leader and this is what happened at the moment of his death:

> Grabbing a cutlass Comfort [his wife] had dropped earlier, Sunday sprang with a roar at the 'dozer. The policeman let off a shout and a shot, and Sunday fell in a slump before the 'dozer, its metal threads cracking his chest like a timber box as it went straight into the wall of his home.
>
> (287)

Abani's narrative is a realist account of what happened in 1990. Instead of helping the poor, the Nigerian government declared the poor neighborhood of Maroko an eyesore and obliterated it. "Instead of dem to address de unemployment and real cause of poverty and crime, dem want to cover it all up under one pile of rubbish" (248). Ashley Dawson invites us to read *GraceLand* as "a damning allegory for a world in which narratives of development have been abandoned."[33] And Elvis, like the rest of Nigerian youths, is compelled to traverse "a world in which hopes for economic development and political reform are systematically obliterated. By *GraceLand*'s conclusion, spatial egress is substituted for temporal progress. Social and economic transformation on both an individual and collective level... cannot be found within the fictional mega-city [or the 'eternal now'] represented in the novel."[34]

Abani's vantage is typical of African writers in the postcolonial period. We have used the language of trauma, postcolonial incredible, and bad governance to characterize the human conditions in the Nigerian or African postcolony. But earlier writers, especially in the 1960s and 1970s, used the language of waste, excess, or excrementalism to highlight not only subjectivity or the general deplorable condition of human existence in the postcolony. Bringing up the topic of excremental visions may jar upon the nerves of some delicate readers. But the figure of waste, excess, or expulsed offcut of biological processes is important for understanding subjectivity and governance in Nigeria, a postcolony. The metaphor of excrement or excess is a common, governing trope for decoding or characterizing the African postcolony for well over sixty years. African postcolonial political leaders conspicuously consume and waste the resources of their nations with a remarkable indifference to proprietary care, utility, and necessity. Novelists and literary critics have deployed the concept of waste

---

[33]Dawson, "Surplus City," 20.
[34]Dawson, "Surplus City," 20.

to illuminate Africa's social conditions in the post-independence era.[35] "What the excremental texture of postcolonial African literature signals is, as I show, the fundamental immorality of luxury and extravagance in a context of scarcity, and its consequent incompatibility with the ideals of postcolonialism and democracy, whose rhetorical deployment serves to legitimate the political and social hegemony enjoyed by the national elites."[36] Nigerian philosophy will do well to also investigate the scatological insofar as it sheds light on subjectivity and governance in a postcolony. Governance in Nigeria is struggling with incompatibilities. The ideals of its public sector management have moved too far away from actual practices; and what is left of them principally serves as rhetorical devices to legitimate political hegemony and anti-democratic governance structure enjoyed by the political elites. Excremental texture as a configuration of heterogeneities and tensions encapsulates the agonistic struggles, ambivalences, and excremental circumstances of the Nigerian polity. Excrementalism, whether in national politics, postcolonial spirituality, or postcolonial literature, often signifies the intersection of ideals and reality, hope and despair, holiness (beauty) and sin (corruption), autonomy and dependence, national revival and national disillusionment, or desire and its impossible object. This frustrating intersection has epistemological consequences.

Politicians, writers, and pastors are pressing the limits of brutally material reality against what they consider as the magical, fantastic realities of society predicated on epistemological crisis (quest). It is a crisis that identifies or deploys a certain kind of narratives and stories as important components of subjective agency. The agent, whether he is a character in novel, a big-time corrupt politician, or a humble preacher, often crafts personal life stories with magical (spiritual) realist visions, emphasizing a preternatural mode of seeing or supernatural endowment of charisma and charismata. While individuals may give different and conflicting reasons for engaging in this practice, it is arguably one of the common ways the postcolonial subject

---

[35]There are often surprising similarities between writers and spiritualists in the context of contemporary theories of national failures, nationalist ambition, ways of seeing, analogies, and so on. For example, as Srdjan Smajić has shown, there is connection between the narrative techniques of popular forms of fiction and spiritualism in Victorian England. Literature—detective fiction and ghost stories—in the nineteenth century both embraced and rejected alternate ways of knowing. In doing this English writers were drawing from contemporary view theories of vision and sight as spiritualists also did. (See Smajić, *Ghost-Seers, Detectives and Spiritualist: Theories of Vision in Victorian Literature and Science*. Cambridge: Cambridge University Press, 2010). In the postcolonial Nigeria and Africa, there is similarity in excremental vision in the work of novelists and spiritualists. Pentecostalism and narrative fiction have a common feature: both attempt to explain the fiendish failure of economic and political development in Africa.

[36]Sarah Lincoln, "Expensive Shit: Aesthetic Economics of Waste in Postcolonial Africa." PhD dissertation (Duke University, 2008), 8–9.

deals with the radical disruptions in the economy, the grotesqueries of networked political power, and the ubiquitous invisible spiritual forces that not only permeate and frame daily existence, but also undermine systemic order of knowledge.

What I intend to do in the remainder of this chapter is to situate the excremental character of governance in Nigeria within what Joshua D. Esty calls "excremental postcolonialism."[37] Put differently, I will place the analysis of the human condition in Nigeria and Africa in the postcolonial "discursive arena saturated by the tropes of... 'belly politics'" and within the context of national politics "characterized by an 'aesthetics of vulgarity.'"[38] We will describe the discursive arena by focusing on postcolonial literature, novels by Nobel Prize winner Wole Soyinka (*The Interpreters*, 1965), Gabriel Okara (*The Voice*, 1964), Ayi Kwei Armah (*The Beautiful Ones Are Not Yet Born*, 1968), Kofi Awoonor (*This Earth, My Brother*, 1972), and Ngũgĩ wa Thiong'o (*Devil on the Cross*, 1987 and *Wizard of the Crow*, 2005). All these will enable us to understand how the general social environment and shared metaphors affect or condition analysis of governance and shed light on the historico-political context of the production of bad governance. By relating the problem that is posed in governance to the general problem of political economy and postcolonial literature, I bring together governance (governmentality) and social ecology in a theory that identifies excreta (waste, excess) as a concept that mediates the political, biological, and economic spheres of Nigerian citizens' existence.[39] Another benefit of this approach to the study of postcolonial governance is that we will be able to demonstrate that in contemporary Nigerian politics "scatology has a formative (and underexamined) significance in the development"[40] of key leaders, in the metaphorics of their narratives and narratologies of power and government, and in the articulation of their public policies.

Excremental Postcolonialism and Literature

The Kalabari (Niger Delta, Southern Nigeria) has a proverb which goes like this: "The dog is walking behind the man with the fat, sagging belly because it thinks the man will soon vomit or defecate." Fela Kuti-Anikulapo, the late musician and social critic, in his album "Expensive Shit" (1974) describes his experience of the police waiting for him to defecate. The

---

[37]Joshua D. Esty, "Excremental Postcolonialism," *Contemporary Literature* 40, no. 1 (Spring 1999): 22–59.
[38]Esty, "Excremental Postcolonialism," 23.
[39]This sentence is inspired by Lincoln, "Expensive Shit," 9.
[40]Esty, "Excremental Postcolonialism," 22.

police had gone to arrest him for marijuana possession. On seeing them he swallowed the exhibit. They took him to the prison and wanted him to defecate so they would examine it for the incriminating evidence, the possession of illegal substance.

Both Fela and the big man "ate" something; the police and the dog are waiting to possess their excrements. In the eyes of the police and the dog, Fela and the big man are corrupt because they had eaten what they were not meant to eat. (Fela on his own may be thinking that the police represent corrupt big men who should regurgitate their stolen wealth.)

"Eating" (illegally or immorally incorporating something into one's being or possession) is a common metaphor for corruption in Nigeria. Eating and excrement are the two sides of the same coin, end points of consumption. Sometimes, one person, the "villain" eats and defecates alone. Other times, the mouth that eats is separated from the anus that excretes. The big man eats and the impoverished masses bear his excrement and tolerate his thunderous farts. This kind of spectacle of enjoyment of extravagant bodily pleasures—performance of wealth or "politics of the belly"—is essential to acquiring power and keeping authority in Africa. Achille Mbembe in *On the Postcolony*, writes: "To exercise authority is, furthermore, for the male ruler, to publicly demonstrate a certain delight in eating and drinking well, and, again in Labou Tansi's words, to pass most of his time in 'pumping grease and rust into the backsides of young girls.'"[41] This kind of separation of the flip sides of the same process of consumption has its roots in the colonial process when Africans, the colonized, were at the butt end of exploitative consumption of white colonizers. Frantz Fanon brings this out in a striking passage:

> The zone where the natives live is not complementary to the zone inhabited by the settlers. The two zones are opposed, but not in the service of a higher unity.... The settlers' town is a strongly built town,... the garbage cans swallow all the leavings, unseen, unknown and hardly thought about.... The settlers' town is a well-fed town, an easygoing town; its belly is always full of good things.... The native town is a hungry town, starved of bread, of meat, of shoes, of coal, of light. The native town is a crouching village, a town on its knees, a town wallowing in the mire. It is a town of niggers and dirty Arabs.[42]

South African scholar Sarah Lincoln's comment on this passage powerfully expresses this idea of an oppressive system that has conveniently separated

---

[41] Achille Mbembe, *On the Postcolony* (Berkeley: University of California, Press, 2001), 110.
[42] Frantz Fanon, *Wretched of the Earth*, trans. Constance Farrington (New York: Grove, 1963), 39.

the consuming mouth/body from dealing with its evacuation of waste. She writes:

> In Fanon's Algiers, as throughout colonial Africa, "natives" and their quarters function as trash heaps and sewers for society's wastes, the end point of the economies of circulation that generate profit (financial as well as symbolic) for the mobile subjects. If Fanon is here describing the colonial body politic, complete with mouth, "belly," feet, skin, eyes and knees, then the "native town" is surely its anus—or, more accurately still, its toilet.[43]

Indeed, the language of excrement is very common in postcolonial Nigeria or Africa. This is not because Africans have no refined metaphors that will describe their existential conditions without jarring upon delicate nerves. It is only because the putrefying environment of corruption, waste, and degradation of human dignity that rapacious African leaders have foisted upon their own people generates this kind of language. On the one hand, the use of the language by social critics, writers, novelists, and scholars reflects the critical consciousness of injustice and destruction of the continent's resources; on the other, it is a tool of African leaders who treat their land and people as the trash heap of the global economy. And again, on the one hand, novelists and others protesting the excesses of the state use excremental language and imagery to challenge official discourse. Their works and protests operate counterdiscursively. On the other, the state deploys the excremental in the theatrics and display of political power. It is a strategy of power by the political elites. The excremental visions of those in power are often calculated to portray them as capable of evacuating the filth and "yama-yama" in the systems that will not allow Africans to have flourishing life, while they are actually consuming and defecating more on the faces of the people. The visions are also to conceal their love of power and are calculated to artfully tell the masses that they the leaders have the divine right to stay above the mess, while the people have the devilish

---

[43]Lincoln, "Expensive Shit," 24. In another section of her dissertation (pp. 79–80), she expands her comment: Colonialism is defined, in this passage, according to an unequal economy of consumption and destruction: one group eats (and is "always full") while the other starves; one group sets itself apart from its own wastes, while the other "wallows" in the mire of abjection. This is, for Fanon, simultaneously literal and symbolic—the "town" he describes is both a real place (Algiers, Dakar, Nairobi, Johannesburg...) and a figure (perhaps a metonymy or an index) for the structural organization of colonial life more generally. The colonized ("niggers and dirty Arabs") are in fact posited as the excremental remainders of colonialism as a system of production and consumption: they are the racialized and disavowed waste products of the accumulation, enjoyment, and subjective self-possession that the West has secured for itself through colonial enterprise.

privilege to wallow in excrement of poverty. On these points, Mbembe states it well when he writes:

[D]efecation, copulation, pomp, and extravagance are classical ingredients in the production of power, and there is nothing specifically African about this; the obsession with orifices results from the fact that, in the postcolony, the *commandement* is constantly engaged in projecting an image of itself and of the world—a fantasy it presents its subjects as a truth beyond dispute, a truth to be instilled into them so that they acquire a habit of discipline and obedience.[44]

African novels produced even before the era of independence adopted the scatological form to convey the brutalization of the life of the masses in the hands of their rulers or to portray fear as the vernacular language of the bond that exists between those who deploy and manifest powers (spiritual, political, and economic) and those who are deprived of countervailing powers. Here I have in mind the novels of Amos Tutuola, *The Palm-Wine Drinkard* (1952) and *My Life in the Bush of Ghost* (1954), which feature excremental settings and characters. Tutuola's scatology is embedded within the ghostliness of everyday realities. A good part of the experiences of his characters are rooted in fear, terror of hunger, and horror of poverty. Connecting Tutuola's insights about the terror of quotidian life in Africa, Mbembe describes the African postcolony as characterized by "forms of social existence in which vast populations are subjected to conditions that confer upon them the status of living dead (ghosts)."[45]

If Tutuola's scatology is embedded within the ghostliness of everyday life, then Kenyan Ngũgĩ wa Thiong'o's novels as satirical commentaries on the postcolony throw turds and urine on the postcolonial elite to unmask their corrupt economics and desecrate their assumed sanctity. In his novel, *Devil on the Cross* (1987), reportedly written on toilet paper while he was in prison, he portrays African rulers as corpulent figures and cohorts of Satan's friends who are competing with one another to determine which of them is the greatest thief and robber. His argument is that these men whose ongoing conspicuous consumption, exploitation, and "verbal diarrhoea" (196) ruin the continent have "shat and farted beyond the limits of tolerance" (158). In Ngũgĩ's next novel, *Wizard of the Crow* (2006), it appears the corrupt elites have reduced the whole of Africa into a giant dumpsite or slum: his protagonist comes back from dead atop of a garbage heap at a slum (41). A character portraying the rich businessman fights his state-sponsored

---

[44]Mbembe, *On the Postcolony*, 108–9.
[45]Achille Mbembe, "Life, Sovereignty, and Terror in the Fiction of Amos Tutuloa," *Research in African Literatures* 34, no. 4 (Winter 2003): 1–26; quotation, 1.

abductors at a police camp with his own bucket of shit and urine (386–92). The president of the fictional totalitarian country of Aburĩria suffers from a mysterious sickness, which monstrously inflates and distends his body (469–70). The various descriptions of the monstrous and foul-smelling body bring to mind the body of dead goat in extreme stages of putrefaction under the tropical sun.

In these two novels, there is an ongoing discussion of the human body as it relates to the body politic. Ngũgĩ counters how the rich convey their bodies as different and superior to those of the masses. He argues that owing to their corruption, grotesque appetites, and excessive consumption, their bodies and by extension the body politic they command are in worse shape than the bodies of the poor. He described the breath of the corrupt leaders-thieves as smelling "worse than the fart of a badger or of someone who has gorged himself on rotten beans or over-ripe bananas" (*Devil on the Cross*, 182). As Lincoln noted about these novels:

Rotting teeth and farting anuses defetishize the dignified integrity of bourgeois bodies by bringing to sensory attention the suppressed modes of abjection on which such dignity is constructed. Shit, farts, rotten breath and vomiting not only satirically highlight, in general, the all-too human bodies of the elites, complete with animal needs like the rest of the population, but more importantly also serve specifically as metonymic traces of the overconsumption, excessive appetites, and "poor taste" that quite literally take food out of the mouths of other postcolonial subjects.[46]

Postcolonial literature uses excrement as a discursive resource to interrogate ruling class idea and the failure of national development in Africa. In Ghanaian Ayi Kwei Armah's *The Beautiful Ones*, the Teacher, a character disillusioned with the performance of Ghana's political leaders expressed his disgust in scatological terms:

We were ready here for big and beautiful things, but what we had was our own black men hugging new paunches scrambling to ask the white man to welcome them onto our backs…. How were these leaders to know that while they were climbing up to shit in their people's faces, their people had seen their arseholes and drawn away in disgusted laughter.

(81–2)

In another place, Armah (one of the early intellectual elites of independent Ghana) describes disgustedly the behavior of the African elites, kowtowing to the white ex-colonizers instead of working to create economic

---

[46]Lincoln, "Expensive Shit," 48.

development and raise the dignity of the black Africans. He portrays them as scavengers: "eating what was left in the teeth of the white men with their companies" (81).

Here a thought urges itself upon us. I am thinking of the ubiquitous narratives of leading Nigerian pentecostal pastors about their exceptional cleanliness amid the excremental postcolony.[47] Instead of taking them seriously at their words that they are above the muck of the postcolony we should do the opposite. Each pastor's loud claim of his or her unique holiness is only a confirmation of the general rottenness of their brand of Christianity. Each narrative of avoidance of defilement is perhaps an indirect, knuckles-in-white-gloves attack on or deprecation of fellow pentecostal ministers. In the telling and retelling of such narratives—often set within spiritual visions of avoiding contamination by excrement—the particular man or woman of God is indicting pastors who think that they are clean, gleaming, but actually are dirty, matters out of place. In Armah's novel a prosperous government minister, Koomson appears to be living a "clean life," but a protagonist, a railway clerk thinks otherwise, "Some of that cleanliness has more rottenness in it than the slime at the bottom of a garbage dump" (44). Thus, in a certain sense each pentecostal pastor's excremental visions may have something to do with his or her disillusionment with pentecostal believers' "assignment of clean and dirty" to their leaders. Or the visions may have something to do with big pastors drawing fat tithes from fraudulent big politicians and businesspersons but pretending to be floating above the excremental source of such money as a *chichidodo*. As the wife of the railway clerk puts it: "Ah, you know, the chichidodo is a bird. The chichidodo hates excrement with all its soul [heart, mind, and strength]. But chichidodo only feeds on maggots, and you know the maggots grow best inside the lavatory. This is the chichidodo" (45).

Commenting on the social ordure that prevents Nigeria from making progress in development, Wole Soyinka through one of the characters in *The Interpreters*, Sagoe, walking through a city and encountering filth and night-soil men, declared: "God is spring-cleaning in heaven, washing out his bloody lavatory .... Next to death, shit is the most vernacular atmosphere of our beloved country" (107–8).

The visionary hero, Okolo in Gabriel Okara's *The Voice*, in a matter reminiscent of great religious figures, offers himself as a martyr in the hands of his own people in an attempt to rid his society of moral pollution and evil imaged as human dirt and excrement.[48] Okolo's vision is not wasted—and

---

[47]Nimi Wariboko, *Nigerian Pentecostalism* (Rochester: University of Rochester Press, 2014), 56–63.

[48]For a discussion of the scatology in *The Voice*, see Derek Wright, "Scatology and Eschatology in Kofi Awoonor's *This Earth, My Brother*," *International Fiction Review* 15, no. 1 (1988): 23–6.

"time finishes" for the corrupt order—as his deeds and words take root in the communal conscience.

If Okara's novel casts a vision of communal redemption based on a messianic figure's death, Ghanaian Kofi Awoonor seems to block this possibility or, at least, refuse to vouchsafe a cheap messianicity. The novel, *This Earth, My Brother*, despite its Christological tone refuses an exit from the dunghill world of corruption as in Okara's *Voice*. "Woman, behold thy son; son, behold thy mother. This revolting malevolence is thy mother. She begat thee from her womb after a pregnancy of a hundred and thirteen years. She begat thee after a long parturition, she begat you in her dust, and you woke up after the eighth day screaming on a dunghill" (28). Ghana after a century of white rule was born as an independent nation, but found herself on the dunghill of precolonial, colonial, and neocolonial accumulated evils. There appears to be no great possibility of "regenerative deliverance in the present," only unalleviated suffering. There is no cheap hope carrying itself forward by wishing that out of the dung and decay there will be a new flowering in the present. The hero's (Amamu's) death at best provides eschatological transformation in the ancestral, unseen world rather than social regeneration in the present. Change is coming, but it is in the approaching eschaton.

> In this novel the dunghill and the butterfly, the night soil dump and the regenerative chrysalis, are antithetical, not contemporary images. The wry refrain "Fear death by shit trucks," with its ironical echoes of *The Waste Land* and *The Tempest*, mocks the idea of a miraculous sea change with a young officer's unambiguous death under heaps of the waste which is society's end product… Material and magical transformation, death as finality and as process, scatology and eschatology, all seem to be working in opposition.[49]

Yet the novel refuses fatalistic resignation and nudges the reader toward revolutionary spirit.

By way of reaching conclusion, let me state that in general the African writers we are studying in this section of the chapter use excrement as a figurative guise of wasted energies and aborted promises. "Excremental allegory works to release the constipated energies of societies, like postcolonial Africa's, that are based on consumption at the expense of production, returning to circulation those energies—libidinal, material, and semiotic—that have been monopolized by greedy elites."[50]

---

[49]Wright, "Scatology and Eschatology," 25.
[50]Lincoln, "Expensive Shit," 55.

In these eight novels (by Soyinka, Okara, Armah, Awoonor, Ngũgĩ, and Tutuola) that focus on the problems inherent in building a postcolonial economy/polity, the scatological form serves to point us to the "constant unfinished character" of the task of nation-building or forging "the uncreated conscience of a new nation."[51] This is not all. The scatological form reveals other dimensions of the state of the postcolony.

Overall, what do we make of the retreats to lavatory (excremental metaphors and language) by Nigerian politicians, protagonists, and preachers? We can make the case that at a deep level, the retreats by these disparate groups indicate that Nigeria as a nation is stuck at the level of physiological necessity and solipsistic withdrawal. Its gaze is fixated on its alimentary canal. In Hannah Arendt's terms, to invoke a more delightful metaphor, the country is gummed up at the "labor stage." It is in dire need of *actors* who can transform it and liberate it from imprisonment in the pre-creation blind, rotary drives of Schellingian nothingness, void. The accent on excrementalism reflects, by and large, Nigeria's people existence as metabolism with nature. The laboring activity, as Arendt informs us, is concerned with extracting food from nature and giving dung back to the earth. Man, woman as the laboring animal (*animal laborans*) is caught in the treadmill history of consumption, excretion, and disposal.

To add another dimension to the alimentary problems of Nigeria, let us continue our deployment of the Arendtian-Marxist metaphor at a slightly different angle. It will further suggest that the use of excremental language and scatological form of narration (cloacal obsession, if you like) reflects Nigeria's entrapment in metabolic relationship with nature or foreign institutions. For more than sixty years, Nigeria has engaged in hyperactive metabolism with the global economy, modernization, or any other foreign matter. This has led to rapid accumulation of ancient and contemporary feces and history (as an ongoing process of life) that has become particularly excrementable. In this nightmare of history in the postcolony, excrementalism "surfaces at the pressure points of engagement"[52] with the imperatives of the foreign *apparatuses*.[53] Excrementalism designates the imperfection of digestion.

Nigerian Literature as cultural criticism is, arguably, better than African philosophy in offering us a robust description of the Nigerian socio-political environment that helps to engender, sustain, and define the versatility of excrement in postcolonial postcolonialism. As I stated in the introductory chapter, literature has something to offer philosophy. Nigerian Literature

---

[51]Esty, "Excremental Postcolonialism," 53, 51.

[52]Esty, "Excremental Postcolonialism," 51, inspired the last two sentences.

[53]For the specific meaning of apparatus being used here, see Giorgio Agamben, *What Is Apparatus?*, trans. David Kishik and Stefan Pedatella (Stanford: Stanford University Press, 2009).

can help Nigerian philosophers in their tasks of cultural criticism and the theorization of their nation. The next chapter offers another pertinent lesson to philosophers. It combines history and literature to shed light on how Nigerian citizens can interrupt the ongoing process of corruption and bad governance so as to extricate themselves from the vicious webs of their leaders and the banality of evil that now define their country.

4

From Executed God to Ozidi Saga: Ethos of Ijo Democratic Republicanism

Introduction

Long before Friedrich Nietzsche's madman in the market shouted, "God is dead…. And we have killed him," the Kalabari people (Izon, Niger Delta, Nigeria) on September 27, 1857, announced to Africans and Europeans in the Niger Delta that they had just killed one of their gods (Owu Akpana, the Shark-god) and proceeded to celebrate the deicide and its ensuing freedom.[1] This act, which was not metaphysical but historical, involved eating the divine flesh and drinking the blood of the god, incorporating the divine into the human and thus recognizing sovereignty in the people. Like a mole, they burst asunder the carapace of spiritual-political hegemony that divided them from their sovereignty, so that the hegemony crumbled away. All gods in Kalabari—except one, the supreme being Tamuno/Tamarau—became vulnerable to death at the hands of their worshippers as a community.[2] Put differently, in

---

[1]Friedrich Nietzsche, *The Gay Science* (Liepzig: E. W. Fitzsch, 1887), 125 and Friedrich Nietzsche, *Thus Spake Zarathustra* (New York: Barnes & Noble, 2005), 10. For a discussion of the killing of the Shark-god, see Liverpool merchant William Oates, diary notes, September 28, 1857, D/0/18, National Museums of Liverpool, Maritime Archives and Library, Liverpool, England. [International Slavery Museum, Liverpool, United Kingdom. See https://www. liverpoolmuseums.org.uk/international-slavery-museum]. See also G. I. Jones, *The Trading States of the Oil Rivers: Study of Political Development in Eastern Nigeria* (Oxford: Oxford University Press, 1963), 217.

[2]This exception does not signify a sovereign's power to overdetermine reality; rather, it is a symbol of a cultural creativity that puts absence of divine vulnerability at the same level as presences of divine vulnerability. Simply put, the exception points to a logic of differentiality.

Jacques Lacan's felicitous phrase, the gods were always already dead; they just did not know it.[3] The Shark-god found out the hard way. Indeed, the killing illuminates three ethico-political elements: human beings are the immanent obstacle that prevents the sacred from achieving full self-identity; the political is the immanent Spirit of the community; and materialization of some higher or untouchable power or reality could be cast down to *nothing*.

Before Nietzsche's madman threw his lantern on the ground on seeing the astonishment on the faces of his listeners and declared, "I have come too early, my time has not come yet," the death of God was already functioning as a *concept* in Kalabari, and not as a mytho-poetic thought to awaken people from their slumber of transcendence. With the execution of Owu Akpana, the preconceptual thought of deicide instantly transformed from thought to material act to an *ideal entity*. This is precisely the moment two revelations traversed Tamarau herself: (a) the people as *demos* as well as Spirit (a community of organized believers as divine, sacred energy, *amatemeso*) is a disruptive, interruptive power, and (b) *natality* as a political notion that haunts all claims of exception and givenness.[4] The divine-human relationship became scarred by traces of this "hubris," social antagonisms/agonisms, or trauma. And its scarred character is, arguably, the interpretative frame through which they perceive and relate to the dense network of relationships that define or mark human existence. More specifically, interactions that appear to Kalabari people as hierarchic relationship, "big other," "objective order," or "hyperobject" are "already transcendentally constituted through a horizon of meaning sustained by" the metonymic 1857 event, the volcanic core of divine-human interaction.[5]

The people (an emancipatory political collective), at least for a moment in 1857, hovered "above the entire life of the state" and all forms of realization of the divine.[6] How can this tradition be retrieved to illuminate democratic politics or counter the politics of near-divine impunity by leaders in Nigeria? What social-ontological power did the revolutionary act of deicide recognize, reveal, or portray? (Perhaps, it is the capacity to initiate something new amid ongoing social-political processes, the possibility of radical new beginning.) What is the implication of all this for democratic sovereignty in Nigeria?

In this chapter, I endeavor to provide a fuller narrative, explanation, and analysis of the 1857 event and deploy it to offer a diagnostic of Nigerian's

---

[3]Lacan quoted in Slavoj Žižek, *Absolute Recoil: Towards a New Foundation of Dialectical Materialism* (New York: Verso, 2014), 273.
[4]Nimi Wariboko, *Ethics and Time: Ethos of Temporal Orientation in Politics and Religion in the Niger Delta* (Lanham, MD: Lexington, 2010), 60–1n13.
[5]Slavoj Žižek, *Disparities* (London: Bloomsbury Academic, 2016), 70.
[6]Carl Schmitt, *Political Theology: Four Chapters on the Concept of Sovereignty*, trans. George Schwab (Cambridge, MA: MIT Press, 1985), 49.

present political situation under late capitalism. To accomplish this, I bring in themes from the *Ozidi Saga*, a highly acclaimed Izon national epic,[7] to critically accentuate the disruptive effects of an awakened demos marked by *the capacity to begin*.[8] According to Isidore Okpewho, who is arguably the most distinguished expert on African oral literature, "The Ozidi story is easily the best known of tales told among the Ijo of Nigeria's delta country, who have drawn worldwide attention to themselves for resisting what they consider the collusion between the country's federal government and some multinational corporations in the exploitation of the area's petroleum resources."[9]

The Ozidi story paints a portrait of people with a restless subjectivity, republican polis, and emancipatory politics of interruption. In a sense, void resides always at the core of power in Izon society, and the *Ozidi Saga* can be interpreted to point to the passion of natality/rebellion, rage for justice/ withdrawal of consent that swirls around established (enchanted, entrusted, or heteronomous) power as a form of concealment or occultation of the void. The killing of god and Izon republicanism (in the sense that political power belongs to no one person) suggest there is a disincarnation of power: political leadership depends on the consent of the citizens, and no leader can function as an incarnation of the divine. A leader can refer neither to an *outside* (to a god or sacred mandate) nor to an *inside*, singular appropriation of the democratic power of the community to privilege his or her authority. Power is groundless and unfounded, and thus open to endless interrogation and alteration.[10]

In the *Ozidi Saga*, we encounter an Izon community questing for its own democratic foundation while also raising questions about divine-human relationship. Ozidi, the hero of the saga, killed all men in politico-military power and some supernatural beings (gods) to rid himself of the burden of justice placed upon him after the assassination of his father at the hands of his father's political rivals. In his victory, we see the rapture that makes two bodies of power (political and divine) vanish and "replaces them with no body at all."[11] He becomes neither a ruler (monarch) nor a materialization (or a moderator) of the divine. The political throne of the community becomes void, an empty space of power, which it was already

---

[7]J. P. Clark-Bekederemo, *The Ozidi Saga: Collected and Translated from the Oral Ijo Version of Okabou Ojobolo* (Washington, DC: Howard University Press, 1991).

[8]See also Nimi Wariboko, *The Pentecostal Principle: Ethical Methodology in New Spirit* (Grand Rapids, MI: Eerdmans, 2012).

[9]Isidore Okpewho, *Blood on the Tides: The Ozidi Saga and Oral Epic Narratology* (Rochester, NY: University of Rochester Press, 2014), 1.

[10]Stathis Gourgouris, *Lessons in Secular Criticism* (New York: Fordham University Press, 2013), 130–7, inspired these lines. His comments are on Claude Lefort's contribution to political theory.

[11]Gourgouris, *Lessons in Secular Criticism*, 141.

always in a democratic, republican polis, except that it became visible. His action and his very identity are now marked by the void, revealing power as an empty place (to be occupied by the polis in its entirety, in its differential multiplicity) and as "the capacity of human beings to alter radically the forms and structures they inherit."[12]

What do all the preliminary analyses and discussions I have so far set forth mean for comprehending Nigeria's current political situation? Preparing the reader to adequately respond to this question through the lens of an historically derived political theory is the main task of this chapter. Putting aside theoretical ruminations for a moment, I now delve into the historical event, the politico-religious earthquake of 1857, which anchors my deliberations today and animates the political philosophy I am constructing in this chapter.

The Executed God

Monday, 28th [September 1857]

> [I] went up to [New] Calabar town this morning and while there heard that the chiefs had a meeting in their palaver house yesterday, in consequence of several of the natives having been killed lately by their big Jew Jew [juju, god], the Sharks, they came to the conclusion that it no be use for have wowo jew jew [useless god] all same shark no more and it is therefore no longer held as such, but the natives are catching them as fast as possible and now allow "white men" to do the same if they like which of course we shall do whenever we have a chance as the shark is the sailor's greatest enemy.[13]

William Oates, a trader from Liverpool who was in New Calabar (Elem Kalabari, the headquarters of the Kalabari people at the time), recorded this event in his diary. When growing up as child in the 1970s, I heard the elders in my town, Abonnema, talk about this event and later, I read about the same story recorded as oral history by British anthropologists such as P. Amaury Talbot, G. I. Jones, and Robin Horton. People in my town had always been suspicious about whether the event actually happened—our people could not have killed their god. Furthermore, no written record existed to support the tale.[14] But there were enough insights into the native

---

[12]Gourgourris, *Lessons in Secular Criticism*, 143, quotation on xvii.
[13]Oates, diary notes, D/O/18.
[14]Until I discovered Oates's diary in July 2009 at the International Slavery Museum, Liverpool, UK.

worldview or philosophy that were repeated often as proverbs to suggest that my Izon ancestors were capable and even prone to killing their gods.[15] According to a popular Kalabari aphorism: If a god becomes too furious or demanding, we will tell it from which wood it was carved (*agu nsi*[16]*owi baka kuma en ke o kara sin en dugo o piriba*). In other words, a community can unanimously annul a god's power by refusing it worship.[17] Horton interprets the aphorism this way:

> Literally, if a spirit's demands become too burdensome, the whole congregation can join together to destroy its cult objects, and by this unanimous act of rejection render it powerless to trouble them further.... Broadly, then, the more people lavish offerings, invocations, and festivals upon any spirit, the more powerful it becomes both to reward and punish them. And conversely, the less they attend to it the less powerful it becomes—up to the point at which unanimous rejection results in the complete loss of power. Generally, of course, a single man cannot reject a spirit at will; for while he is only one among a congregation of many, it will have the power to punish him.[18]

The idea that when a people stop praying or worshipping a god, the god ceases to exist can be interpreted through the lens of two principles in Izon political philosophy. First, is the indigenous conception of freedom. In the light of the traditional African spirit of communality, freedom is something enjoyed in public not in private; free people participate in public actions for the common good with one's peers. Freedom is the power to act together, to initiate new possibilities in the community, to think and act in new ways.

---

[15]The people of Bonny, another Izon group, also killed two gods that they considered wicked. "Kunbuyana and Tolofari ... were wicked and capsized many Bonny canoes, going and coming from market, unless a small offering of palm-oil was thrown into the river. They so molested Bonny that my [B. M. Pepple] ancestor, King Dappa Pepple, went off and cut off their heads, which he brought back to Bonny. This happened long years ago." P. Amaury Talbot, *Tribes of the Niger Delta: Their Religions and Customs* (London: Frank Cass, 1967), 52. I have heard of another case in Okrika, another Izon community, where the god Kun-ma (which is called *Ogboloma* in Kalabari) was also "disrobed."

[16]*Agu-nsi* is an Igbo word that has been adopted in Kalabari. The Kalabari word for carved or sculptured idol is *ẹkẹkẹ-tamụnọ*; *ẹkẹkẹ* means stone, piece of stone, or rock.

[17]Robin Horton, *Kalabari Sculpture* (Lagos: Department of Antiquities, Federal Republic of Nigeria, 1965), 8–9. See also Robin Horton, "The Kalabari Worldview: An Outline and Interpretation," *Africa* 32, no. 3 (July 1962): 197–219, esp. 204. Horton relates the story of how a spirit who misbehaved was summoned before an assembly of its worshippers, found guilty, and fined. (Robin Horton, "A Hundred Years of Change in Kalabari Religion," in *Black Africa: Its People and Their Cultures Today*, ed. John Middleton [New York: Macmillan, 1971], 194–8).

[18]Horton, "Kalabari Worldview," 204.

It is about appearing to others as a distinct, irreplaceable individual in the public space (the shared world) and performing immortal deeds.[19]

This notion of freedom embeds the idea of the *capacity to do*, to do what a person needs to do irrespective of obstacles, burdens, or circumstances, a striving to achieve the improbable; thus, one can bring something new into an already-existing situation. One way this capacity-to-do is rendered in Kalabari is "*I ye gbaye ye*." This is the pure capacity to do—the "I can." The focus is not on the will—"I will," which can be defeated by interior (mind versus body struggle) and exterior circumstances; nor is it dependent on the intellect, which can be paralyzed by analysis of future desirability of aims. *I ye gbaye ye* is pure doability—it is sufficient to act; to manifest one's being in the presence of others, to manifest the human character as acting with the initiative to begin again, to establish a new reality. *I ye gbaye ye* demands doing or acting to bring in the new, even the unexpected. Usually, a series of events is ongoing, and an action is needed to interrupt it. Within it there is always this freedom to act, to begin afresh, which is the key quality of the intercourse among fellow citizens. The man/woman is free if he/she can disrupt automatic political, historical, and religious processes by persuading other citizens to act collectively with him/her rather than be a slave to them.

Quintessential freedom of the individual in Kalabari involves three dimensions. Number one: the person was not a slave to another human being. Number two: he/she was not a servant of necessities of life. Number three: she/he could act (*ori ine o ye gbaye ye ba*), exhibiting the capacity to begin, to do and act, to start something new in the midst of others (world). To be free is to thrive on the basis of the unprecedented. Kalabari say, "*ala-okolo poku pilamaa*," which literally means "a chief's (great person's) feces do not pollute the holy." The phrase is generally understood to mean that a great man or woman is above the law. But the inherent meaning of the saying goes beyond seeing chiefs as above the law. Law, in general, imposes limitations of action and such containment is founded on precedent, but every action (which law is attempting to police or contain) is inherently boundless and unpredictable, and thus thrives in the realm of the unprecedented.[20]

The divine-human relationship is not above these sentiments of freedom or the belief in the human capacity to begin something new. As the event of 1857 in Elem Kalabari and other similar stories in Izon communities in the nineteenth century demonstrate, Izon people are willing to start afresh with their gods. If a god initiates a process that is not conducive to human flourishing, humans can disrupt the process to start something new. If a god becomes too violent, humans will cause it to cease to exist.

---

[19]See Nimi Wariboko, *The Depth and Destiny of Work: An African Theological Interpretation* (Trenton, NJ: Africa World Press, 2008) for the role legacy and social immortality play in the ethical formation of subjects in an Izon community.
[20]Wariboko, *Ethics and Time*, 46–9.

This brings me to the second political principle in Izon political philosophy with which to interpret the event of 1857: the withdrawal of worship from or worshipful dependence on the god deprives the god of its power and authority to act on humans or control human activities. Once we grasp the importance of relations as constitutive of both society and personhood in Kalabari communities, the 1857 deicide is not at all surprising. Worship is not just reverence, obeisance, praise and exaltation, or an appropriate response to deity, but the dynamic maintenance of a deep social bond with a deity. All forms of power, be it political or spiritual, are predicated on the strength of social bonds between and among persons, and the fracture or rupture of the bond or the displacement of harmony within the bond means erosion of power and authority.

The idea that the holy emerges from social practice has long been taken for granted in traditional Izon culture. Among the Kalabari of the Niger Delta in Nigeria, the holy—godliness—is an emergent phenomenon of human worship; like social systems, it realizes itself through practices. The holy emerges from and is ensconced in the social practice of worship. The gods arise from such practice insofar as their power of being is in it. The gods are conceived as a source of tremendous power. But the power that the gods possess is believed to depend on the social practice of human worship, and as such, humans can reduce or completely efface the power of any god by withdrawing worship.[21] The Kalabari believe that spirits and gods do not have intrinsic powers of their own, maintaining that an unworshipped god loses its power.

Politics of Interruption: The Volcanic Core of Social Relations

I have so far deployed Kalabari understanding of freedom and relationship to frame the 1857 deicide. A third factor—action as an interruptive force—expands this framing. Kalabari people interpret action as the capacity to interrupt; disrupt the power dynamics or to lob in a voice or do something that halts or diverts an ongoing system or process. Persons or institutions that have this kind of power to maximally interrupt others' lives become gods. In the early twentieth century, for instance, the British colonial imposition as consulate authority in the life of the Kalabari people caused so many disruptions in their everyday lives and in how local institutions functioned that the consulate became a "god." In the 1970s, years after Nigeria's independence, old folks were still invoking this terrible god

---

[21]Wariboko, *Depth and Destiny of Work*, 37–9.

against an adversary: "*Konsin bere ibu paka*," may you be persecuted by the consulate. The consulate as a god that interrupted local power dynamics was now called upon to visit its form of interruption on an adversary, to deploy its wickedness and impunity to interrupt a person's ongoing life.

Gods are interruptive forces, but human beings can also interrupt gods. British colonial governors knew well that under the influence of a local deity, the people they controlled could summon enough collective energy to disrupt their oppressive imperial rule. Thus, under the guise of Christian "civilization" that frowned on the worship of local gods, colonial rulers proceeded to discredit them. In some cases, colonial authorities destroyed the shrines of deities and even passed laws against people invoking the name of their gods against their opponents in a dispute. In the early 1940s, Kalawanyi Wariboko Young-Jack, a Christian widow in her thirties, invoked the name of a local deity against a powerful chief of her Jack compound in Abonnema. The chief's son had severely flogged her ten-year-old daughter while playing a masquerade during a festival in the public square.[22] Young-Jack wanted the young man to be punished for the infraction, but his father refused. Having no political power to bring the chief and his son to justice, she summoned (*oru gbo*) one of the local deities to punish the chief, to interrupt his smugness and unassailable power. He dragged the aggrieved woman to the colonial native authority court (in which he was one of the judges) and charged her with breaking the law by invoking the name of a local god against him (though it was still common in the town to call down the judgment of gods in disputes). Another man, Chief Graham Douglas, a cousin of Young-Jack from a different compound and a member of the native authority court, saved the woman from the wrath of the colonial authority by interrupting the power-drunk chief's plan to convict her. After she was cleared, Young-Jack changed her name back to its maiden form, Kalawanyi Daketima Douglas, thus interrupting her shared belonging (through their common last name) to the overbearing chief's kinship group.

The key principle I want to highlight here is that oru gbo, calling on a god, is a way Kalabari culture gives voice or speech to persons who are not supposed to be heard among the powerful. The rupture of Mrs. Young-Jack, her calling up a deity to secure justice for her regardless of the colonial ban, is publicly interruptive of the hegemonic order symbolized by her rich and powerful adversary. The part-of-no-part speaks when they are expected to be silent, providing a way for the gods to become involved in politics, the politics of interruption, and the dissensus of the uncounted and excluded as French philosopher Jacques Rancière informs us.[23]

---

[22]My mother was the daughter who was flogged. My grandmother told me this story.
[23]Jacques Rancière, *Disagreement: Politics and Philosophy*, trans. J. Rose (Minneapolis: University of Minneapolis Press, 1999).

The power of community to interrupt powerful people or agents is asserted or enacted in the ceremony of becoming chiefs. One of the questions a would-be chief must answer is, If you are with a beautiful woman, a new woman and you are about to have sex or already engaged in it, will you interrupt the coitus and come when the community calls?[24] If the aspirant is not capable of resisting libidinal impulses to promptly leave for community services when he hears a clarion call for action in the face of a new naked lover who is alone with him in the room, then he does not qualify for leadership and he has exhibited a failure to understand a basic requirement of citizenship. The man is questioned so the community can learn something about his willingness to consciously move from the private realm to the public, to interrupt his private interests for sake of the public.

This penchant to interrupt or gauge the preparedness of citizens for interruption is also evident in one of the primordial relations, Kalabari Izon believe, existing between God (the supreme being, Tamarau/Teme-órú/ Tamuno) and them. Here, I am talking about the tension between *fiyeteboye* and *bibibari*. In the Kalabari theory of personhood, the individual is believed to have a two-part personality. The component parts of this personality act as separate "persons." One is conscious, the other unconscious. Before the person is born, the unconscious part (the soul) decides on the person's destiny (*so* or *fiyeteboye*), the life course of the whole person on Earth. When a soul (spirit) is about to come to Earth, the would-be soul of the person goes before Teme-órú and decides on a set of possibilities for the life of the individual it is going to inhabit. The conscious part of the personality—that is, the physical embodiment of the soul—works to actualize the chosen set of possibilities in history. If a person does not like the course of her life on Earth, she may go to a diviner to change her *so* or *fiyeteboye*. The process of changing destiny is called *bibibari* (altering or nullifying the spoken word, recanting). Through the diviner, the person tells Teme-órú that she would like to change her life course on Earth. Once the change of destiny is effected, the new *so* conditions the person's life course for the remainder of her life.[25]

What does this example add to the portrait of the Izon political philosophy I am developing in this chapter? If *fiyeteboye* is the "timeless," ontological structuring of the range of possibilities within a person's life, then *bibibari*, is the radical temporality of subjectivity as an openness to the future in Kalabari thought. The individual has the opportunity or right to interrupt the primal voice, the preexistent speech in her life. Here the person is actually interrupting the voice speaking from the throne room of the supreme being. Yes, in the beginning was the word, but there is always

[24]See a reinstatement of this question in the form of a public announcement in J. P. Clark, *Ozidi* (Ibadan, Nigeria: Oxford University Press, 1966), 18.
[25]Wariboko, *Ethics and Time*, 66–70.

a re-beginning of the beginnings. And owing to the disruptions caused by interruptions, beginning does not stop itself from occurring more than once.

The Kalabari-Izon person is culturally formed to interrupt not only his speech-agreement with God but also his very being or own desire. This is enacted in a set of practices I have named elsewhere as *counterfoil choice*.[26] The characteristic feature of counterfoil choice is that whenever A is offered, the Kalabari offer its negative (non-A) to the person, to deter the person from a specific decision or to gauge the person's willingness to interrupt their desire. During rites of passage or in situations in which citizens must rethink their actions or behavior, the community gives them a forced choice between A or non-A. Another question asked of a would-be chief is, Are you willing to pick yam or cannonball? Yam represents the ability to feed his household and cannon ball represents taking risks on behalf of the community and using his capability and financial resources to defend it in times of war and uphold its freedom. The man knows he must pick cannonball to make it through the ceremony, going against his self-centered well-being. His upbringing has prepared him for how to respond to tests like this. Fathers tell their sons and nephews that if given the forced choice of freedom or death, you choose death to keep your freedom of choice. Choosing freedom under the threat of death is unmanly and cowardly, offering no proof of freedom. Young men learn that when a proper Kalabari man faces such a condition (a kind of declaration of war), he should be able to quietly cut off his breath instead of "eating phlegm." In such a condition, he should be willing to sacrifice the very thing that he cares most about—he should betray his own paramount interest in life. It is this very natural desire to preserve and promote life that makes the forced choice so palpable, personal, and painful in order to demonstrate that he has the freedom of choice. He chooses freedom by choosing its negation (non-A). He interrupts the flow of his life so as not to give up on who he is.[27] He interrupts his very being, the innermost desire that brings him to the point of sacrifice in the first place.

This idea of interruption runs so deep in the culture that as we have already seen, the very gods that could be used to interrupt the speech of powerful men who govern can, in turn, be interrupted or put out of existence, experiencing the ultimate interruption. As a matter of fact, Kalabari say that they create sculptures for their gods as a means to interrupt the flow of their movement and exercise control over them. An informant told anthropologist Robin Horton, "If you invoke a spirit without sculpture to act against someone who had wronged you, where will you call it off? Maybe, the place

---

[26]Nimi Wariboko, *Pattern of Institutions in the Niger Delta: Economic and Ethological Interpretations of History and Culture* (Port Harcourt, Nigeria: Onyoma Research Publications, 2007), 301–37.
[27]I am indebted to Bonnie Honig for the language to interpret Izon counterfoil choice. See Bonnie Honig, *Antigone, Interrupted* (New York: Cambridge University Press, 2013), 177–9.

where you invoke, the spirit will not be there: and the place where you do not invoke, the spirit will be there."[28] The Kalabari say gods come and go in their names, and a wooden sculpture (*oru fubara*, literally, "forehead of the god"[29]) is a form of a name of the god that confines it for interactions in a shrine. In this way, a sculpture of a god "enjoys the same intimate link with the spirit it represents as would any other kind of name: whatever is done to the one *ipso facto* affects the other."[30]

The politics of interruption I have laid out is akin to the notions of freedom and relationship that also define interactions between gods and humans. They all point to the limitations of power, whether supernatural or natural, and that the citizens, worshippers, or subjects under authority must always have something to disrupt ongoing social processes, to overturn overbearing power. So when Kalabari say, "if a spirit becomes too violent, they will tell him from which stick it was carved" in everyday speech, it is a reminder, as Horton informs us, about the limitations not only of supernatural power, "but also the pitfalls that lie in wait for the overbearing human being. Its use is based on the fact that 'the stick they carved him' is a figure of speech for the instrument of their power over him."[31] The people as a collective always have something through which they can control or successfully revolt against a god or person in authority. This "something" is their action or their capacity to begin. The generative impulse of the political is that the actions of human beings work to eliminate the impossible by creating new possibilities. Simply put, coexistence (among humans and between human beings and gods) carries a high-voltage charge of disruptive possibility and is delicately balanced on a fragile consensus in which each actor has agreed not to overstep their bounds.

The Shark-god transgressed its limits and was killed; portions of its blood and flesh put into the town's drinking well for the citizens to consume. The mixing of shark's blood in the town's well says to the people as a collective, "This is the blood of Owu Akpana shed by us for us. Drink this in remembrance of our triumph and liberation and in fidelity to our collective destiny and our collective guilt." The political theological, the political economic, and the democratic all intersect here. The political theological and the democratic do not need to delay me here as I have been shedding light on them and will say more about them below. The Akpana lineage (surviving remnants of the ancient Amabiame house of Elem Kalabari) that produced the priests for the shark cult (Owu Akpana) refused to partake

---

[28]Quoted in Horton, *Kalabari Sculpture*, 8.

[29]"Now the forehead is that part of the person associated with the *so* [destiny] that rules the fortunes of his life; hence *oru fubara* implies not just something which is intimately linked to a spirit, but something which exercises a kind of control over it" (Horton, *Kalabari Sculpture*, 8).

[30]Horton, *Kalabari Sculpture*, 10.

[31]Horton, *Kalabari Sculpture*, 8.

in the communion and eucharistic feast on the flesh of the Shark-god. For their refusal, members of the lineage were tried and heavily fined. Unable to pay the sum, "King Karibo redeemed its members by paying the fine and they thus became absorbed into his house and the independence of the [Amabiame] house finally came to an end."[32] The divine flesh secured by the citizens acting in concert was commodified.

The transformation from the political theological and democratic to the political economic took place against the background of international trade with European merchant capitalists. The wrong for which the Shark-god was executed and consumed cannot be adequately understood apart from the slave trade and so-called legitimate commerce among the people of the Niger Delta and Europeans from the fifteenth through the nineteenth century. The unanswered question here is, What caused the increased contact between human beings and sharks that led to the increased shark attacks on children that fueled the decision to commit deicide? Historians inform us that sharks followed European ships (during the slave and legitimate trades) along the coasts to feed on scraps and dead bodies thrown into the waters. Thus, it is arguable that European ships coming into the Niger Delta brought the sharks closer to areas of human residence and play.

Indeed, the shark's flesh teems with signification, standing at the junction between the normative, the somatic, and the democratic.[33] The flesh provokes a quest for meaning and justice; generates a feeling of satisfaction at the process of killing the deity, consuming its divine meat, and accepting redemption money; and enacts the praxis of coming together with others and acting in concert.

The deicide also gestures in other directions; apropos to the political theological and the democratic. First, it points to a devouring relation, feasting on carrion of the god, and to the deed as a sponge that wiped away an entire horizon of religious meaning, so to speak.[34] The people were called to accept the deicide with enjoyment (instead of the usual horror) even though it removed the protective powers, the spiritual umbrella of a god. Second, the eating and drinking of the substance of the god symbolizes communal decision, a collective action; no one individual can defeat a god, but the community can with a triumphant yes-saying to itself. The power of the defeated god is now incorporated into the human body. The sacred in

---

[32]Jones, *Trading States*, 217.

[33]Eric L. Santner, *The Weight of All Flesh: On the Subject Matter of Political Economy* (New York: Oxford University Press, 2016).

[34]We only need to read Captain Crow's account of Kalabari relationship with the Shark-god decades before they murdered it to appreciate the enormity or radicality of their deed. This was a very powerful god in their world and riverine environment. Captain Hugh Crow, *Memoirs of the Late Capt. Hugh Crow* (London: Longman, Rees, Orme, Brown, and Green, 1830).

this case is no longer an external force that rules over them but a mark of their capacity to create new possibilities by altering the form and structure of the sacred they inherit. Finally, the story of the 1857 deicide offers a productive way of thinking about religion and political theory creatively through a critical lens of the politics of interruption.

Indeed, the story of the Izon people that I have narrated here offers the reader a way to imagine Rancière's characterization of the political being-together as "a community of interruptions, fractures, irregulars and local, through which egalitarian logic comes and divides the police community from itself."[35] I further explore this characterization of Izon political community through a critical discussion of the famous epic, *Ozidi Saga*, which explores the issues of interrupting establishments, challenging natural and supernatural powers, and initiating something new amid ongoing social processes. Engagement with this text enables me to further explore the practice and concept of interruption for both religion and political theory. I seek to explore not because I want to excavate deep truths others do not know about the Izon spirit, but rather to revivify the epic for the present African political moment; learn more about initiating something new amid increasing vulnerability, fragility, and mortality on the continent; and seek ways of reorienting political imagination toward the politics of interruption. As Hannah Arendt put it, "The lifespan of man running toward death would inevitably carry everything human to ruin and destruction if it were not for the faculty of interrupting it and beginning something new, a faculty which is inherent in action like an ever-present reminder that men, though they must die, are not born in order to die but in order to begin."[36] The *Ozidi Saga* points us to where to look for the source of new, the impulse for the capacity to begin, to initiate something new in the space of responsibilities. In this epic, the community is made "right" (mainly) from inside. The hero, Ozidi, and his grandmother, Oreame, rely less on Tamarau, the transcendental power for their success, than one might expect to find in a traditional gods-drenched African society. It is from within (immanent) rather than from outside that the source of the new lies. As the story goes, in the performance of their herculean tasks, they relied more on people, flora, fauna, and forces of nature within the natural Izon world than on God (Tamarau).[37]

---

[35]Rancière, *Disagreement*, 137.
[36]Hannah Arendt, *The Human Condition* (Chicago: University of Chicago Press, 1958), 246.
[37]Okpewho, *Blood on the Tides*, 19, 33. See J. P Clark-Bekederemo, *The Ozidi Saga: Collected and Translated from the Oral Ijo Version of Okabou Ojobolo* (Washington, DC: Howard University Press, 1991).

The Weight of Ozidi: Long Live the People!

The *Ozidi Saga* is the story of a boy hero named Ozidi who set out to avenge the assassination of his father (Ozidi Sr.). Ozidi Sr., a brave warrior, died at the hands of some of the most powerful generals of the city-state of Orua of the Tarakiri-Orua Izon (Ijo, Ijaw) clan in Nigeria's Niger Delta. His killers also desecrated his body. His colleagues conspired to murder him when they all went to secure a human head to honor the installation of a new king, Temugedege, a mentally challenged man and the elder brother of Ozidi Sr. The right to rule has come to the lineage of Ozidi by rotation based on the Izon notion of republicanism—govern and be governed—but the other leaders in the town resented the coronation of Temugedege because he was an "idiot." In resisting the right of Temugedege to rule, the aristocratic generals were contesting the very foundation of the notion of democracy, the complete absence of distinguishing quality or entitlement to govern. "Democracy," Rancière teaches us, "is the specific situation in which it is the absence of entitlement that entitles one to exercise *arkhè*."[38]

In his play, *Ozidi*, which is based on the saga itself, John P. Clark interprets the military generals' reluctance to go through with the coronation rites by giving gifts to Temugedege as also based on the fear that a fool made a leader might turn out to be too demanding, like a god. One of the citizens of Orua in conversation with others on the issue makes this connection clear, as well as points to the fecundity of the tension in any divine-human or hierarchic relation.

> I have no water in my mouth as I stand
> Here speaking. You all know a god is
> A god once you make him so. After
> The ceremony, he ceases to be mere wood. Give him
> Palm oil then, and he'll insist on blood.[39]

I also interpret this conversation in light of a political philosophy that founds the immanence of sovereign power on resistance to any political paradigm which facilitates a creator becoming enslaved to her creation, an effect "transfiguring" into its own cause.

Seven months after the assassination of Ozidi Sr., his widow, Orea, bore a son, and the son's maternal grandmother, Oreame, a famed and powerful sorceress, carefully trained him. She raised him to wreak vengeance on all who conspired to kill his father and any supernatural being or force

---

[38]Jacques Rancière, *Dissensus: On Politics and Aesthetics*, trans. Steven Corcoran (London: Continuum, 2010), 31.
[39]Clark, *Ozidi*, 15.

of the community that would oppose his lineage claim to kingship and prominence in the land. Altogether, Ozidi the hero fought fourteen epic battles during which he vanquished all foes, humans and nonhumans alike, "who constitute[d] a menace to life and leadership in his society."[40] The fights were marked by revolutionary terrors and horrors. In all his fights, he was ably supported by Oreame, whose words encouraged and energized Ozidi in moments of weakness and equipped him with supernatural powers. In the first eight clashes, they battled human figures who had a hand in the assassination of Ozidi Sr. In the last six, the Izon warrior battled nonhuman figures in a spirit of interruptive impulse. "Having disposed of the assassins, Ozidi and Oreame emerge[d] as the supreme powers in the society. They therefore incur[red] the resentment of other forces, of far less human order, who long claimed such a position and will not brook any competition."[41] The reputation of the Ozidi-Oreame team reached the supernatural beings from the citizens of Orua who were running into the bush to escape the bloodshed occurring in their city.

The Ozidi story is suffused with magic and the supernatural. One gets the impression that the boy-grandmother team won their fights because of the unrivaled magic prowess of Oreame, even as we know they were propelled by a sense of justice. Magic or the supernatural in this context should not be conflated with powers from beyond-history space, a transcendental realm. The noumenal is often an *intensification* of the phenomenal. As Nigerian novelist Isidore Okpewho explained, "The supernatural power quite often consists in exploiting the virtues [the pharmacological qualities] inherent in the surrounding nature."[42] Tamarau herself plays a minor role in the story. For instance, in the midst of a pitched battle, Oreame flies to heaven to meet God (Tamarau). Seeking confirmation of the justice of their mission, a disappointed Oreame receives no such reassurance from Tamarau.[43] According to Okpewho, "It is clear that the Oreame-Ozidi team owes its triumph far less to whatever aid the higher beings might offer than to the occult power of magic derived from exploiting the latent qualities of the flora and fauna of the natural Ijo world."[44]

Ozidi and Oreame accomplished great feats in the name of justice; yet, I am somewhat reluctant to declare them as champions of the Izon republican spirit. Were the victories of the Ozidi-Oreame team really a triumph if their rise to power caused the citizens of Orua to flee in terror from them? Was it

---

[40]Isidore Okpewho, "Performance and Plot in the Ozidi Saga," *Oral Traditions* 19, no. 1 (2004): 63–95, quotation on 64.
[41]Okpewho, *Blood on the Tides*, 124.
[42]Okpewho, "Ozidi Saga: A Critical Introduction," xiii.
[43]Clark-Bekederemo, *Ozidi Saga*, 82–3.
[44]Okpewho, *Blood on the Tides*, 33.

not the fleeing of Orua citizens into the bush that provoked the nonhuman forces to challenge Oreame and Ozidi? And what does this in some ways ironic (and tragic) saga mean for the theory of democratic sovereignty, Izon republicanism, and politics of interruption I am attempting to craft in this chapter?

In the Ozidi story, the details of the reality of republicanism, the wresting of power from hegemonic forces, are spectralized, and the moment or the realism of liberation is experienced as a nightmarish dream. Herein lies a crucial difference between the 1857 historical revolutionary act and the fictional (historical) account of revolution. While Ozidi, the main protagonist in the epic, fights to sustain Izon republicanism through asserting his historical destiny as an authentic son of Orua, his calling fails politically (in a sense) because of his inability to expand his work—the conjunction of his authentic existence and historical destiny—onto collective modes of being. Yet, the failure of Ozidi (individual) and the success of the Kalabari (community) are not two different things; rather, they are two sides of the same process. They interpret one another. His failures are part of the identity of Izon emancipatory political praxis. Ozidi accepted the basic premise of Izon emancipatory politics; his failures are only its unexpected or disavowed consequences. Excess revolutionary terror and the emergence of an individual who directly embodies the political collective are just two of the consequences. (Is the elimination of all gods—higher powers and not just the Shark-god—not an immanent utopian vision of the 1857 multitude? Is revolutionary terror to correct all wrongs at once not an inherent fantasy of every successful emancipatory struggle?) A third consequence is that the singular leader can be "sublated" in the "living spirit of the community": his very failure does not signal a renunciation of the community or its ethos but "functions as a founding gesture of universal mobilization."[45] Ozidi (or rather what this fictional character represents) has come to function as a master signifier of the collective national praxis of freedom in the social imaginary of the Izon people.

In summary, the failure and success we are speaking about here are of one thing because Ozidi's revolutionary horrors are the result of the immanent antagonisms of the Izon praxis of freedom. Ozidi, an innocent boy, "directly embodies/assumes the excess," the surplus violence that makes an act revolutionary.[46] A revolutionary act mobilizes two elements of the praxis or decisionism of freedom; this is the source of its inherent imbalance.[47] The exercise of freedom in a novel, revolutionary context is marked by a tension between these: (a) The ensuing decisions are unpredictable, marked

[45]Žižek, Disparities, 271.
[46]Žižek, Disparities, 268.
[47]Žižek, Disparities, 249–54.

by non-knowledge insofar as it is unprecedented, and the actors are guided by their audacity. But once the decision or action is taken, it retroactively changes the reality within which the actors acted. As described by Jean-Pierre Dupuy, "If an outstanding event takes place, a catastrophe, for example, it could not have taken; nonetheless, insofar as it did not take place, it is not inevitable. It is thus the event's actualization—the fact that it takes place—which retroactively creates its necessity."[48] And (b) there is a recognition of the domain of objective knowledge or experience of reality. Constant tension between these two elements and the opposition between them can break down, allowing the first element to dominate and appear as the capriciousness (abyss) of human will and power of a leader.

There is another dimension to the immanent antagonisms of freedom in the Izon praxis of freedom: Ozidi's story reveals the passage from republic to empire, from emancipatory politics to totalitarian temptation. Although Ozidi, aided by his grandmother, fulfills his historical destiny (at least in part), in so doing, he drives away almost all members of the community when he takes control of the mythical city of Orua. And yet, after killing the mentally challenged old king (his uncle, Temugedege), Ozidi cannot crown himself the new king. Paradoxically, it is both impossible for Ozidi to become king and impossible for him to rid himself of the desire to be king. According to the republican rules of the Izon community—which include "partake in ruling and being ruled" and rotating leadership—Temugedege's successor cannot come from the same lineage. But since Ozidi has eliminated all rivals and emptied the town of its citizens, he is de facto king. When there are no citizens or equals to recognize him, reigning as master is worthless. This is the fundamental deadlock of desire and structural reason in the relationship between Ozidi and Orua. Furthermore, the empty town of Orua symbolizes the impossibility of a person representing, assuming, or embodying the people. Ozidi cannot be a "leader who *is* the people"; he cannot be a singular leader who is not sublated in the spirit of the people.[49]

Okabou Ojobolo's narration succinctly captures the deep Izon impulse for republicanism and equality by not depicting the people of Orua dancing and celebrating their freedom under Ozidi, the Great Leader. The genius of Ojobolo is to keep the city empty, resisting filling the city square with an adulating, ululating crowd, and with ideological projections of harmonious organic unity of the city under a hero. Ojobolo's deep appreciation of Izon homebred political philosophy is further revealed in the dialectical shift he makes in the character of Ozidi and the flow of the story itself. He moves us from the chaotic abyss of Ozidi's killing, the void of destructive fury, "which

---

[48] Jean-Pierre Dupuy, *Petite metaphysique des tsunamis* (Paris: Seuil, 2005), 19, quoted in Žižek, *Disparities*, 249–54.

[49] Žižek, *Disparities*, 368–9, inspired this insight.

swallows everything to [a] Frame within which the New can emerge."[50] Ozidi's seven-pronged killing sword moves from being magically stored in his *inside*, his inner being, to being given physically to his grandmother, Oreame. Additionally, he learns to have sex, pointing to future children, natality, a new beginning. Perhaps, then, Ozidi's failure or impossibility to represent the people opens a new space, a "zero-point of a new beginning," the space for sublation.[51]

Conclusion

In sum, this chapter has described key dimensions of the theological revolution (the killing of the Shark-god) of Izon religion that have implications for political theory. First, members of Izon society, like people in many traditional cultures, believe that their social norms preexist them and were substantially given to them. But there is tension such that, given the Izon politics of interruption, Izon citizens also see their social norms as expressions of their spirit, their capacity to begin. They make their norms or institutions real by taking them as real, by weaving the spirit of the new out of the old. Clark-Bekederemo, armed with the metaphor of dance, illustrates the appearance or finding of the new through a process of making the old.

Traditional Ijo dance, as seen in the story of Ozidi, apparently has no beginning, no middle, no end within a time structure. The dancer, submerged in the stream of everyday chores, rises spontaneously to the beat of the drum, to the sound of the song, and the dance flows on for as long as there is a tidal wave of drum and song sweeping through the town. In the seeming monotony and fixity of such experiences, a dancer may in fact attain a new fluidity of movement, achieving freedom of spirit from this material world. This surely is transfiguration, whether pejoratively termed "a state of possession" or "auto-intoxication" by those outside such an area of experience.[52]

Second, in most religions, when the relation between god and human beings has been severely fractured because of sin, the adherents strive to purify themselves in order to overcome the alienation from god and restore the relationship. In Izon religion, on the contrary, the god is likely to be abandoned, rejected, or killed. The alienation of human beings from god is projected into god as disparity within the god: as a gap between immortal

---

[50]Žižek, *Disparities*, 371.
[51]Žižek, *Disparities*, 372.
[52]Clark-Bekederemo, *Ozidi Saga*, li.

divine and finite mortal supernatural being, as a gap between the glory of power and its foundationless void, as an alienation between godliness and worshipful fidelity within the god itself.

Third, the place of power is empty. Izon recognize that in this perspective of seeing the gods and power against the background of nothingness is the supreme gift of freedom. This should not be construed to mean that freedom or democratic sovereignty emerge from the void that is in the very heart of power, but from constraints on void. "Constraints means here an inner obstacle or limit which prevents some possibilities of being realized, some roads not to be taken, not accidentally but necessarily (even if it appears that it happens only by accident)."[53]

In this chapter, I have made explicit some of the norms of emancipatory politics that are implicit in Izon divine-human relationship and democratic tradition, which are always incomplete. The question for students of Nigerian politics is: How do Nigerians grapple with this ethos and attempt to follow it in order to craft a democratic governance that is accountable to the people? I suggest we think along the lines of politics of interruption and seek to disrupt the usual flow of things as a form of resistance. This requires enacting social practices of freedom and radical emancipatory politics at the grassroots, as well as building popular institutions for massive political organization and mobilization to adequately respond to Nigeria's current political moment. Two *Nigerias* currently exist: a subjugated Nigeria that is an instrument of global capital and an incipient Nigeria of emancipatory politics. Stasis (mortality) versus natality. For those of us who hitch the wagon of Nigeria's development only to emancipatory radical politics there is another choice. We can choose natality to demand both what is possible within the current system and what is impossible. Izon religious acts and political theory gesture to the impossible as the soul of politics, which is a subjective openness to swerve from equilibrium—an inclination to being otherwise.

---

[53]Žižek, *Disparities*, 39.

5

Comedy as Dialectics: Laughing Nigeria to Human Flourishing

Introduction

This chapter elucidates the style and dialectics of the jokes by a Nigerian comedian with the stage name Mc Edo Pikin (Mr. Gbadamasi Agbonjor Jonathan is his real name). It takes his comedic style and elevates it to the dignity of a philosophical template for analyzing the contemporary social situation in Nigeria. His comedy offers a remarkable dialectics of cultural criticism, and in this chapter I situate it within the rigors and systematicity of a philosophical discourse. As Walter Benjamin might put it, this chapter is an image wherein Mc Edo Pikin's (preexisting) dialectics come together in a flash with the now of my philosophical ruminations to form a constellation.[1] In other words, this chapter is a signature (in the Agambean sense) or constitutes a set of signatures of Mc Edo Pikin's remarkable dialectics of cultural criticism.[2] It demonstrates how we can transfer ideas of the comedian into serious philosophical reflection. According to Giorgio Agamben, a signature makes it possible for us to grasp the internal logic, the distinguishing mark of a situation (or thing, being, world). It is a process of transference that allows us to move knowledge (concept or discourse) from one domain to another. Signature makes the sign of situation (being, thing, world) intelligible, allowing meaning to happen.[3] This chapter not only manifests the hidden virtues of Mc Edo Pikin's narrative style but also

---

[1]Walter Benjamin, *The Arcades Project*, trans. Howard Eiland and Kevin McLaughlin (Cambridge, MA: Belknap Press, 1982), 462–3.
[2]Giorgio Agamben, *The Signature of All Things: On Method*, trans. Luca D'Isanto with Kevin Attell (New York: Zone Books, 2009).
[3]Agamben, *Signature of All Things*, 35, 42, 64.

makes it intelligible in a philosophical discourse. Let me quickly add that the ideas, concepts, and discourses of the preceding chapters of the book are neither the essence of Mc Edo Pikin's dialectics nor something foreign to it.

The Comedy of Mc Edo Pikin

Comedian Gbadamasi Agbonjor Jonathan (stage name, Mc Edo Pikin) was born on January 2, 1990 in Edo State, Nigeria. He obtained his first degree in theater and media arts from Ambrose Ali University, Ekpoma, Nigeria. His comedy caught my interest because of its structural dialectics, its comparative definitions. He has a series in which the whole comedy is about comparative definitions of everyday terms, events, and reality in Nigerian society, and in this way he forces into active awareness what others have not noticed or simply ignored. In each of the series he offers hilarious definitions of three related terms, functions, or offices that portray the actions of his fellow Nigerians. His comparative definitions are always in response to the question, "What's is the difference between X, Y, and Z?" The first definition focuses on *deeds in themselves*. He defines for his audience what Nigerians in a particular function, office, or status usually do (the "X"). The second definition emphasizes *deeds for themselves* (the "Y"). He explores how the people understand their actions, their engagement in functions, in the practice of their statuses, or in the performance of their deeds. Finally, he comes down to the *idea of the deed* (the office, function, or reality; the "Z"). He would say the "Z" does not exist or live in Nigeria. The idea of the deed is about the practices and commitments of the deed (office, reality, event, function) that make it transhistorical; that is, make it applicable and meaningful in all historical epochs. Transhistorical here does not mean beyond history. When he says the Z does not exist in Nigeria, I take it to mean not that he is saying the idea is too abstract or beyond concrete application in the Nigerian polity, positing that it is not yet embodied in material, social, and institutional practices in the country. His well-crafted comparative definitions are held together by a tripartite movement of an original dialectic, which I am naming here as thesis, antithesis, and transfinite thesis (novuthesis).

As the four examples of his comedy that I have transcribed from his YouTube collections will demonstrate, the movement from thesis to transfinite is "predictable" by the infractions of conventional, descriptive syntax.[4] In a Cubist manner the descriptive contours of each definition are distorted. This is done so well that each figure (symbol, subject matter) being

---

[4]Note that it is the forward moving impulse toward an ideal that we might predict, and not necessarily the ideal.

defined is conceptually obliterated through a deliberate distortion of our background (taken-for-granted understanding of it). In this way, a figure (new conceptualization) emerges within the distorted spaces around the definition (defined figure) and coincides and clashes with spaces around it. Shifting and displacing shapes of definitions or subject matter, suddenly all these movements appear in new contours, new relations, and new figures. This new, emergent figure appears to take a further step, breaking out of the frame of the criticism (logic) of the thesis and antithesis as the boy in the painting of Pere Borrell del Caso, *Escaping Criticism* (1874), who is stepping out of the painting with eyes wide open in wonder.

Let me illustrate this point with his 2019 skit on the voter's card.

Question: Please, what is the difference between a voter's card and PVC?

Mc Edo Pikin: "Voter's card is an ordinary PVC. PVC is a very powerful voter's card. PVC is a permanent voter's card, a powerful voter's card. The one that cannot be bought by any political party. Voter's card is the one where you stand under the sun for weeks to struggle to get it. After getting it, you now go on the day of election to sell it for 2,500 naira. How much is the subscription? How can you say voter's card that is your right and you go across the road to buy akpu and egusi soup [local delicacy]? Some people will sell their voter's card to buy igbo [marijuana]. Will you be high for four years? The most shameful thing [is that] you will see your voter's card and you will go and carry ashawo and buy condoms. Will you have sex for the next four years?

Ogakpakpata [the supreme chief] of them all is your conscience. Conscience is the general overseer. Conscience is the one that will tell you to vote for the individual but not the political party. Conscience is the one that will tell you to vote for competency, competency that cannot be sacrificed on the altar of mediocrity, weakness, and failure. The problem I have with this country, the people that are voting, they don't have conscience. The people that we are voting for, they don't have conscience. The people that are counting the vote, they don't have conscience. In fact, conscience does not live in Nigeria. In 2019, we need to go and borrow a conscience to vote. Make sure you don't sell your conscience. In 2019 vote your conscience, thank you."[5]

His definitions interrupt, challenge, and shake up the discursive stability of the words or concepts and thus raise the possibility of an alternative, enlarged understanding. The result is that the third word is shot through with the meaning of resistance to the prevailing ethos or status quo and has the impulse of forward movement into the not-yet. The moral weight of

---

[5]https://www.youtube.com/watch?v=WbuHYLPqOvQ

the third word is not all about maintaining order, but about disrupting and interrogating order in the name of a new and better Nigeria.

The third figure (the transfinite thesis) always bursts from nowhere, so to speak. At the beginning, he is comparing only two items, but suddenly, as if moved by the powerful logic of his comparative analysis, a figure or idea that was not in the cards jumps out. (Did you notice how conscience jumped out, seemingly from nowhere, when the two initial comparative terms only related to forms of the voter's card?) A figure that is neither part of the "was" nor of the "is," but is that which is to come. It is not the new that flows from the trajectory of the past and the present. It is the new that asks for, creates, and sustains the alternative possibilities, the unexpected path.[6]

Below is one of his sets of triune comparative definitions that also clearly brings this point out:

> *Question:* Please, what's the difference between an artiste and a musician?
>
> *Mc Edo Pikin:* The difference is very clear …. A musician is a responsible artiste. An artiste is an irresponsible musician. A musician is the one that gets their inspiration from God, but an artiste gets his inspiration from igbo [marijuana]. A musician is the one that sings for the love of the people, that sings what the people can understand, but an artiste sings for yansh, breast; an artiste sings just for women to twerk. A musician is the one that sings what people will go home and think about. An artiste sings to make money. A musician sings for the love of music …. A musician is the one that can perform with a live band, but the artiste runs away from a live band.
>
> But the ogakpatakpata [the supreme chief] of them all are legends. Legends are the ones that understand the rudiments of music. They sing for the people and the world. They sing to highlight the ills in the society. They sing against maladministration or bad governance. Legends when they die, their music is passed from generation to generation. Some of the legends are like prophets, they sing to tell you what will happen in the nearest future. Like Bob Nesta Marley, like Fela Anikulapo Kuti, like Lucky Dube, like Michael Jackson. In fact, legend does not live in Nigeria; we only have few legends in Nigeria and one of them is 2Face Innocent Idibia. He is the ogakpatakpata of them all. His music will live on from generation to generation.[7]

Given the way the joke is structured, the movement starts from the artiste (#1), moves to the musician (#2), and ends or points toward the legend (#3).

---

[6]Jürgen Moltmann, *The Coming of God: Christian Eschatology*, trans. Margaret Kohl (Minneapolis: Fortress Press, 1996), 23–8.
[7]https://www.youtube.com/watch?v=BZYUkYDdPJc

Mc Edo Pikin clearly establishes a formal relationship between the first two parts and the third one. The properties or objective features of musician and artiste are combined in contingent ways relative to the perception and intent of the agent (in this case, the comedian) or the needs of the (Nigerian) symbolic network in which the features are embedded. The movement from #1 to #2 is not a matter of the etymology of #1 and #2, nor of their functions, designs, or regnant practices. The dynamic he sets in motion or the logic he presents is not about the unfolding of inherent potentials. It all depends (not in any way deterministic) on the perceiving and acting agent's interaction with, interpretation, and ethical assessment of his or her situation or the particularities of her surroundings. All these afford him or her the capacity or opportunity to discover the path from point A (#1 and #2) to point B (the *nuvothesis*).[8] The connection between points A and B, the movement from A to B, is one way of showing how the features of thesis (artiste) and antithesis (musician) might be combined in a distinctive way to envision a site that exceeds ordinary synthesis, a site that mimics what happens in an *emergent process*. Novuthesis (an *ideal*) shows how the features or properties of an existing system, institution, or object can be taken up and elaborated, improvised, critiqued, etiolated, or exceeded within shifting paradigms.

This novuthesis involves each of the two definitions' (#1 and #2) relationships to each other and to an ideal one that evaluates, critiques, or disturbs them. In a definitional triangle, the comedian (interlocutor) brings two functions (capacities, roles, offices) together with respect to similarities and incongruencies and points them toward an ideal to which they are also positioned as failed performances and thus subject to transformation. This is a highly stylized and dramatic style of interlocution in which the ordinary articulations of "what a thing is" are saturated with ethical descriptions and evaluations.

Occasionally the ethical evaluations can be burdened by an archaic view of women that borders on misogyny. Take, for instance, this episode of girl, babe, and lady that highlights not only his distorted views about the role of women in modern Nigerian society but also the triangular formation of his skits:

Questioner: "What is the difference between girl and babe?"

Mc Edo Pikin: The difference is very, very clear. A girl is a responsible babe. And a babe is an irresponsible girl. A girl is the one that still gets permission [excuse] from her parents before she leaves the house. A babe is the one that is outside for a long time and even her parents are begging

---

[8]Webb Keane, *Ethical Life: Its Natural and Social Histories* (Princeton: Princeton University Press, 2015), 27–32 inspired this thought.

her to come back home. A girl is the one that goes to church, weekly services and every Sunday. A babe is the one that waits for Shiloh [yearly service] until she now goes to church. A girl can quote all the verses in the Bible, but a babe can quote all the wines in the bar and their alcoholic percentage. A girl can cook four different soups in a day, but a babe can visit four different clubs in the night. Even some boys learned how to smoke and drink from their babes.

But the ogakpatakpata [the supreme chief] of them all, the general overseer of them all, is a lady. A lady is the girl who makes a madman feels like a gentleman. A lady has got the tenacity to work. A lady believes that responsibility in a relationship is for both sides, not 100 percent on the boyfriend. A lady is a mentor to other girls. A lady is a decent woman with the fear of God. A lady is a well-cultured woman who carries the parental upbringing of her parents to the husband's house. A lady works so hard that she even puts men on the payroll. In fact, ladies put to bed [give birth to children], while babes have abortions. Ladies end up getting married, while babes end up getting frustrated.... Do we still have ladies in Nigeria? Ladies do not live in Nigeria.[9]

This episode of girl, babe, and lady illustrates the "triangle" that animates his comparative definitions and the hilarity of his comedy. The top of the triangle harbors his third thesis, the transfinite thesis. The triangle appears to point beyond itself, beyond reality. The third thesis ("lady" in this case) is not an immutable Platonic standard, not an infinite object that Nigerians are seeking to grasp. It is a directing principle and not a constituting concept. It asks what lies beyond the finite, corrupt substandard form of living that Nigerians celebrate or have attained. And in this way it directs them to the quest for the unlimited potentialities of their minds and sociality. As Mc Edo Pikin directs the minds of Nigerians to experience their own potentialities, his listeners feel a tension in his definitions.

There is a tension between internal transcendence and external transcendence in his conceptualization of the third term. If it does not exist in Nigeria, does this imply that it does not exist in history? Does it exist only in that peculiar Nigerian sense of only God can do it or save us? He settles this tension or forestalls anyone taking the external, extrahuman notion of transcendence when, in the episode of gentleman or preacher/teacher, he points to actually existing Nigerians that fit the transcendence of the third term.

Question: What is the difference between a preacher and a teacher?

Mc Edo Pikin: The difference is very clear. A preacher is the one that will tell you about knowledge, while a teacher will impart knowledge into

---

[9]https://www.youtube.com/watch?v=k45wAxRcHa8

you. A preacher is the one that will tell you about the kingdom of God, while a teacher will show you the kingdom of God. A teacher is the one that will tell you that money is the root of all evil, while a preacher will tell you the blessings of God make rich and add no sorrow.... Preachers are always close to the rich members in the church, while teachers are close to the poor members, so that they can make them rich....

But the ogakpatakpata of them all is Pastor Kingsley Okonkwo. Pastor Kingsley Okonkwo is a great servant in the vineyard of God Almighty.... Pastor Kingsley Okonkwo, the ogakpatakpata of DCC, David Christian Center, you don't live in Nigeria, you live in DCC, David Christian Center, Lagos.[10]

Here Mc Edo Pikin says Pastor Okonkwo does not live in Nigeria when DCC is clearly in Lagos, Nigeria. This is an interesting revelation of the dialectics or the philosophical depth of the comedian. Pastor Okonkwo lives in DCC, a stand-in for the ideal site or thought. This ideal place might be physically located in Nigeria, but it does not really *belong* to the situation of Nigeria. DCC belongs to the Nigerian situation as a set but does not belong to any part of the situation. It is an excluded part that does not fit normally or properly into the Nigerian situation; it is unrepresentable. In the language of French philosopher Alain Badiou, DCC is akin to a singularity, a void that bears potential for a revolution in a situation. DCC, in this case, is the generic name for the disruptive element from which an event, Nigeria's transformation, can emerge. DCC is the ideal, the consistent multiplicity that can disrupt or interrupt the order of things.

We were led to the episode of preachers and teachers because we observed a tension between internal transcendence and external transcendence in his conceptualization of the third term. We stated that the episode of gentleman or preacher/teacher demonstrates that his notion of transcendence is not something from beyond history. Yet his various episodes occasionally play at the boundary between internal and external transcendence. This does not necessarily represent a deficiency of his philosophical thought or a display of the vexing Nigerian tendency to look beyond the immanent realm for social transformation of their nation. The line between the two forms of transcendence is not always clear-cut in social analysis. What the American philosopher Martha Nussbaum says about sorting out the lines of demarcation between the two forms of transcendence is apt:

The line between the appropriate (internal) sort of transcending and the other sort (external, extrahuman) is not and can never be a sharp one. For human striving for excellence involves pushing, in many ways, against

---

[10]https://www.youtube.com/watch?v=Ph5ko_4n-Tc

the limits that constrain human life. It is perfectly reasonable, within the human point of view, to want oneself and others not to be hungry, not to be ill, not to be without shelter, not to be betrayed or bereaved, not to lose any of one's faculties—and to strive as hard as one possibly can to bring all that about in life. In fact, one of the merits of focusing on the internal sort of transcendence is that it tells us that such things really matter, that these jobs are there for human beings to do, for politics to do.... What is recommended is a delicate and always flexible balancing act between the claims of excellence, which lead us to push outward, and the necessity of the human context, which pushes us back in. It is not easy... to say where the line is drawn.[11]

From Format of Comedian's Joke to Philosophical Methodology

In this section, I want to capture the philosophical format of Mc Edo Pikin's comedy to show how I can view it as methodology. Mc Edo Pikin's first thesis (definition) states the "what is" of a situation. The antithesis is the opposite of the what is. It is more powerful than the thesis; the opposite arises because its inherent nature is to exceed or defeat the performance or the glory of the thesis condition. Finally, we have novuthesis (that is, a new thesis, that which exceeds the synthesis of the thesis and antithesis; hence, it is a transfinite thesis). It is not a synthesis, a higher combination of the previous two or the realization that the antithesis has always been part of or embedded in the thesis, but an ideal that transcends the positivity of both the thesis and the antithesis and is not subject to their antagonism. This is the sense of novuthesis as "beyond." It is a paradigm shift.

The juxtaposition of the two theses forces the mind to conceive that which is beyond them—the new thing, *the novum*; hence the *novuthesis*. The commonplace definition of synthesis of Hegelian dialectics presents it as a combination of thesis and antithesis. An alternative interpretation, which also emphasizes combination, offers a twist. It says the combination is always already present—in the thesis. The synthesis, or rather the idea that harmonizes the thesis and antithesis, is already in the thesis and emerges only by recognition of what is already there. Novuthesis is not a combination of the thesis and antithesis, but a paradigm shift. It is about that which is to come. That which is when it is present moves along with its antagonistic opposite to a new site in Being.

---

[11]Martha C. Nussbaum, *Love's Knowledge: Essays on Philosophy and Literature* (New York: Oxford University Press, 1990), 380–1.

This new site has some similarity with the "abandoned" (superseded) site(s) such that the reader can see the new site as being a plausible reality of the future. They see it as a not-yet. Let us quickly add that the envisaged new site is never a reified, dehumanized world. It is in history. Novuthesis employs the logic of cognitive estrangement. It encourages new ways of thinking about the thesis and antithesis that not only offer an alternative way of thinking of the theses individually or collectively, but also subversively undermine the ground (spatial, temporal, and social), status quo, paradigm, or framing that undergirds or nurtures both the thesis and antithesis.[12] The aim is to estrange the reader or the listener from the familiar reality and help her look toward an alternative form of social existence.

The ethos of cognitive estrangement informs how Mc Edo Pikin even describes or explains both the thesis and the antithesis. They are presented in ways that jar their commonplace, assumed meaning. Their very definitions immediately begin to destabilize, to cognitively disturb the configuration of concept (word) and its normal ground. They seem to harbor an *event*.

Novuthesis is a kind of a "jump" from obvious reality. It comes off as an *event*. You cannot predict it from the thesis and antithesis. The engine for the jump here is like emergence. By emergence I mean novel properties, traits that arise from a given set of matter in the right sort of organized complexity. The properties are novel because they not only cannot be found at lower levels of complexity but are also unpredictable phenomena produced by the interactions between preexisting elements or parts. Emergence names the process whereby "the underivable"[13] can be birthed amid many derivable conditions.

We can examine the novuthesis from another angle, in terms of affirming or negating a predicate. The novuthesis (the idea that comes after the thesis and antithesis) does not negate a predicate but affirms a non-predicate. Let us take an example from a simple format of philosophical argument to clarify this point. "The soul is mortal" is a positive judgment. This statement can be negated in two ways: (a) "the soul is not mortal" and (b) "the soul is non-mortal." In the first instance, the predicate ("mortal") is negated, but in the second case, a non-predicate is asserted. "The indefinite judgment [as per Kant] opens up a third domain which undermines the underlying distinction."[14] This occurs in the same vein when we say a

---

[12]Eviatar Zerubavel, *Hidden Rhythms: Schedules and Calendars in Social Life* (Berkeley: University of California, 1981), 1–30.

[13]Emergence, as I understand it, reminds me of Paul Tillich's concept of the kairos and "the underivable." See his *Systematic Theology, Vol. 3.* (Chicago: University of Chicago Press, 1963), 324.

[14]Slavoj Žižek, *Less Than Nothing: Hegel and the Shadow of Dialectical Materialism* (London: Verso, 2012), 166.

"person is inhuman" instead of "he is not human," a new space beyond humanity and its negation is opened up. "He is not human' means simply that he is external to humanity, animal or divine, while 'he is inhuman' means something thoroughly different, namely that he is neither human nor not-human, but marked by a terrifying excess which, although negating what we understand as 'humanity,' is inherent to being human."[15] Novuthesis is neither thesis nor antithesis, but marked by a terrifying (not-terrifying) excess that, although negating what we know as thesis/antithesis, is inherent to being a thesis of the situation. It is always about a state of condition that is unlike the ones that came before it yet does not escape or transcends them.

The insights of novuthesis can structure the way we seek solution to a social problem. Take for example this case: a farmer's income is limited because of illiteracy. The typical "antithesis" in development programs is to provide the farmer what is missing, an extension officer to help him measure and prepare his harvest for sale, so he would get a better price in the market. But the novuthesis will demand that we take a different approach. This approach is not about aiding the farmer but about changing the unfreedom that thwarts his human flourishing. The different approach demands that we should not just provide the illiterate farmer with a field extension worker to help him properly weigh and trade agricultural produce, but that we also make his illiteracy go away by educating him. This is the ethical thing to do in order to ensure that he is an agent and beneficiary of economic development, that he fosters his own flourishing.

Embedded in the dynamics of the movement from thesis to transfinite thesis there is always an articulated notion of what is just. Mc Edo Pikin takes for granted a shared moral universe with his audience and a certain disposition of faith. In addition to the sheer joke and the connective of reason that reveals the incongruities of the simple but profound definitions of terms, there is also a capacity for faith for what Nigeria could become in the vision of the third (transfinite) thesis. Thus, the goals of ethical transformation run through the definition of the triangle, which speaks to human flourishing.

Thesis #3 (transfinite thesis) is what it means for the thesis and antithesis each to function well—to best express, authenticate, reveal its "essence" (that is, its central function). Transfinite thesis is thesis cutting into thesis to lift it up to a higher plane, just as *agape* is love cutting into love to lift all forms of love into a higher level, beyond the ambiguities of self-centeredness. According to Paul Tillich, "in the holy community the *agape* quality of love cuts into *libido*, *eros*, and *philia* qualities of love and elevates them beyond the ambiguities of their self-centeredness." In another place in

---

[15] Žižek, *Less Than Nothing*, 166.

the same book he writes, "*agape* is love cutting into love, just as revelation is reason cutting into reason and the Word of God is the Word cutting into all words."[16]

The third term or thesis gives us a glimpse of native psychoanalytic insights that Mc Edo Pikin has about Nigerian citizens and their desire for economic development. According to the psychoanalytic literature, when a desire cannot be satisfied, society or subject turns "the *inherent impossibility* of its satisfaction into a *prohibition*."[17] This way they convince themselves that they would have succeeded if only the rules of the social order were different. Nigerians seem to have convinced themselves that economic development, a corruption-free society, or corruption-free economic development are inaccessible. This is so because Nigerian leaders and elites deliberately refuse to seek means of accessing them. Mc Edo Pikin subtly captures this refusal or the impasse constitutive of the desire for corruption-free economic development by the tripartite scheme of definitions. In this schema, that which will satisfy the desire of Nigerians for economic development or a corruption-free society is declared impossible, nonexistent in the country. His point—or, at least, my interpretation of his underlying theory—is that if not for the existence of the first and second definitions, which represent the current rules, norms, and practices of the social order and its *abjected* figures, the third definition, which represents the satisfaction of national desire, would be attainable. In Mc Edo Pikin's comedic representation the symbolic order of the nation is split. And there is a celebration of failures of the two "figures" around the traumatic cut that represents the hindrance to the country's progress. This writer considers economic development in the mood and mode of the transfinite thesis. He refuses to accept that economic development in Africa is impossible.[18]

---

[16] Paul Tillich, *Love, Power and Justice: Ontological Analyses and Ethical Applications* (London: Oxford University Press, 1954), 33, 116.

[17] Slavoj Žižek, *For They Know Not What They Do: Enjoyment as a Political Factor* (London: Verson, 2008), 266–7.

[18] See Nimi Wariboko, *The Split Time: Economic Philosophy for Human Flourishing in African Perspective* (Albany, NY: SUNY University Press, 2022, forthcoming).

6

Literature and Ethics

Introduction

This book has not presented a single thesis about literature in Nigeria. Rather, it has provided a series of essays exploring the philosophical ideas of four Nigerian writers and a comedian. My purpose when I embarked on this book was limited to giving a philosophical account of handful of Nigerian plays, novels, and possibly a comedy. Such a task required that I take each artist seriously as a thinker and each work as a potentially philosophically rich text. Now that I have executed this task, the question now is how do the interpretative possibilities of the works that I have illuminated help the average Nigerian citizen engage in public policy debates or help us to learn to live well in our various communities?

In this chapter, I want to explore the connections between literature and ethics: the relationship between creative imagination and moral imagination; the nature of moral attention and moral vision; the role of context-specific judging in ethical decisions. The chapter will help citizens to deepen and broaden their ethical understanding in ways that involve and give priority to compassion, *similar possibilities, similar vulnerabilities*, and eudaimonistic judgment, rather than abstract general principles. I rely on the thought of philosopher Martha Nussbaum to help us develop the competence relevant for the use of moral imagination and narrative works of art in ethical reasoning. Overall, using Nussbaum's insights we will learn how to make the vital connections between the novelist's art, literary imagination, and our ethical reasoning.

Nussbaum explores the traditional novelist's attention to the particular and concrete in ways that can enrich Nigerians' ethical vision. A crucial part of that vision is sensitivity to the particular problem at hand, and concrete reasons for action as derived from a particular philosophical-theological-ethological perspective of a particular social group. Another important part of this sensitivity is the capacity of agents to move from the particulars to the universal or, more precisely, from the particular to the particular (the particular as an exemplar of the universal). The novelist through attentiveness to particularity in the narrative of characters is often able to invoke in the reader identification with and sympathetic understanding of fictional characters. Nussbaum articulates a procedure by which we can make the connection between the novelist's art and our ethical reasoning (methodology).

The literary imagination or the novelist's art enables ethicists, ordinary citizens, or students to pay close attention to particulars in the life of individuals struggling under a social problem and to respond to the persons with sympathetic understanding and mercy. Literature invites immersion and critical conversation, nudging the reader to put herself in the place of the character, and thus enabling the reader to see similar possibilities between her own experience and the character. The identification and sympathy of one reader can also be compared with those of other readers, and with their responses and arguments to the same text. This kind of imagination and response is highly relevant to public reasoning in a democratic society.

When ethics is taught in the classroom through literature, the student acquires important skills for public reasoning. For one, she learns the comparative assessment of situations. The practice of matching her reading of narratives against others, some of which are challenging and others that are affirming, mimics the kind of public discourse in a democratic and pluralistic society. Through this process, she learns the art of critical conversation which must be preceded by immersion, an engagement with the characters to understand their concrete circumstances, hopes, and all that thwarts or supplements their dreams and aspirations.

The question that imposes itself is this: Why do novels serve this purpose while historical and biographical works do not? Aristotle and Nussbaum offer very insightful responses to the query. Aristotle is forthright that literary arts are better sources of philosophy than histories and biographies, which are also narratives. He argues that unlike history, which only shows us "what happened," a literary art shows us what might happen in a human life.[1] Nussbaum's answer to the question flows from this Aristotelian insight:

Literature focuses on the possible, inviting readers to wonder about themselves.... Unlike most historical works [histories and biographies], literary works typically invite their readers to put themselves in the place of people of many different kinds and to take on their experiences. In their mode of address to their imagined reader, they convey the sense that there

---

[1]Aristotle, *Poetics*, translated by S. H. Butcher (London: Macmillan and Co, 1895), chapter 9. See also Martha C. Nussbaum, *Poetic Justice: The Literary Imagination and Public Life* (Boston: Beacon Press, 1995), 5, 9.

are links of possibility, at least on a very general level, between characters and the reader. The reader's emotions and imagination are highly active as a result, and it is the nature of this activity, and its relevance for public thinking, that interests me.[2]

Nussbaum's thought as it relates to our project is that the ethicist should draw on the resources of the novelist's art so as to remain capable of *suggnômê*.[3] "The novelist's structure is a structure of *suggnômê*—of the penetration of the life of another into one's own imagination and heart. It is a form of imaginative and emotional receptivity in which the reader, following the author's lead, comes to be inhabited by the tangled complexities and struggles of other concrete lives."[4] The public intellectual needs this kind of imaginative capability to reason properly about public policy.

Any discussion of the task of ethics and solutions to the problems that threaten the moral fabric of society often involves talks about searching, imagining, and developing alternatives to ongoing social situations. Indeed, social ethics requires that human capability that Mr. Thomas Gradgrind deprecates in Charles Dickens's *Hard Times* as "fancy." But according to Nussbaum, such fancy leads to certain postures of mind, creating the "ability to imagine nonexistent possibilities, to see one thing as another and one thing in another, to endow a perceived form with a complex life."[5]

The novel, by enabling readers to imagine possibilities, thinking about worlds that do not yet exist, is an aid to acknowledging the present world and its limitations and to making choices in it more reflectively. Readers form bonds of identification and sympathy with characters in the novel, taking on their pains, problems, possibilities, and aspirations. There are readers of Ayn Rand's *Atlas Shrugged* who completely identify with the vision of America that John Galt wants to create. Galt wants an American economy that is completely market-and-entrepreneurism driven, one that cuddles innovators, and is supplemented with a very lean government and a fiscal-policy regime that is aimed at maximizing economic growth and innovation and never focused on income redistribution. Some of those readers may have joined the Tea Party as a means of realizing such a vision. In certain segments of the Tea Party, *Atlas Shrugged* is the "Bible" of the movement and Rand is the "goddess" of rationalism, freedom, and pro-growth economic philosophy. On the other hand, there are other readers who reject the visions of Galt and Gradgrind (*Hard Times*) for a more communitarian, humanist

---

[2]Nussbaum, *Poetic Justice*, 5.
[3]Martha C. Nussbaum, *Sex and Justice* (Oxford: Oxford University Press, 1999), 183.
[4]Nussbaum, *Sex and Justice*, 170.
[5]Nussbaum, *Poetic Justice*, 4.

social existence. There is no doubt that literature influences reasoning about public policies in the United States and other countries.

I share the conviction with Nussbaum that narrative literature has an important contribution to make in public reasoning about ethical issues of our times. Narrative literature helps us to develop the competence to imagine how people who are not like us live and to not resort to a reductive approach to concrete issues. Many students come to college or master's degree ethics classes as Mary Dalton in Richard Wright's *Native Son*. Ms. Dalton (white upper class liberal) cannot imagine how people are different from her even though poor black folks in Chicago live just ten blocks away from her. Because of this lack of understanding, telling her why black Bigger Thomas acted the way he did "would have involved an explanation of his entire life."[6]

Reading narrative literature will not erase all deficiencies in public reasoning, but will surely help readers to develop an expanded conception of life and the disadvantages suffered by those who are in different class, status, race, and gender from them. This kind of competence or sensitivity is of practical and public value where social ethics requires us to think in terms of the common good which must of necessity involve persons who are different and distinct from us. How policymakers or ethicists think about the common good is based on some implicit or explicit notion of human nature, of its desires and sociability. What kind of human nature is presupposed in their ethical analyses? Whatever is supposed cannot be taken for granted in our analysis of public policy.

Thus, an important dimension of any ethical methodology is the capacity to model human behavior. Often policymakers and scholars rely on technical models such as economic utilitarianism, patterning processes of inanimate objects, or ideal heavenly scenarios. This they often do to the exclusion of literary imagination. Public discourses and ethical arguments are therefore left bereft of stories, narratives, parables, and mythos that should enrich the search for alternatives to current bad situations. Nussbaum deploys storytelling and imaginings as essential ingredients of rational arguments, public debates, and ethical methodology.[7] For her, philosophical discussions of literature, art, and music are part of public policy, business, law, medicine, race relations, and gender relations. Nussbaum uses literature to illumine discussions on the connection between "compassion and mercy, the role of emotions in public judgment, [and] what is involved in imagining the situation of someone different from oneself."[8] In doing this, she is relentless in her effort to inform the reader that narrative, storytelling, and their philosophical analyses are good forms of ethical methodology.

---

[6]Nussbaum, *Poetic Justice*, xiv.

[7]Nussbaum, *Poetic Justice*, xiii.

[8]Nussbaum, *Poetic Justice*, xiv.

Literary Analysis as Ethical Methodology

Ethical methodology, as I understand it, is a means of interpreting, addressing, and responding to social problems that threaten the social fabric of existence so that we can answer afresh these broad questions: How should human beings live? How should we live together? Literary imagination or the novelist's art is a relevant piece of equipment that can and does provide illumination concerning these questions. The novelist's art—that capacity to present characters or situations in their color and singularity—is very relevant in the work of deliberation, in the kind of practical wisdom and *phantasia* Aristotle insists the ethicist must have.

By not artificially demarcating the moral life ahead of any dialogue into, for instance, how to maximize utility or "what is my moral duty," instead of focusing on moral and non-moral goods that enable individuals and socialities to flourish, we open the ethical methodology to much of what novels present as relevant in understanding how lives hang together. Of course, not every novel or narrative is useful in this respect. According to Nussbaum, ethical analysis is best enriched, enlarged, and endorsed by the content and form, styles and structures, and sense of life of the realist novel.[9] The novelist's attention to particulars and proficient use of imagination to illumine concrete social situations are some of the skills a public policymaker needs to have in order to adequately grasp the complex issues of our time. Cultivating imagination, Dickensian "fancy" (as in the *Hard Times*), is one of the pathways to the faculty that grapples with the generation and evaluation of the alternatives that human complexity, non-monolithic sociality, and dynamic social justice require. Such competence must also encompass the capability to balance or accommodate the concrete and the general.

The narrative literature or novel is good at helping us to see how concrete circumstances shape the life of characters. This is often set against general human aspirations, hopes, desires, dreams, and needs. According to Nussbaum, the particular and concrete of narrative literature can promote empathetic reasoning without discarding rule-governed moral reasoning.

This play back and forth between the general and the concrete is, I claim, built into the very structure of the genre, in its mode of address to its readers. In this way, the novel constructs a paradigm of a style of ethical reasoning that is context-specific without being relativistic, in which we get potentially universalizable concrete prescriptions by bringing a

---

[9]Martha C. Nussbaum, *Love's Knowledge: Essays on Philosophy and Literature* (Oxford: Oxford University Press, 1990), 25–7.

general idea of human flourishing to bear on a concrete situation, which we are invited to enter through the imagination. This is a valuable form of public reasoning, both within a single culture and across cultures.[10]

In the hands of Nussbaum, ethical methodology becomes not a procedure of mathematical clarity or certainty, not a kind of explanation of complex human problems as reduced to simplified statements or logic of decision-making. But it is both a release to say what needs to be heard and interpreted about how humans ought to live together and how each person needs to live well, and it is a clarification of the particulars of social existence that inform what human beings are to each other. For her this is what it means for ethical methodology to be both empirical and practical.

> Empirical in that it is based on and responsible to actual human experience…. Practical in that it is conducted by people who are themselves involved in acting and choosing and who see the inquiry as having a bearing on their own practical ends. They do not inquire into a "pure" or detached manner, asking what the truth about ethical value might be as if they were asking for a description of some separately existing Platonic reality. They are looking for something in human lives, something, in fact, that they themselves are going to try to bring about in their lives. What they are asking is not what is the good "out there," but what can we best live by, and live together as social beings? Their results are constrained, and appropriately constrained, by their hopes and fears for themselves, their sense of value, what they think they can live with. This does not mean that inquiry cannot substantially modify their antecedent conception of their "target," specifying goals that were vague before and even convincing them to revise in substantial ways their conception of their goals. But their end is practice, not just theory. And inquiry is valuable because it contributes to practice in two ways: by promoting individual clarification and self-understanding, and by moving individuals toward communal attunement.[11]

It is important to mention that Nussbaum's use of literary imagination as ethical methodology and her analyses of movements in fiction as moments of ethical analysis are anchored to her understanding of the role of compassion and mercy in ethical or public reasoning. Compassion and the cultivation of it are key to not only public reasoning, but also issues of social justice in a democratic, pluralistic society. Compassion serves as an important bridge between persons and between persons and community. Compassion

---

[10]Nussbaum, *Poetic Justice*, 8.
[11]Nussbaum, *Love's Knowledge*, 173.

is deeply connected to individuals as moral agents in society. Nussbaum's conceptualization of compassion is very illuminating.[12] For her, compassion broadens, educates, and stabilizes elements of concern that we already have. It widens one's own circle of concern. She explains at length that compassion expands the boundaries of the self as it is often set in motion by "painful emotion occasioned by awareness of another person's underserved misfortune."[13] The citizen who feels compassion suffers painful emotion, and now the original pain is doubled due to fellow feeling. Compassion is a process in which the suffering of one citizen is shared by another— hence the doubling. This co-sharing, which can and often does prompt us to treat others justly and humanely, is based on an evaluative judgment of the sufferer's condition.

Though compassion is an emotion, Nussbaum argues that it is rational (based on reasoning) and not driven by irrational sentimentality. She rejects any understanding of emotion that opposes it to reason. The emotion of compassion has a cognitive (thought) structure. It involves the appraisal that the person's suffering is not trivial. It is serious; it matters for the person's flourishing. And thus there is a desire to relieve the person of the suffering. In addition, the person does not deserve it. Implicit in all of this evaluation is the conception of human flourishing and what constitutes a substantive obstacle to it. The evaluation is not all detached and clinical. Either because of shared citizenship, class, race, religion, gender, ethnicity, or sexual orientation, the citizen acknowledges not only some community between herself and the sufferer, but inhabits a sense of similar possibilities and vulnerabilities. The possibilities of the person who experiences suffering are similar to hers and her loved ones. She does not think that she is above suffering and has gotten everything to protect her from all contingencies of life.

In addition to the issue of the *size* of the person's suffering and *non-desert* (undeserved nature of suffering), there is a third element to the cognitive structure of compassion: *eudaimonistic judgment*. The person is part of your scheme or goals and so as such the person's ill condition affects your own flourishing. Similar possibility is an epistemological aid to forming eudaimonistic judgment.

Based on this succinct analysis, Nussbaum concludes that compassion is a motivation for helping actions and an essential part of the social justice project of any society. Literature helps in this process of broadening the self. What Nussbaum teaches us is that we cannot afford to ignore the role of emotion in public reasoning. Emotions are built into the very structure of Nussbaum's philosophical-ethical analysis. She gives emotions a carefully

---

[12]Martha Nussbaum, "Compassion: Tragic Predicaments," in *Upheavals in Thought: The Intelligence of Emotion* (Cambridge: Cambridge University Press, 2001), 297–353.
[13]Nussbaum, *Upheavals in Thought*, 301.

demarcated role in her discourse. This writer here is not just talking about the emotions that the beauty, form, style, and brilliance of her work arouses in the careful reader, but how her sophisticated discourse solicits attention for the ideal of full equality, human dignity, and draws the readers' ire against social systems or philosophy that reduce the actual functional capabilities of any human being.

One key impact of Nussbaum's work is that it has redefined the ethical task in the public square. She has shown that the task involves drawing analysts and citizens to see their own possibilities in the lives of others, enabling all of us to acknowledge that we are not self-sufficient, and as human beings we are not accessible only to reason but also to compassionate influence. Plato also recognized that literature could play this role well—all too well. Hence, he banned the poets, literary artists from his *Republic* (the ideal city), from the public realm. But for Nussbaum the very ability of literature to arouse emotions, to teach and lead into bonds of identification and sympathy, to see our own incompleteness and vulnerability is what makes it a great tool of both ethical training and analysis.

> Literature is in league with emotions. Readers of novels, spectators of dramas, find themselves led by these works to fear, to grief, to pity, to anger, to joy and delight, even to passionate love. Emotions are not just likely responses to the content of many literary works; they are built into their very structure, as ways in which literary forms solicit attention.[14]

To imitate her rhetorical flourish, I will say that emotions are not just likely responses to the often painstaking, insightful, and moving philosophical analyses of Nussbaum, they are built into the very structure and flow, as ways in which ethical discourses solicit attention. Although it is common knowledge that all ethical analyses no matter the methodology that undergirds them want to change human behavior toward a particular goal, the use of literary analysis as ethics by Nussbaum appears to be personally, frontally directed at the reader herself, eliciting her desires and giving her a paradigm on how to live her life—or at least emotionally engage with the other as an essential element of her own flourishing. In this way, Nussbaum hopes to bind the moral imagination of the reader to particular, concrete social problems by bringing them close to the (reader's) person's self, giving the reader a first-person reference.

This advantageous feature of Nussbaum's ethical analysis is not about the *content* of her work, although this is very important and worthy of attention, it is about *form*. The very shape of her analyses is subversive of the common attempt to dismiss the ill condition of the other as not affecting

---

[14]Nussbaum, *Poetic Justice*, 53.

one's own flourishing. Indeed, both the content and form of her philosophical-ethical analyses—that is, to say her ethical methodology—constitute an epistemological aid for forming individual eudaimonistic judgment. In her hands, we do not have just an ethical methodology, but a story-formed methodology.

From a Story-Formed Community to Story-Formed Methodology

Other scholars, ethicists and philosophers also tell stories. But there is a difference between theirs and Nussbaum's. Stanley Hauerwas is another American ethicist who is well known for his ethics of narrative-formed community. The difference between Nussbaum and Hauerwas is that she explicitly develops a form of ethical methodology for public discourse that relies on the form, beauty, and style of narrative literature, while he does not. No doubt Hauerwas often relies on novels (such as *Watership Down* and *The Brothers K*),[15] but I am not aware of his work that developed literary imagination as an essential methodology of ethical discourse in a pluralistic, democratic society. Besides, as Gloria Albrecht argues, though his narrative approach rejects a universal, foundationalist epistemology it often "becomes the new foundation for the assertion of universal truth" or it presses for belief in a single truth.[16] Nussbaum goes beyond narrative ethics (theology) to argue that the very structure of literary works is the format for proper ethical analysis. Hauerwas's work relies on novels to buttress his predetermined ethical treatise, but they are not meaningfully employed to show his readers how they can expand their imaginative capabilities so as to make better choices about the lives they live and make better judgments about the demands of public life upon them.

Nussbaum's work not only teaches us that literary imagination is an ethical methodology but goes further to elucidate the *tripartite method of ethical analysis*.[17] Her philosophical analysis of fiction-making imagination embodies in it a form of ethical methodology and a certain sort of moral/political

---

[15]See Stanley Hauerwas, *A Community of Character: Toward a Constructive Christian Social Ethic* (Notre Dame: University of Notre Dame Press, 1981); and *In Good Company: The Church as Polis* (Notre Dame: University of Notre Dame Press, 1995).

[16]Gloria H. Albrecht, *The Character of Our Communities: Toward an Ethic of Liberation for the Church* (Nashville, TN: Abingdon Press, 1995), 26.

[17]This is (a) Statement and Analysis of the Moral Problem; (b) Resources for Reflecting of the Problem, or Philosophical/Ethological/Theological Framework, and (c) Ethical Solution (Responses, Paradigm) and Payoff. See Nimi Wariboko, *Methods of Ethical Analysis: Between Theology, History, and Literature* (Eugene, OR: Wipf and Stock, 2013), 19–35.

vision—democratic, compassionate, committed to complexity, choice, and qualitative differences. Her work on literary imagination does not merely represent an ethical methodology, "but also enacts it in its structure, in its ways of conversing with its hypothetical reader."[18]

What her work shows is exactly what she likes about narrative literature, especially the novel, as a supreme way of teaching ethics.[19] Thus her ethical methodology is formed and in-formed by the very subject she studies. The convergence has occurred not because she merely wants to stay close to fiction writers, but because like writers of realistic fictions she believes that "life is painting a picture not doing a sum."[20] Fiction writers and Nussbaum approach public reasoning not content to show what has happened, but to show us, as Aristotle believes, "things such as might happen." The genre of novel, according to her, is important for public reasoning because "on account of some general features of its structure, generally constructs empathy and compassion in ways highly relevant to citizenship. Adam Smith was correct when he found in the experience of readership a model of attitudes and emotions of the judicious spectator."[21]

When Nussbaum analyzes a fiction she carefully lays out the viewpoint, the stance, ideology, or behavior that is the source of the problem that is fracturing the social relationship, threatening the moral fabric of society. She will then employ her humanistic viewpoint or Aristotelian framework to define the problem and set the reader up for sourcing or funding solutions, suggestions, and responses to the problem. Finally, she will give the reader her opinion on how best to address or rescue the problem.[22]

In *Hard Times*, the problem she identified was the utilitarian, rational choice model that Mr. Gradgrind promotes. Ethics and its methodology in Gradgrind's world are reduced to "some sort of 'sum-ranking' and maximizing procedure, a clear and present solution for any human problem."[23] In the opening scene of the novel Mr. Gradgrind declares: "In this life, we want nothing but facts, sir; nothing but facts." The problem with the economical-mind of Gradgrind is that the utilitarian picture of human beings and of rationality is taken

---

[18]Nussbaum, *Poetic Justice*, 36.

[19]Nussbaum, *Poetic Justice*, 36.

[20]Nussbaum, *Poetic Justice*, xix.

[21]Nussbaum, *Poetic Justice*, 10.

[22]For example, see her analyses of Charles Dickens's *Hard Times*, in her *Poetic Justice*, 13–78; Richard Wright's *Native Son*, in her *Sex and Social Justice*, 154–83; Sophocles's *Antigone*, "The Antigone: Conflict, Vision, and Simplification," in *The Fragility of Goodness: Luck and Ethics in Greek Tragedy and Philosophy*, ed. Martha C. Nussbaum (Cambridge: Cambridge University Press, 2007), 51–82; Euripides's *Hecuba*, "The Betrayal of Convention: A Reading of Euripides' *Hecuba*" in her *Fragility of Goodness*, 397–421.

[23]Nussbaum, *Poetic Justice*, 23.

not just as a way of writing reports, but as a way of dealing with people in daily encounters; not just as a way of doing economics, but as a way of defining a horse or talking to a child; not just as a way of appearing professionally respectable, but as a commitment that determines the whole content of one's personal and social life.[24]

In this world, all qualitative differences, mystery, and complexity with each life are ignored when public decisions are made, and human beings are added up as data "to weigh and measure any parcel of human nature, and tell you exactly what it comes to."[25]

She identifies the problem, interprets it, and attempts to resolve it all within a tightly argued philosophical framework. The most prominent features of her philosophical framework are given in *Love's Knowledge*. They are (1) "the noncommensurability of valuable things"; (2) "the priority of perceptions" and "priority of the particular"; (3) the "ethical value of emotion" and the imagination; and (4) "the ethical value of uncontrolled happenings."[26]

Let me explain what she means by these features. The first one requires that in doing ethics, we should not place all values on a single scale of ranking or comparison without regard to qualitative distinctions. Values are often incompatible. Second, we must develop the capacity to discern accurately and responsively the salient features of particular situations in making moral judgment. She argues that moralities that are based exclusively on general rules are ethically crude. Third, emotions have a cognitive structure and that practical reasoning must be accompanied with emotion to reach full rational judgment and practical wisdom. Fourth, rules do not enable us to respond well to chance, contingency, and the unexpected that necessarily bedevil all moral life. So the best way to proceed is to understand the particular situation and improvise accordingly.[27]

Now see the way she interprets how Dickens resolves the ethical tension (utility, self-interest as the measure of life that ignores individual particularity) in *Hard Times*. Her interpretation of the resolution fits with her own philosophical framework. It pays to quote her at some length here:

In its engagement with a general notion of the human being, this novel (like many others) is, I think, while particularistic, not relativistic. That is, it recognizes human needs that transcend boundaries of time, place, class, religion, and ethnicity, and it makes the focus of its moral

---

[24]Nussbaum, *Poetic Justice*, 17.
[25]Dickens, *Hard Times*, 11.
[26]Nussbaum, *Love's Knowledge*, 36–44.
[27]For a good review of *Love's Knowledge*, see Kalin, "Knowing Novels," 135–51.

deliberation the question of their adequate fulfillment. Its criticism of concrete political and social situations relies on a notion of what it is for a human being to flourish, and this notion itself, while extremely general and in need of further specification, is neither local nor sectarian. On the other hand, part of the idea of flourishing is a deep respect for qualitative difference—so the norm enjoins that governments, wherever they are, should attend to citizens in all their concreteness and variety, responding in a sensitive way to historical and personal contingencies. But that is itself a universal injunction and part of a universal picture of humanness. And it is by relying on this universal ideal that the novel, so different from a guidebook or even an anthropological field report, makes readers participants in the lives of people very different from themselves and also [makes readers] critics of the class distinctions that give people similarly constructed an unequal access to flourishing.[28]

Concluding Remarks

As we have demonstrated above, Nussbaum does approaches ethical analysis with skeptical detachment. In this regard she is like many other prominent ethicists in the academy. But she also differs in certain key areas. Many top social ethicists neither deem ethical reasoning as akin to formal reasoning in the sciences, nor maintain that the ethicist should be neutral by distancing him or herself from the particulars. But Nussbaum is among the few ethicists in the world whose approach raises the concern with particulars as a methodological highpoint. By not using an approach that provides a fine-tuned perception of particulars, as the novelist is wont to do, the other scholars portray the ethical as only a collective mode of action, social pattern of events indistinguishable from the political. Nussbaum's ethical methodology not only invites us to engage with broad patterns, but also focuses on individuals and their particular circumstances.

Not that the other scholars lack commitment to the individual, but their variant of the ethical methodology leaves the individual "lives as drops in an undemarcated ocean."[29] Their variant of the methodology is not supple enough or pushed far enough to focus on the social issue (problem, misery) as well as on the individual. Their forms do not promote the habit of the heart and mind that sheds light on an individual shrouded in darkness of poverty or neglect. In Walt Whitman's word, their forms of ethical methodology do not let us see "the sun falling around a helpless thing."

---

[28]Nussbaum, *Poetic Justice*, 45–46.
[29]Nussbaum, *Poetic Justice*, 21.

Nussbaum has gained this edge over the others because of her deft use of literature. Literary imagination and the novel's ability to focus on the particulars, on individuals and their particular circumstances, is a major aid to ethical judgment. As she puts it:

> I have argued that the experience of novel reading yields a strong commitment to regard each life as individual and separate from other lives. This way of seeing is highly relevant to the questions of well-being.... Group hatred and the oppression of groups is very often based on a failure to individualize. Racism, sexism, and many other forms of pernicious prejudice frequently ground themselves in the attribution of negative characteristics to the entire group.[30]

Before I offer my concluding remarks let us revisit the tripartite method of ethical analysis mentioned earlier in the light of what we have learned from Nussbaum. There is something subtle and compelling about this ethical methodology when it is executed well. The methodology works through major alternative positions on how we should live together in the face of a social problem or crisis. These positions are examined and held against one another at three levels: at the stage of analysis of the problem from multiple angles, so as to give full recognition to the nature of the practical situation in its particularity. Next it situates the problem within a philosophical (or theological, ethological) framework, which is likely to fund ways of reasoning about the solution. Finally, there is the search for relevant solutions. The requirement here is that the ethicist should treat approaches to its solution as non-homogenous, and should not arrive at solutions by using a single qualitative or quantitative standard of value in the faulty thinking that all values are commensurable. This requirement, hopefully, will force the ethicist to rigorously engage with other citizens' perspectives on the problem in order to find solutions in the spirit of democratic pluralism. The form or spirit of pluralism—as against totalitarianism—does not go from the particular to the general, but from particular to particular, linking "particulars without dispersing with their particularity."[31]

Indeed, the overall approach or tenor of the ethical reasoning taught in this book arguably dovetails into what Nussbaum calls "perceptive equilibrium." This is "an equilibrium in which concrete perceptions 'hang beautifully together,' both with one another and with agent's general principles; an equilibrium that is always ready to reconstitute itself in

---

[30]Nussbaum, *Poetic Justice*, 92.
[31]Nussbaum, *Love's Knowledge*, 78.

response to the new."[32] The literary imagination teaches this kind of perception with compelling subtlety and vigor.

Let me conclude this book by restating what I said in the introductory chapter and in the introduction to this chapter. I deliberately did not develop an overarching thesis of Nigerian literature; I have only engaged in the philosophical analysis of one work from each of the four writers and a comedian. I do not have the competence and temperament of Ahab to engage in an unyielding pursuit of the Moby Dick of a single brilliant thesis to make sense of Nigerian literature. Given the color, dynamics, and the sheer productivity of writers in the current Nigerian literary scene any scholars who propounds a single, reductive theory of Nigerian literature deserves to be taken down into the abyss as Ahab and the whale.

The last time I checked I got the joyful feeling that it was better for my scholarly hubris to go down into the abyss than for me to do so. In Nigeria a scholar can still get into the abyss even if he or she is not as stubborn, foolhardy, or revengeful as Ahab. I know there are those who will disagree with my thesis if I stated one because I did not follow their "literary village" consensus knowledge. Such might be too willing to send a man and his book (his lover) into the abyss for disagreeing with them. This is the picture Gabriel Okara paints of the Ijaw in his pathbreaking novel, *The Voice*.[33] The characters Okolo and Tuere challenged the consensus knowledge, the received wisdom of their community, and for this they were hogtied, put in a small canoe to drift far offshore—and were eventually sucked into the abyss of the sea. "Down they floated from one bank of the river to the other like debris, carried by the current. Then the canoe was drawn into a whirlpool. It spun round and round and was slowly drawn into the core and finally disappeared. And the water rolled over the top and the river flowed smoothly over it as if nothing had happened."[34]

---

[32]Nussbaum, *Love's Knowledge*, 182–3.
[33]Gabriel Okara, *The Voice* (New York: Africana Publishing Company, 1964).
[34]Okara, *Voice*, 127.

BIBLIOGRAPHY

Abani, Chris. *GraceLand*. New York: Farrar, Straus, and Giroux, 2004.

Adebayo, Sakiru. "The Black Soul Is (Still) a White Man's Artefact? Postcoloniality, Post-Fanonism, and the Tenacity of Race(ism) in A. Igoni Barrett's *Blackass*." *African Studies* 79, no. 1 (2020): 143–59.

Adebiyi, Rasheed Ademola. "Communicating Indigenous Knowledge through Exogenous Channel: A Comparative Content Analysis of Adelakun's *Under the Brown Rusted Roofs* and Achebe's *Things Fall Apart*." *Journal of Culture, Society, and Development* 12 (2015): 1–12.

Adelakun, Abimbola Adunni. *Under the Brown Rusted Roofs: Fiction*. Ibadan: Kraft, 2011.

Adepoju, Oluwatoyin Vincent. "Spatial Navigation as a Hermeneutic Paradigm: Ifa, Heidegger and Calvino." In *Palgrave Handbook of Africa and the Changing Global*, 987–1024. Edited by Samuel Ojo Oloruntoba and Toyin Falola. New York: Palgrave Macmillan, 2022.

Afolayan, Adeshina. *Philosophy and National Development in Nigeria: Toward a Tradition of Nigerian Philosophy*. London: Routledge, 2018.

Agamben, Giorgio. *The Signature of All Things: On Method*. Translated by Luca D'Isanto with Kevin Attell. New York: Zone Books, 2009.

Agamben, Giorgio. *The Time That Remains: A Commentary on the Letter to the Romans*. Stanford, CA: Stanford University Press, 2005.

Agamben, Giorgio. *What Is Apparatus?*. Translated by David Kishik and Stefan Pedatella. Stanford: Stanford University Press, 2009.

Albrecht, Gloria H. *The Character of Our Communities: Toward an Ethic of Liberation for the Church*. Nashville, TN: Abingdon Press, 1995.

Apter, Andrew. *Black Critics and Kings: The Hermeneutics of Power in Yoruba Society*. Chicago: University of Chicago Press, 1992.

Arendt, Hannah. *Between Past and Future: Eight Exercises in Political Thought*. New York: Penguin Books, 1968.

Arendt, Hannah. *The Human Condition*. Chicago: University of Chicago Press, 1958.

Aycock, Amanda. "Becoming Black and Elvis: Transnational and Performative Identity in the Novels of Chris Abani." *Safundi* 10, no. 1 (2009): 12–25.

Bakare-Yusuf, Bibi, and Jeremy Weate. "Ojuelegba: The Sacred Profanities of a West African Crossroad." In *Urbanization and African Cultures*, 323–40. Edited by Toyin Falola and Steven J. Salm. Durham, NC: Carolina Academic Press, 2005.

Bakhtin, Mikhail. *Problems of Dostoevsky's Poetics*. Minneapolis: University of Minnesota Press, 1984.

Bantum, Brian. *Redeemed Mulatto: A Theology of Race and Christian Hybridity.* Waco, TX: Baylor University Press, 2010.

Barber, Karin. "Yoruba *Oriki* and Deconstructive Criticism." *Research in African Literatures* 13, no. 4 (1984): 497–518.

Barnett, Clive. "Review of African Literature as Political Philosophy by M. S. C. Okolo." *African Affairs* 109, no. 436 (July 2010): 503–5.

Barrett, A. Igoni. *Blackass.* Minneapolis, MN: Gray Wolf, 2015.

Beals, Corey. *Levinas and the Wisdom of Love: The Question of Invisibility.* Waco, TX: Baylor University Press, 2007.

Benjamin, Walter. *The Arcades Project.* Translated by Howard Eiland and Kevin McLaughlin. Cambridge, MA: Belknap Press, 1982.

Boenisch, Peter M. "Who's Watching? Me!: Theatrality, Spectatorship, and Žižekian Subject." In *Žižek and Performance*, 48–60. Edited by Broderick Chow and Alex Mangold. New York: Palgrave Macmillan, 2014.

Borges, Jorge Luis. "The Secret Miracle." In *Ficciones*, 143–50. Translated by Anthony Kerrigan. New York: Grove, 1962.

Brecht, Bertolt. *The Threepenny Opera.* New York: Grove, 1994.

Brook, Peter. "Does Nothing Come from Nothing?" *British Psycho-Analytical Society Bulletin* 34, no. 1 (1998), reprinted at Centre de International Recherches Etudes Transdisciplinaires. https://ciret-transdisciplinarity.org/bulletin/b15c1.php

Brook, Peter. *The Empty Space.* New York: Penguin, 1990.

Brook, Peter. *The Open Door: Thoughts on Acting and Theatre.* New York: Random House, 2005.

Butler, Judith. *Bodies That Matter: On the Discursive Limits of "Sex."* New York: Routledge, 1993.

Butler, Judith. *Frames of War: When Is Life Grievable?* London: Verso, 2016.

Butler, Judith. *Gender Trouble: Feminism and the Subversion of Identity.* New York: Routledge, 2007.

Callender, Elizabeth Jarrell. "A Theology of Spatiality: The Divine Perfection of Omnipresence in the Theology of Karl Barth." PhD dissertation, University of Otago, Dunedin, New Zealand, 2011.

Caputo, John D. *The Weakness of God: A Theology of the Event.* Bloomington, IN: Indiana University Press, 2006.

Carr, Karen L. *The Banalization of Nihilism: Twentieth-Century Responses to Meaninglessness.* Albany, NY: SUNY Press, 1992.

Cavanaugh, William T. *Torture and Eucharist.* Malden, MA: Blackwell, 1998.

Clark-Bekederemo, J. P. "Ibadan." In *Collected Poems, 1958–1988: J. P. Clark-Bekederemo*, 14. Washington, DC: Howard University Press, 1991.

Clark-Bekederemo, J. P. *Ozidi.* Ibadan, Nigeria: Oxford University Press, 1966.

Clark-Bekederemo, J. P. *The Ozidi Saga: Collected and Translated from the Oral Ijo Version of Okabou Ojobolo.* Washington, DC: Howard University Press, 1991.

Cobb, John B. Jr., and David Ray Griffin. *Process Theology: An Introductory Exposition.* Louisville, KY: Westminster John Knox, 1976.

Copeland, Rebecca L. *Created Being: Expanding Creedal Christology.* Waco, TX: Baylor University Press, 2020.

Critical Theory Library. "Slavoj Žižek: Key Ideas." *Cultural and Critical Theory Library*. Accessed July 16, 2021. http://criticaltheorylibrary.blogspot. com/2011/02/slavoj-zizek-key-ideas.html?m=1

Cross, Terry. "Tillich's Picture of Jesus as the Christ: Toward a Theology of the Spirit's Saving Presence." In *Paul Tillich and Pentecostal Theology: Spiritual Presence and Spiritual Power*, 71–83. Edited by Nimi Wariboko and Amos Yong. Bloomington, ID: Indiana University Press, 2015.

Crow, Captain Hugh. *Memoirs of the Late Capt. Hugh Crow*. London: Longman, Rees, Orme, Brown, and Green, 1830.

Dawson, Ashley. "Surplus City: Structural Adjustment, Self-Fashioning, and Urban Insurrection in Chris Abani's *GraceLand*." *Interventions* 11, no. 1 (2009): 16–34.

Derrida, Jacques. *Positions*. Translated by Alan Bass. Chicago: University of Chicago Press, 1981.

Dickens, Charles. *Hard Times*. New York: Pocket, 2007.

Dingome, Jeanne. "Soyinka's The Road as Ritual." *Kunapipi* 2, no. 1 (1980): 30–41.

Dupuy, Jean-Pierre. *Petite metaphysique des tsunamis*. Paris: Seuil, 2005.

Ellis, Simon, and Collin Poole. "Collaboration, Violence, and Difference." In *Žižek and Performance*, 209–23. Edited by Broderick Chow and Alex Mangold. New York: Palgrave Macmillan, 2014.

Erekosima, Tonye V. W., H. Kio Lawson, and Obeleye Macjaja. *Hundred Years of Buguma History in Kalabari Culture*. Lagos: Sibon Books Limited, 1991.

Esty, Joshua D. "Excremental Postcolonialism." *Contemporary Literature* 40, no. 1 (Spring 1999): 22–59.

Falola, Toyin. *In Praise of Greatness: The Poetics of African Adulation*. Durham, NC: Carolina Academic Press, 2019.

Fanon, Frantz. *Black Skin, White Masks*. New York: Grove, 1952 and 2007.

Fanon, Frantz. *Wretched of the Earth*. Translated by Constance Farrington. New York: Grove, 1963.

Fatunmbi, Awo Fa'lokun. "Esu-Elegba: Ifa and the Spirit of the Divine Messenger." Unpublished essay, July 2021.

Ferguson, James. *Global Shadows: Africa in the Neoliberal World Order*. Durham, NC: Duke University Press, 2009.

Freud, Sigmund. *The Interpretation of Dream*. New York: Macmillan, 1913.

Garuba, Harry. "Explorations in Animist Materialism: Notes on Reading/Writing African Literature, Culture, and Society." *Public Culture* 15, no. 3 (2003): 261–85.

Gourgourris, Stathis. *Lessons in Secular Criticism*. New York: Fordham University Press, 2013.

Green, Chris E. W. *All Things Beautiful: An Aesthetic Christology*. Waco, TX: Baylor University Press, 2021.

Hägglund, Martin. *Dying for Time: Proust, Woolf, Nabokov*. Cambridge, MA: Harvard University Press, 2012.

Hall, Stuart. "Who Needs 'Identity'?" In *Questions of Cultural Identity*, 1–17. Edited by Paul Du Gay and Stuart Hall. London: Sage, 1990.

Hallward, Peter. *Badiou: A Subject to Truth*. Minneapolis: University of Minnesota Press, 2003.

Haney, William S. II. "Soyinka's Ritual Drama: Unity, Postmodernism, and
the Mistake of Intellect." *Research in African Literatures* 21, no. 4 (1990):
33–54.

Harrison, Sarah K. "'Suspended City': Personal, Urban, and National Development
in Chris Abani's *GraceLand.*" *Research in African Literatures* 43, no. 2 (Summer
2012): 95–114.

Hauerwas, Stanley. *A Community of Character: Toward a Constructive Christian
Social Ethic.* Notre Dame: University of Notre Dame Press, 1981.

Hauerwas, Stanley. *In Good Company: The Church as Polis.* Notre Dame:
University of Notre Dame Press, 1995.

Hegel, G. W. F. *Phenomenology of Spirit.* Translated by A. V. Miller. Oxford:
Oxford University Press, 1977.

Hegel, G. W. F. *The Science of Logic.* Translated by George Di Giovanni.
Cambridge: Cambridge University Press, 2010.

Hodges, Hugh. "No, This Is Not Redemption: The Biafra War Legacy in Chris
Abani's *GraceLand.*" In *Writing the Nigeria-Biafra War*, 380–99. Edited by
Toyin Falola and Ogechukwu Ezekwem. New York: James Currey, 2016.

Honig, Bonnie. *Antigone, Interrupted.* New York: Cambridge University Press,
2013.

Hook, Derek. "Death-Bound Subjectivity: Fanon's Zone of Nonbeing and the
Lacanian Death Drive." *Subjectivity* 13, no. 28 (2020): 355–75.

Horton, Robin. "Ekineba: A Forgotten Myth." *Oduma* 2 (1975): 33–6.

Horton, Robin. "A Hundred Years of Change in Kalabari Religion." In *Black
Africa: Its People and Their Cultures Today*, 194–8. Edited by John Middleton.
New York: Macmillan, 1971.

Horton, Robin. "Igbo: An Ordeal for the Aristocrats." *Nigeria Magazine*
(September 1966): 168–83.

Horton, Robin. "The Kalabari Ekine Society: A Borderline of Religion and Art."
Africa 33 (1963): 94–114.

Horton, Robin. *Kalabari Sculpture.* Lagos: Department of Antiquities, Federal
Republic of Nigeria, 1965.

Horton, Robin. "The Kalabari Worldview: An Outline and Interpretation." *Africa*
32, no. 3 (July 1962): 197–219.

Iromuanya, Julie. "'White Man Magic': A. Igoni Barrett's *Blackass*, Afropolitanism,
and (Post) Racial Anxieties." In *Afropolitan Literature as World Literature*,
71–84. Edited by James Hodapp. New York: Bloomsbury Academic, 2020.

Jameson, Frederic. *The Ideologies of Theory.* London: Verso, 2008.

Jantzen, Grace M. "'Death, Then, How Could I Yield to It?': Kristeva's Mortal
Visions." In *Religion in French Feminist Thought: Critical Perspectives*, 117–30.
Edited by Morny Joy, Kathleen O'Grady, and Judith L. Poxon. London: Routledge,
2003.

Jones, Gwilym Iwan *The Trading States of the Oil Rivers: Study of Political
Development in Eastern Nigeria.* Oxford: Oxford University Press, 1963.

Kafka, Franz. *Collected Stories.* London: Everyman's Library, 1993.

Kafka, Franz. *The Great Wall of China, Stories, and Reflections by Franz Kafka.*
Translated by Willa Muir and Edwin Muir. New York: Schocken, 1946.

Kant, Immanuel. *The Metaphysics of Morals.* Cambridge: Cambridge University
Press, 1996.

Keane, Webb. *Ethical Life: Its Natural and Social Histories*. Princeton: Princeton University Press, 2015.

Keller, Catherine. *Face of the Deep: A Theology of Becoming*. New York: Routledge, 2003.

Keynes, John Maynard. *General Theory of Employment, Interest, and Money*. San Diego: Harcourt Brace Jovanovich, 1964.

Lacan, Jacques. *The Four Fundamental Concepts of Psychoanalysis*. Translated by Alan Sheridan. New York: Norton, 1981.

Lacan, Jacques. *The Seminar of Jacques Lacan Book XVII: The Other Side of Psychoanalysis*. Translated by Russell Grigg. New York: W. W. Norton, 2007.

LaCapra, Dominick. *Writing History, Writing Trauma*. Baltimore: Johns Hopkins University Press, 2001.

Lehman, Paul L. *Ethics in a Christian Context*. Eugene, OR: Wipf and Stock, 1998.

Levinas, Emmanuel. *Totality and Infinity*. Translated by Alphonso Lingis. Pittsburgh, PA: Duquesne University Press, 1961.

Lincoln, Sarah. "Expensive Shit: Aesthetic Economics of Waste in Postcolonial Africa." PhD dissertation, Duke University, Durham, NC, 2008.

Lorey, Isabel. *State of Insecurity: Government of the Precarious*. London: Verso, 2015.

MacIntyre, Alasdair. *After Virtue: A Study in Moral Theology*. 2nd ed. Notre Dame, IN: University of Notre Dame Press, 1984.

Mangold, Alex. "Introduction: Performing Žižek: Hegel, Lacan, Marx and the Parallax View." In *Žižek and Performance*, 1–12. Edited by Broderick Chow and Alex Mangold. New York: Palgrave Macmillan, 2014.

Marx, Karl. *Grundrisse*. Translated by Martin Nicolaus. New York: Penguin Classics, 1973.

Mbembe, Achille. "Life, Sovereignty, and Terror in the Fiction of Amos Tutuloa." *Research in African Literatures* 34, no. 4 (Winter 2003): 1–26.

Mbembe, Achille. *On the Postcolony*. Berkeley: University of California Press, 2001.

McGowan, Todd. *Capitalism and Desire: The Psychic Cost of Free Markets*. New York: Columbia University Press, 2016.

McKittrick, Katherine, ed. *Sylvia Wynter: On Being Human as Praxis*. Durham, NC: Duke University Press, 2015.

Moltmann, Jürgen. *The Coming of God: Christian Eschatology*. Translated by Margaret Kohl. Minneapolis: Fortress Press, 1996.

Mosès, Stéphane. *The Angel of History: Rosenzweig, Benjamin, and Scholem*. Translated by Barbara Harshav. Stanford, CA: Stanford University Press, 2009.

Nancy, Jean-Luc. *Being Singular Plural*. Translated by Robert D. Richardson and Anne E. O' Byrne. Stanford, CA: Stanford University Press, 2000.

Nancy, Jean-Luc. *Birth to Presence*. Translated by Brian Holmes et al. Stanford: Stanford University Press, 1993.

Nancy, Jean-Luc. *The Inoperative Community*. Translated by Peter Connor, Lisa Garbus, Michael Holland, and Simona Sawhney, foreword by Christopher Fynsk. Minneapolis: University of Minnesota Press, 1991.

Nietzsche, Friedrich. *The Gay Science*. Liepzig: E. W. Fitzsch, 1887.

Nietzsche, Friedrich. *Thus Spake Zarathustra*. New York: Barnes & Noble, 2005.

Nussbaum, Martha C. *The Fragility of Goodness: Luck and Ethics in Greek Tragedy and Philosophy*. Cambridge: Cambridge University Press, 2007.

Nussbaum, Martha C. *Love's Knowledge: Essays on Philosophy and Literature*. Oxford: Oxford University Press, 1990.

Nussbaum, Martha C. *Poetic Justice: The Literary Imagination and Public Life*. Boston: Beacon Press, 1995.

Nussbaum, Martha C. *Sex and Justice*. Oxford: Oxford University Press, 1999.

Nussbaum, Martha C. *Upheavals in Thought: The Intelligence of Emotion*. Cambridge: Cambridge University Press, 2001.

Oates, William. Diary notes, September 28, 1857, D/0/18, National Museums of Liverpool, Maritime Archives and Library, Liverpool, England (International Slavery Museum, Liverpool, United Kingdom. https://www.liverpoolmuseums.org.uk/international-slavery-museum).

Ochonu, Moses. "How Not to Defend Buhari." *USA Africa Dialogue Series*. Wednesday, February 17, 2016. https://groups.google.com/forum/#!topic/usaafricadialogue/P4LqeenuytQ

Oha, Obododima. "The Esu Paradigm in the Semiotics of Identity and Community." Unpublished essay.

Okara, Gabriel. *The Voice*. New York: Africana Publishing Company, 1964.

Okolo, Mary S. C. *African Literature as Philosophy*. London: Zed Books, 2007.

Okpewho, Isidore. *Blood on the Tides: The Ozidi Saga and Oral Epic Narratology*. Rochester, NY: University of Rochester Press, 2014.

Okpewho, Isidore. "The Ozidi Saga: A Critical Introduction." In *The Ozidi Saga: Collected and Translated from the Oral Ijo Version of Okabou Ojobolo*, vii–xxviii. Edited by J. P. Clark-Bekederemo. Washington, DC: Howard University Press, 1991.

Okpewho, Isidore. "Performance and Plot in the Ozidi Saga." *Oral Traditions* 19, no. 1 (2004): 63–95.

Olaniyan, Tejumola. *Arrest the Music!: Fela and His Rebel Art and Politics*. Bloomington: Indiana University Press, 2004.

Pemberton, John. "Eshu-Elegba: The Yoruba Trickster God." *African Arts* 9, no. 1 (1975): 20–92.

Rambo, Shelly. *Spirit and Trauma: A Theology of Remaining*. Louisville, KY: Westminster John Knox Press, 2010.

Rancière, Jacques. *Disagreement: Politics and Philosophy*. Translated by Julie Rose. Minneapolis: University of Minnesota Press, 1998.

Rancière, Jacques. *Dissensus: On Politics and Aesthetics*. Edited and Translated by Steven Corcoran. London: Continuum, 2010.

Riddell, Barry. "Review of African Literature as Political Philosophy by M. S. C. Okolo." *Review of African Political Economy* 35, no. 118 (December 2008): 681–2.

Santner, Eric L. *The Weight of All Flesh: On the Subject Matter of Political Economy*. New York: Oxford University Press, 2016.

Schaub, Michael. "An Audacious Transformation Bogs Down in *Blackass*." March 6, 2016. https://www.npr.org/2016/03/06/468941255/an-audacious-transformation-bogs-down-in-blackass

Schmitt, Carl. *Political Theology: Four Chapters on the Concept of Sovereignty*. Translated by George Schwab. Cambridge, MA: MIT Press, 1985.

Smajić, Srdjan. *Ghost-Seers, Detectives and Spiritualist: Theories of Vision in Victorian Literature and Science*. Cambridge: Cambridge University Press, 2010.

Soyinka, Wole. *Myth, Literature, and the African World*. Cambridge: Cambridge University Press, 1976.

Soyinka, Wole. *The Road in Collected Plays*. London: Oxford University Press, 1973.

Steiner, George. *Real Presences*. Chicago: University of Chicago Press, 1989.

Taiwo, Olufemi. *Africa Must Be Modern: A Manifesto*. Bloomington: Indiana University Press, 2014.

Talbot, P. Amaury. *Tribes of the Niger Delta: Their Religions and Customs*. London: Frank Cass, 1967.

Tanner, Norman P. (ed.). "Council of Chalcedon—451." In *Decrees of the Ecumenical Councils*, Vol. 1, *Nicaea 1—Lateran V*. London: Sheed and Ward, 1990.

Taylor, Mark C. *Altarity*. Chicago: University of Chicago Press, 1987.

Taylor, Mark Lewis. "Tillich's Ethics: Between Politics and Ontology." In *The Cambridge Companion to Paul Tillich*, 189–207. Edited by Russell Re Manning. Cambridge: Cambridge University Press, 2009.

Thatamanil, John. *The Immanent Divine, God, Creation, and the Human Predicament: East–West Conversation*. Minneapolis, MN: Fortress, 2006.

Thomas, Philip S. *In a Vision of the Night: Job, Cormac McCarthy, and the Challenge of Chaos*. Waco, TX: Baylor University Press, 2021.

Tibebus, Teshale. *Hegel and the Third World: The Making of Eurocentrism in World History*. Syracuse, NY: Syracuse University Press, 2011.

Tillich, Paul. *Love, Power and Justice: Ontological Analyses and Ethical Applications*. London: Oxford University Press, 1954.

Tillich, Paul. *Systematic Theology, Vol. 1*. Chicago: University of Chicago Press, 1951.

Tillich, Paul. *Systematic Theology, Vol. 2: Existence and Christ*. Chicago: University of Chicago Press, 1956.

Tillich, Paul. *Systematic Theology, Vol. 3: Life and the Spirit, History and the Kingdom of God*. Chicago: University of Chicago Press, 1965.

Trilling, Lionel. *The Moral Obligation to Be Intelligent: Selected Essays*. Edited by Leon Wieseltier. Evanston, IL: Northwestern University Press, 2008.

Verene, Donald Phillip. *Hegel's Recollections*. Albany: SUNY Press, 1985.

Wagner, Richard. *Jesus of Nazareth and Other Writings*. Lincoln: University of Nebraska Press, 1995.

Wariboko, Nimi. *The Charismatic City and the Resurgence of Religion: A Pentecostal Social Ethics of Cosmopolitan Urban Life*. New York: Palgrave Macmillan, 2014.

Wariboko, Nimi. "Between Community and My Mother: A Theory of Agonistic Communitarianism." In *The Palgrave Handbook of African Social Ethics*, 147–63. Edited by Nimi Wariboko and Toyin Falola. Cham, Switzerland: Palgrave Macmillan, 2020.

Wariboko, Nimi. *The Depth and Destiny of Work: An African Theological Interpretation*. Trenton, NJ: Africa World Press, 2008.

Wariboko, Nimi. *Economics in Spirit and Truth: A Moral Philosophy of Finance*. New York: Palgrave Macmillan, 2014.

Wariboko, Nimi. *Ethics and Time: Ethos of Temporal Orientation in Politics and Religion in the Niger Delta.* Lanham, MD: Lexington, 2010.

Wariboko, Nimi. "Excellence as a Moral Vision for Political Leadership." In *Nigeria: Leadership and Development. Essays in Honor of Governor Rotimi Amaechi*, 61–80. Edited by Eme Ekekwe. Bloomington, IN: Authorhouse, 2011.

Wariboko, Nimi. "Kalabari: A Study of Synthetic Ideal." *Nordic Journal of African Studies* 8, no. 1 (1999): 80–93.

Wariboko, Nimi. *Methods of Ethical Analysis: Between Theology, History, and Literature.* Eugene, OR: Wipf and Stock, 2013.

Wariboko, Nimi. *Nigerian Pentecostalism.* Rochester: Rochester University Press, 2014.

Wariboko, Nimi. *Pattern of Institutions in the Niger Delta: Economic and Ethological Interpretations of History and Culture.* Port Harcourt, Nigeria: Onyoma Research Publications, 2007.

Wariboko, Nimi. *The Pentecostal Principle: Ethical Methodology in New Spirit.* Grand Rapids, MI: Eerdmans, 2012.

Wariboko, Nimi. *The Principle of Excellence: A Framework for Social Ethics.* Lanham, MD: Rowman and Littlefield, 2009.

Wariboko, Nimi. "Senses and Legal expression in Kalabari Culture." In *The Foundations of Nigeria: Essays in Honor of Toyin Falola*, 305–31. Edited by Adebayo Oyebade. Trenton, NJ: African World Press, 2003.

Wariboko, Nimi. *The Split Time: Economic Philosophy for Human Flourishing in African Perspective.* Albany, NY: SUNY University Press, 2022.

Weheliye, Alexander G. *Habeas Viscus: Racializing Assemblage, Biopolitics, and Black Feminist Theories of the Human.* Durham, NC: Duke University Press, 2014.

Whitehead, Anne. *Trauma Fiction.* Edinburgh: Edinburgh University Press, 2004.

Wright, Derek. "Scatology and Eschatology in Kofi Awoonor's *This Earth, My Brother.*" *International Fiction Review* 15, no. 1 (1988): 23–6.

Zerubavel, Eviatar. *Hidden Rhythms: Schedules and Calendars in Social Life.* Berkeley: University of California, 1981.

Žižek, Slavoj. *Absolute Recoil: Towards a New Foundation of Dialectical Materialism.* London: Verso, 2014.

Žižek, Slavoj. *Disparities.* London: Bloomsbury Academic, 2016.

Žižek, Slavoj. *Event: A Philosophical Journey through a Concept.* London: Penguin, 2014.

Žižek, Slavoj. *In Defense of Lost Causes.* London: Verso, 2009.

Žižek, Slavoj. "The Eclipse of Meaning: On Lacan and Deconstruction." In *Interrogating the Real*, 190–213. Edited by Rex Butler and Scotts Stephen. London: Continuum, 2006.

Žižek, Slavoj. "Freud Lives!" *London Review of Books* 28, no. 10, (May 25, 2006). http://www.lrb.co.uk/v28/n10/slavoj-zizek/freud-lives

Žižek, Slavoj. *Incontinence of the Void: Economico-Philosophical Spandrels.* Cambridge, MA: MIT Press, 2017.

Žižek, Slavoj. *Less Than Nothing: Hegel and the Shadow of Dialectical Materialism.* London: Verso, 2012.

Žižek, Slavoj. *Living in the End Times.* London: Verso, 2010.

Žižek, Slavoj. *Looking Awry: An Introduction to Jacques Lacan through Popular Culture*. Cambridge, MA: MIT Press, 1991.

Žižek, Slavoj. *Organs without Bodies: On Deleuze and Consequences*. New York: Routledge, 2012.

Žižek, Slavoj. *The Parallax View*. Cambridge, MA: MIT Press, 2006.

Žižek, Slavoj. *The Plague of Fantasies*. London: Verso, 1997.

Žižek, Slavoj. *The Puppet and the Dwarf: The Perverse Core of Christianity*. Cambridge, MA: MIT Press, 2003.

Žižek, Slavoj. "The Sexual is Political." Accessed July 16, 2021. https://thephilosophicalsalon.com/the-sexual-is-political/

Žižek, Slavoj. *The Sublime Object of Ideology*. London: Verso, 2008.

Žižek, Slavoj. *Tarrying with the Negative: Kant, Hegel, and the Critique of Ideology*. Durham, NC: Duke University Press, 1993.

Zumhagen-Yelpé, Karen. "The Everyday's Fabulous beyond: Nonsense, Parable, and the Ethics of the Literary in Kafka and Wittgenstein." In *Philosophy and Kafka*, 73–93. Edited by Brendan Moran and Carlo Salzan. Lanham, MD: Lexington, 2013.

INDEX